AMERICAN WOMEN

images and realities

AMERICAN WOMEN
Images and Realities

Advisory Editors
ANNETTE K. BAXTER
LEON STEIN

A Note About This Volume

From her mother, Sarah Josepha Buell Hale (1788-1879) received a classical education at home. Married at 25, she bore five children in nine years before being widowed. She then turned to writing, became editor in 1827 of the *Ladies' Magazine* and in 1836 of *Godey's Lady's Book,* published in Philadelphia. *Manners; or Happy Homes and Good Society All the Year Round* summarizes the credo that established her as arbiter of good conduct for half a century: the home, not the public arena, was woman's battleground; her weapons were education, conversation, delicacy, femininity, and the power to persuade; and her role was that of God's moral agent on Earth.

MANNERS;

OR,

HAPPY HOMES AND GOOD SOCIETY

ALL THE YEAR ROUND

Sarah J. Hale

ARNO PRESS

A New York Times Company
New York • 1972

Reprint Edition 1972 by Arno Press Inc.

American Women: Images and Realities
ISBN for complete set: 0-405-04445-3
See last pages of this volume for titles.

Manufactured in the United States of America

Publisher's Note: This volume was reprinted
from the best available copy.

- - - - - - - - - - - - - -

Library of Congress Cataloging in Publication Data

Hale, Sarah Josepha (Buell) 1788-1879.
    Manners.

    (American women: images and realities)
    Reprint of the 1868 ed.
    1. Etiquette. I. Title. II. Series.
BJ1852.H17 1972   395   72-2606
ISBN 0-405-04461-5

MANNERS;

OR,

HAPPY HOMES AND GOOD SOCIETY

ALL THE YEAR ROUND.

BY MRS. HALE,

AUTHORESS OF "NORTHWOOD," "DISTINGUISHED WOMEN," "THE VIGIL OF
LOVE," ETC., ETC.

"Manner is everything with some people, and something with everybody.
Bishop Middleton.

BOSTON:

J. E. TILTON AND COMPANY.
1868.

STEREOTYPED BY C. J. PETERS & SON, NO. 5 WASHINGTON STREET, BOSTON.

PRESS OF JOHN WILSON & SON, CAMBRIDGE.

To

Young People Particularly,

AND TO

ALL WHO SEEK FOR HAPPINESS IN THIS LIFE, OR FOR THE HOPE
OF HAPPINESS IN THE LIFE TO COME,

THIS BOOK

IS OFFERED AS A FRIEND IN THEIR PURSUITS.

PREFACE.

————

EVERY new book must have, in the consciousness of its author, a private history that, like the mysteries of romance, would if unfolded have an interest for the reader, and by unveiling the inner life of the volume show its character and tendencies. As the preface is the proper place for explanations, it seems to me that a sketch of the origin of this book will be the most fitting testimony of my endeavors to make it worthy of approval.

Long ago, when I was a little girl at school, one of the poetic selections in my reading-book stamped itself into my heart and mind as my country's photograph : it ran thus, —

> "Columbia, Columbia, to glory arise,
>   The queen of the world, and the child of the skies!
>   Thy Genius commands thee; with rapture behold;
>   While ages on ages thy splendors unfold!"

The word "splendors" struck me with awe and delight. I longed to know what these glories would be. I wondered if it would ever be possible for me to do any thing to aid in this "unfolding" of national greatness. Then came Independence Day, with the Fourth-of-July orations and their patriotic burden, all tending to prove that American citizens had the "inalienable right to life, liberty, and the pursuit of happiness."

These ideas seemed grand, but not satisfying. Who gave these rights? and what could I do to obtain happiness? were questions to be answered. I did not apprehend

3

their full scope until the deep waters of affliction had gone over my soul; from that baptism of sorrow I learned to distrust the abstract and ideal as guides in the duties of life. The value of things seems to me greatest when their right uses produce the greatest good; and thus human rights have their true interpretation when subordinated to the laws of God, which are the highest good. In this light, it seems to me that the value of all material things is in proportion to the degree in which they minister to the good of human beings; and that human nature finds its best happiness in obedience to the Divine Exemplar of all goodness.

An illustration may help us to apprehend these lessons. Take a wide prairie: in its luxuriance of wild fertility it can only furnish food for buffaloes. Are not its uses immeasurably exalted when its same broad, ocean-like surface is seen in waving wheat-fields, dotted with human habitations? The beneficent changes have been wrought out by obedience to God's law of labor, — that man should subdue the earth before he could become its ruler. Thus we find the reason why the man who makes two blades of wheat grow where only one grew before is a public benefactor. This power of doing good in little things is a material aid in securing the happiness of life: in short, human rights involve the duty of doing right individually. In "the pursuit of happiness," the first right step is to seek that which is good to do, not merely for one's self, but for others: ultimately we reach the public good.

To illustrate this philosophy of happiness has been the study and aim of my literary life. Dr. Chalmers left on record his experience that repetition was the way of success most effectual in promoting good. I have followed this plan, as the readers of Godey's "Lady's Book" for the last thirty years will testify. "Line upon line, precept upon precept;"

— these are the examples of Nature, and the doctrines of Revelation. Can human reason find better methods?

This seemed my proper plan when I engaged to furnish a series of articles, during 1866, for a family newspaper.* My department, " The Home Circle," was to include the etiquette of social observances, and the philosophy of home happiness. Order, if not Heaven's first law, is the law through which human beings gain their most useful knowledge of Nature; and as Time, which began with the creation, is the first principle of order, I took my plan from the first week of the world's life. Reckoning each week as a day, I divided the fifty-two weeks into seven periods, or parts, of seven weeks each: the seventh number in each part was the *Sunday rest.* The three weeks that make up the full year are given to our three American holidays.

Thus my sheaf has been garnered. Its design is to furnish the varied entertainment of mental food for home happiness which the diversity of conditions in life and of cultivation in taste require. To give this variety, gleanings have been made from the best writers on these subjects; but as no book, excepting the inspired volume of divine truth, is just to *woman,* the foundation principles of love and duty, the pillars of domestic peace and social improvement, have been built up from the Bible.

When we study domestic life in its influence on national characteristics, it seems as if the two Anglo-Saxon Peoples were intrusted with the holy duty of keeping pure the home of woman and the altar of God. Where in all the Old World, but in England, could the family life of Sir Thomas More keep his memory glorious? or the wedded union of

* " The Home Weekly," then published in Philadelphia by Mr. George W. Childs, the well-known editor of " The Public Ledger," and " The American Literary Gazette."

Lord William Russell become sacred as a holy example? and where else would the domestic virtues of a sovereign Queen and a Prince Consort have ennobled their high rank? English literature is rich in these evidences of honor to goodness in home-life. America has all needed means of making her history unparalleled in the reality of happy homes and good society throughout the Great Republic.

Moreover, there are, in the texture of American life, certain threads, that, like telegraphic wires, reach across all obstacles, and awaken the sympathies of the world. These sympathies are drawn to us in our American holidays, that thus become exponents of the heart of humanity. Take, for instance, Washington's birthday. Is there not among all nations the feeling that he is the best example of a perfect hero, and that his name deserves to be honored? Independence Day,—has it not ideas and deeds and results that move the heart and mind of man as no other Holiday can stir them? And our Thanksgiving Day for the mercies of God and His bounteous gifts of harvest — could not every Christian nation and every Jewish family in the world join us in this Thanksgiving, on the last Thursday in November?

The Anglo-Saxon peoples have another bond of unity, — they represent home-life, in its highest characteristics among the nobility of England, and in its best aspects of purity and happiness in America. These characteristics and virtues of the Princely and the Popular are united in the MANNERS that form the most perfect standard for social life and home happiness. This standard it has been my purpose to set forth and illustrate in a fashion that would do good, and not evil; as I believe in Tennyson's estimate of merit, —

" 'Tis only noble to be good."

SARAH JOSEPHA HALE.

CONTENTS.

Preface 3

PART FIRST.

I.   Love 13
II.   Home 19
III. Food 25
IV.   Language 31
V.   Clothing 39
VI.   Recreation 46
VII. The Home Sunday 52
      WASHINGTON'S BIRTHDAY 57

PART SECOND.

I.   Shaping an American Home 65
      Hints 70
II.   Marriage 72
III. How to beautify our Homes 79
IV.   Society 86
      Hints for the Family 91

    V. Amusements 93

             Crowning the Wisest 94

   VI. A Plea for Dancing 99

  VII. Sunday our National Defence 107

PART THIRD.

     I. The Home Circle 115

    II. Engagements and Weddings 121

   III. Foreign Travel 129

             Hints 134

   IV. Letter-writing 136

             Hints 139

    V. Requisites of Good Society 142

             Hints 147

   VI. A Life of Etiquette 148

  VII. Shakspeare's Sunday Book 154

PART FOURTH.

     I. The Glorious Fourth; or, the Home-life of the
         Nation 163

             Song of the Flower Angels 168

    II. Accomplishments of Men 170

             Hints 174

   III. Accomplishments of Women 176

             Hints 180

   IV. Literature. — New Novels 182

             Doctor Norton's Story 183

    V. The Importance of Needlework 189

             The Autograph Bedquilt 192

VI. Young America 196
     Words of Washington 199
VII. The Book, and how to read it 202

PART FIFTH.

I. Heathen Homes 211
II. Private Visits and Social Parties 217
     Social Parties 220
     Hints for Visits 222
     Hints for Social Parties 223
III. Character 225
     The Womanly and the Manly 226
IV. Conversation 231
     Hints 235
V. A Lady's Dress 236
     Hints 241
VI. Pets, and their Uses 243
     The Silk-worm 252
VII. Happy Sundays for Children 253

PART SIXTH.

I. German Home-life 261
II. Dinner-parties 269
     Hints about the Dinner 272
III. Politeness at the Table 275
     Rules for a Dinner-party 278
IV. Balls 280
     Hints for the Ball 286
V. Blots on the Light of Home 287

VI. The Hand and its Work 294
VII. Sunday and its Rest 300

PART SEVENTH.

I. Desolated Homes 307
II. Domestic Etiquette and Duties 316
III. Mistakes in Language 323
IV. Our National Thanksgiving Day 331
V. Evening Receptions 339
        Hints about Receptions 344
VI. Books for Home-reading 345
        List of Books 350
VII. Men and Women 353
VIII. Merry Christmas 361
        The Queen's Book 363
        Christmas Trees 367
        How the Tree was made 368
        Christmas Song 370
IX. Time's Last Visit 371
X. The Three Sceptres 376

MANNERS.

"He that is only real had need have exceeding great parts of virtue; as the stone had need to be rich that is set without foil."

LORD BACON,

On Ceremonies and Respects.

PART FIRST.

———◦◦◦———

I.—LOVE.

Love is a celestial harmony
Of likely hearts, composed of stars' consent,
Which join together in sweet sympathy
To work each other's joy and sweet content.

Spenser.

Love's heralds should be thoughts,
Which ten times faster glide than the sun's beams,
Driving back shadows over lowering hills.

Shakspeare.

LOVE and HOME: these seem inseparable ideas. As regards humanity, they began together; nor can we think of one theme without bringing up some smile or sigh of the other to delight or sadden us: thus memory, or consciousness, proves us to be true human beings.

It is of love that we will, in this number, chiefly confer together. Let us think, first, of the source of love, the Divine Love, that, on Christmas morning, nearly nineteen hundred years ago, came down from heaven to gladden and revivify suffering and dying humanity.

Are you well read in the history of the world before the angels shouted their song of redeeming love, "Glory to God in the highest; on earth, peace, good will toward

13

men "? If so, you will see, in the following rapid sketch, a true outline: —

Had an angel been gifted with power to look over the whole inhabited globe, on the opening of the eventful year 4004 of the old era, what would have appeared? Everywhere the spectacle of demoralization, despair, and death. Rome, representing the Gentile world, had trodden down, with iron heel, alike the civilized Greek and the barbarian Goth, into a passive state called *peace!* The temple of Janus was shut, but the flood-gates of sin were opened wide as those of death; and from the corrupt hearts of wicked men such foul streams were poured forth as threatened to overwhelm the race.

Patriotism, the holiest emotion of the Pagan mind, the loftest virtue of the Roman people, which had given such wonderful power to the men and women of that regal nation, — patriotism had hardly a votary in the Eternal City.

The Jews, the chosen people of God, had touched the lowest point of national degradation, — subjection to a foreign power. Their religion had lost its life-giving faith, and become a matter of dead forms or vain pretences, used by the priests for their own profit, and to foster their own pride. The selfish passions were predominant; the evil, sensual nature triumphed; love had become lust; the true idea of marriage and of home — the hallowed union of one man with one woman, faithful to each other through life — was treated as an idle jest, a mockery of words, never intended to be made true.

Everywhere, sins, crimes, and woes filled the world. There was no faith in God, no hope in man, no trust in woman.

Such was the dark picture of heathenism when the Roman world held its proud day of peace!

Our American world has lately had its day of national thanks for the "blessings of peace." — 1865.

Six millions of households gathered together on the last Thursday in November, 1865, uniting as one great family Republic, whose States and Territories were all enjoying this American festival of Thanksgiving Day. Is not this a spectacle to move the Old World with admiration and respect for the domestic, social, and religious characteristics of the American nation, as well as to impress the idea of an invincible moral power in our political institutions?

Archimedes, with all his mechanical genius and knowledge, was ignorant as a wild Arab of human power in its moral influences. He wanted a *place* to stand upon, and plant his machine, before he could begin to move the world. But this was more than two hundred years before Christ was born. When "God sent forth His Son, made of a woman," the power of moral ideas was revealed; and American men have learned how to use them. Take a newspaper or book as an engine, place it in the homes of the people; let its weapons be truth, love, goodness, usefulness; and the world will not only move, but go on in the right way.

Women, too, have their part in this beneficent sway of moral power. A woman may sit in her own quiet room, and, by her love, that brightens the homes of earth, and her faith, that lifts up human hearts to the hope of their heavenly home, she may send out influences that will not only make the world better and happier, but also help it to rise upward in its onward progress.

Yes: we have many sins as a people, and faults enough as individuals; but, while we make humble confession to God of our sins, and extol his goodness as infinite, and pray to Him for the gift of holiness, our civilization is purified by love of the divine, and exalted by faith in the good: thus our country, as compared with old Rome, is a living proof of the truth of God's word, that, "righteousness exalteth a nation; but sin is a reproach to any people."

Probably we have all seen some picture or representation that brought before the eye, as well as the mind, that tender scene in Bethlehem, "the babe in the manger," or in the arms of his loving mother; while Joseph, the "just man," kept watch over his "holy family." Can you not recall that lowly scene, and its influence on your heart? But did you think of the wonderful changes which that "babe," by His words and deeds as the Christ, has wrought in the condition of men and women? Did you think, that, to this source we must look for all the blessed privileges we enjoy as a nation? American institutions are founded on Christ's Gospel of "peace on earth, and good will to men." It is this influence which has made our land the home of the homeless and poor of all nations, — these people come to live with us because the brotherhood of mankind is the basis of our nationality.

In this way, the United States has won the position Rome had forfeited by her injustice, cruelties, and sins, and which she lost when moral truth was exalted above material force. In eighty years, the sway of Gospel Love has wrought out and built up an empire on this new continent, that, for its power to do good, is as far above the empire which the Romans had reached in seven hundred years as heaven is above earth.

This is only the worldly view of Christ's ministry of love in its national influences. The blessings it has brought to individual life, — family enjoyments, social happiness, and human improvement, — are as much beyond our powers of computation as the round of the universe was beyond the apple that made Newton search for truth.

Lord Bacon, in his " Bible Thoughts," says, —

"The spirit of Jesus is the spirit of a dove. No miracle of His is to be found to have been of judgment or revenge, but all of goodness and mercy, and respecting *man's body ;* for, as touching riches, He did not vouchsafe to any miracle, save only that tribute might be given to Cæsar."

So also, in the words of Christ, the rules and precepts he gave are, in a large measure, intended to regulate life, and its morals and manners, in this world. The gentle-

2

man or lady who will conform their conduct to this perfect pattern of "good will" needs few other rules for the "etiquette of good society." They would need none, were we what we profess to be, — a Christian nation.

One part of my plan is to set forth the "customs and manners of good society." There are in the words of Christ seven precepts for the guidance of life, which Americans should hold as rules of conduct and character. Let us call these *the Gospel etiquette of love and duty.*

1. "Judge not, that ye be not judged."

2. "Love thy neighbor as thyself."

3. "Do unto others as you would they should do unto you."

4. "Give to him that asketh of thee; and, from him who would borrow of thee, turn not thou away."

5. "A man shall leave his father and mother, and cleave to his wife; and they twain shall be one flesh: what therefore God hath joined together let not man put asunder."

6. "Suffer little children to come unto me."

7. "Render to Cæsar the things that are Cæsar's, and unto God the things that are God's."

In these seven rules are set forth the charter of our national privileges, and the sum of our individual duties. We read, in these precepts of Divine Wisdom, the charities that sustain brotherhood, and the amenities that make society a pleasure; the sweet and sacred sympathies of married life; the tender loves of home, and the true culture of childhood; the freedom of private judgment, with obedience to established law; the home, the world, the state, and the worship of the true God, are all drawn into the circle of love and peace.

—

II.—HOME.

The first sure symptoms of a mind in health
Is rest of heart, and pleasure felt at home.
Young's Night Thoughts.

Let me live amongst high thoughts, and smiles
As beautiful as love; with grasping hands,
And a heart that flutters with diviner life,
Whene'er my step is heard.
Procter's Mirandola.

HOME! Where in our language shall we find a word of four letters that stirs all the sweet pulses of life like this of home,— Our Home?

Perhaps you think of love, the master-passion, as it has been styled, of human nature.

But human love owes its beginning and its perfection to its precursor,— *home.* Eden, the divinely prepared abode of the first of our race, was planted before woman was created: with her came love.

The home for the bride was made, and adorned with all the wealth of nature's loveliness, before the Lord God.

drew out, from the *carbon* of *man's* flesh and bones, the pure diamond of feminine purity and beauty, and light of moral perfectness, which he enshrined in the form of *woman.*

This wonderful history of the first home and the first love should be carefully studied by all who wish to apprehend the real glory of human nature, which it is my purpose to set forth in this *Home Book.*

Pray do not quote from Milton. His "Paradise Lost," in regard to the temptation and fall, is fabulous as the story of Proserpine. So we will take the Book of books.

As the Bible is, I trust, in the homes of all where "manners and morals" are cultivated, there is no need that I should quote, as my readers will prefer to look over the sacred text. Pray examine the first three chapters of Genesis carefully. The particular history of the human creation is in the second chapter. You cannot fail to observe that there were care and preparation in the forming of woman which were not bestowed on man.

Why was this recorded, if not to teach us that the wife was of finer mould, and destined to the more spiritual uses, — the heart of humanity, as her husband was the head? She was the last work of creation. Every step, from matter to man, had been in the ascending scale. Woman was the crown of all. Was this last step downward?

It must have been, unless woman was superior in those qualities which raise human nature above animal life, — the link which pressed nearest to the angelic, and drew more delicate beauty and holier power from the spiritual life.

Does it not mark the better nature of woman, that, after the fall even, when she was placed under the control of her husband, she yet held their immortal destiny in her keeping? For her the gracious words of consolation were spoken; to her the promised Seed was given: not a ray of hope can be found in the destiny of the man, save through the hope given to the woman.

Thus they stood together, when, after their sorrowful "fall," they were driven forth from Eden, and sent,— Adam to till the ground, "cursed for his sake" or sin; Eve to become "the mother of all living."

.   .   .   .

And now they have their own *home* to make, their own earthly happiness to secure. Can these blessings be attained in any other way than by obedience to the laws of God? In the plan of redemption, as shadowed forth in that sentence of punishment for their first sin of disobedience, the divine Judge seems to have fixed the human duties thus:—

Man is the worker or provider, the protector and the law-giver; woman is the preserver, the teacher or inspirer, and the exemplar.

Under these laws, Adam, sole sovereign of earth, chose the little plot of ground that was to be their home, where love, in the guise and graces of Eve, would, by her smiles and gentleness, make his hard tasks pleasant for her sake, and, by her goodness and her faith in God, she would draw him from the dark power of the evil Tempter into the sunshine of heavenly love. And thus they would seek to renew the joys of their lost Eden. They would gather into their new garden all the wild flowers of earth, that were like those around their bridal bower. They would drive to their home all the gentle animals; and sweet singing birds would still come at the soft call of the loving mother, who had faith that her first-born son was " a man from the Lord."

But sin was at the door, and the first-born of humanity yielded himself to the evil. From that second fall, there seemed no recovery; when the homes of the sons of God were given up to the pollutions of sin, there was no hope.

You have read, in the sixth, seventh, and eighth chapters of Genesis, the terrible results of this universal wickedness. The flood, which left its history etched over the whole earth, swept the sinners, and the evidences of their sins, into the great deeps: there sixteen centuries lie buried.

.   .   .   .

When Noah, the only righteous man in his generation, and his family, came forth from the ark to re-people the world, then the Eden laws were re-established in all their holiness and purity. The worship of the living and true God, that leads mankind to heaven; the purity of the true marriage, that, in its love and faithfulness, makes the true home, — were both restored. Those four couples held the happiness of the world in their keeping. Each husband and wife had their home to make; not only for their own family, but for their race. Did they do it?

The first act of Noah, when he builded an altar unto the Lord, established the true worship. So also was true marriage, one man with one woman, which only can make the true home, established in all its laws of purity and faithfulness.

Those saved in the ark knew these laws of God: they knew that the Old World had perished for the sins of transgression. Did they not, while looking from Ararat on the wide New World before them, purpose in their hearts to keep these Eden laws, as the only conditions under which they could expect God's blessings of peace, prosperity, and happiness? Did they obey?

.   .   .   .

Stand here with me on this rock, — Plymouth Rock! It is the 22d of December, 1620, two centuries and a half ago. "The sea around is dark with storms, and white the shore with snow." What shall we see?

> "A sail! a sail! o'er yonder wave
>   A freighted bark is sweeping on!
> Land of the learned, the proud, the brave,
>   Mourn'st thou no treasure gone?
> Thou Island Empire, forth from thee,
>   Like Wisdom from the Thunderer's brow,
> Sprung the bright form of Liberty;
> And high-souled men have joined her train,
> Nor fagot's blaze, nor dungeon's chain,
>   Can their firm purpose bow.

They would have held the guarded Pass,
Or shared thy doom, Leonidas,
   Had Faith and Freedom cheered them on.
They come, that Pilgrim band, they come!
This lone land is their chosen home,
   And this New World is won!

.   .   .   .

Do you not perceive a striking similitude between the family on Mount Ararat and the Pilgrim band in the "Mayflower"?

Both had knowledge of the true God and of his laws; and they also had faith in Him. Both were beginning life anew, under like necessities of working to subdue a wild, uncultivated world; and both had those two institutions from Eden — the true marriage and the true home — which only can insure the well-being and improvement of mankind.

Forty-two centuries have gone by since that family from the ark — representing all the families, tribes, and races of mankind — went forth to found their homes and empires. What is the result?

But one race retains the Eden laws of love and home; and in that race only is the faith and worship of the true God. From that race were the families that settled and made our American people. In two centuries and a half, this North-American empire has gained power and place in the great family of nations: compared with her, those old cradles of civilization and centres of knowledge and glory — Asia and Africa — are now only blanks in the lot of humanity.

III.—FOOD.

"ALL the labor of man is for his mouth," says Solomon.

This must mean that the chief aim and purpose of human labor is to make home the place of family enjoyment.

Food is the first requirement of life : it must be had, or we cannot live. It therefore becomes the most pressing necessity of our daily cares; and this want, like all wants for which our wearisome work must be done, comes upon us by the *Fall.*

How we miss our Eden, where the love of God had provided "every tree that was pleasant to the sight and good for food," and given all these for the joy and refreshment of his human children!

"Behold, I have given you every herb bearing seed which is upon the face of all the earth, and every tree in the which is the fruit of a tree yielding seed; to you it shall be for meat," — was the word of God to Adam.

There is nothing in the Bible to show that any other diet was used among those long-lived people, the antediluvians. But this vegetable food did not seem to nourish the whole nature of human beings. The physical propensities must have had an almost overwhelming dominion, and the development of the intellectual powers must have been used to gratify the base animal passions of lust and selfishness: "the whole earth was filled with violence, and the imaginations of men's hearts were only evil, and that continually." The moral sentiments seem scarcely to have been cultivated at all.

And do not similar characteristics — that is, the predominance of animal propensities over moral sentiments — mark even now, in a striking degree, the people of those tribes and nations, where, either from climate, custom, or condition, the mass of the families live on vegetable food?

Have you ever considered the effect of those two important changes in the human condition made after the Flood? One of these was the shortening of man's life; the other, that of eating flesh-meat. I shall refer to the first in a future number. Now let us look into this matter of food.

When, after the destruction of the old world, Noah and his family came forth from the ark, and God promised, that, while earth continued, the race of man should not be again thus destroyed, what new agent of human improvement and civilization was brought to the aid of mankind?

We are told of none, except the change in their diet, — the permission, or rather the command, that Noah and his descendants should eat animal food. Thus it runs: —

" Every moving thing that liveth shall be meat for
you: even as the green herb have I given you all things.
But flesh with the life thereof, which is the blood thereof, ye shall not eat."

Such was the Creator's law, when he had determined
that the character and condition of his rational creatures
should go on till the end of time improving in the arts of
life, in dominion over the earth, and in their knowledge of
Him and His laws.

Here we may remark, that the tribe or nation which vio-
lates the express command of God, *to separate the flesh
from the blood, and not to use the latter, but eats raw
meat*, never improves in character or condition. In truth,
the command *includes* the rudiments of domestic cook-
ery, — the preparation of food by the aid of fire: till this
is the constant habit of communities, they are not civilized.

Another important truth should be noted. Since the
appointment of flesh-meats as a part of human food, no
instance is recorded of its having been prohibited by divine authority. In the Bible, intoxicating drinks were forbidden to certain individuals; and drunkenness is among
the sins of men: but from the time that righteous Abraham dressed a calf to entertain his angel-visitors, till the
coming of John, " whose meat was locusts and wild hon-
ey," no servant of God has been confined to a vegetable
diet. The great prophet who was fed by the express
command of the Lord, had "bread and flesh" twice each
day.

In strict accordance with this divine law, which makes a portion of animal food necessary to develop and sustain the human constitution in its most perfect state of physical, intellectual, and moral beauty, strength, and perfectness, we know that the races of mankind are now to be seen. In every country where a " mixed diet " is habitually used, as in the temperate climates, there the greatest improvements are found, and the best energies of character developed. It is that portion of the human family who have the means of obtaining this food at least once a day who now hold dominion over the world. A hundred thousand of the beef-fed British govern and control a hundred millions of the rice-eating nations of Asia.

In our own country, the beneficial effects of a generous diet, in developing and sustaining the energies of the people, are clearly evident. The severe and great labors of every kind which were required to subdue and obtain dominion over this wide wilderness world would not have been done by a half-fed, vegetable-eating people. A larger quantity and better quality of food were necessary here than would have supplied men in the old countries, where less action of body and of mind is permitted.

Still there is great danger of excess in all indulgences of the appetites, even when a present benefit may be obtained. This danger should never be forgotten. The tendency in our country has been to excess in animal food.

The advocates of "*a vegetable-diet system*" had good

cause to object that too much meat was used; that it was given to infants before they had teeth, and eaten too freely by the sedentary and the idlers. To increase the danger, it is often eaten in a half-cooked state, and swallowed without sufficient chewing. All these things are wrong, and should be reformed.

But, as the spirit of inquiry is abroad, searching out abuses of all kinds, let us hope that the abuses of the good things God has so bounteously dealt out to us as a people may be reformed.

When women are well instructed in physiology, and in the natural laws which govern the health of humanity, and also are taught to understand chemistry and botany in their application to domestic science and family uses, then we may expect that desideratum of Dr. Johnson, — "A Cookery-book on Philosophical Principles."

This philosophy would teach us that " *bread is the staff of life,*" and that *flesh-meats* are indispensable to the perfecting of human life in its best energies, because God has specially appointed these for human food.

We may, then, state, as an established truth in physiology, that man is *omnivorous*, or constituted to eat the four kinds of food — vegetables, fruits, flesh, and fish — which, separately, nourish other living creatures. The human teeth are formed to masticate, and the stomach to digest, this variety of substances. Man can eat and digest these in a raw state: but it is necessary to the health and improvement of human beings that food should be prepared by cooking; that is, by the aid of fire and water. Such is the evidence of nature to the suitableness of a mixed diet for mankind.

Some determined advocates of the "vegetable system" maintain that the teeth and stomach of the monkey correspond, in structure, very closely with those of man; yet it lives on fruits and vegetables. Therefore, if man followed nature, he, too, would live on fruits and vegetables.

But, although the anatomical likeness between man and the monkey is striking, it is not identical and complete. The difference seems to be precisely that which makes a difference of diet indispensable to nourish and develop, in the most perfect manner, the dissimilar animal natures.

Would not those people who live as the monkeys do be most likely to resemble monkeys?

It may be well to consider these matters, when grave philosophers are putting forth learned theories to prove that all human beings are but developments from the oyster, the ape, and the gorilla.

Such foolish theories may become popular in the Old World of nations; but "we, the people of the United States of North America" (as our national title runs), will hold fast to our royalty of race. This dates from Eden, and claims full sovereignty over the earth (which human labor and skill have subdued), by and through the divine charter of Bible truth; and also we thus hold "dominion over the fish of the sea, and over the fowl of the air, and over every living thing that moveth upon the earth."

IV. — LANGUAGE.

TALKING is so very easy, that we are hardly conscious what a wonderful gift language is to the human race. How did we come by it? is the question now being seriously discussed by the new "Science of Language."

I shall give the opinion of one of England's most eminent scholars,* and a large contributor to sacred and secular literature, as the reply that seems to me fully sustained by reason, and corroborated by Scripture.

"The true answer to the inquiry how language arose is this, that God gave man language, just as he gave him reason (for what is man's word but his reason coming forth to behold itself?); that he gave him language, because he could not be man, that is, a social being, without it.

"Yet this must not be taken to affirm that man started at first with a full-formed vocabulary of words; as it were, with his first dictionary and first grammar ready-made to his hands. He did not thus begin the world with names, but with the *power of naming;* for man is not a mere speaking machine. God did not teach him words, as one of us teaches a parrot, from without; but gave

* Richard Chenevix Trench, R.A., now the Archbishop of Dublin.

him a capacity, and then evoked the capacity which he gave him.

"Here, as in every thing that concerns the primitive constitution, the great original institutes of humanity, our best and truest lights are to be gotten from the study of the *first three chapters of Genesis;* and you will observe that there it is not God who interposed the first names of the creatures, but Adam, — Adam, however, at the direct suggestion of the Creator. He brought them all, we are told, to Adam, 'to see what he would call them; and whatsoever Adam called every living creature, that was the name thereof.' — Gen. ii. 19.

"Here we have the clearest information of the origin, at once divine and human, of speech; while yet neither is so brought forward as to exclude or obscure the other.

.   .   .   .

"*How* this latent power evolved itself first, how this spontaneous generation of language came to pass, is a mystery, even as every act of creation is of necessity a mystery; and, as such, all the deepest inquirers are content to leave it.

"Yet we may, perhaps, help ourselves a little to the realizing of what the process was, and what it was not, if we liken it to the growth of a tree springing out of and unfolding itself from a root, and according to a necessary law, — that root being the divine capacity of language, with which man was created; that law being the law of highest reason, with which he was endowed, —

if we liken it to this, rather than to the rearing of a house, which a man should slowly and painfully fashion for himself with dead timbers combined after his own fancy and caprice, and which, little by little, improved in shape, material, and size, being first a log-house, answering his barest needs, and only after centuries of toil and pain growing for his son's sons into a stately palace of pleasure and delight.

. . . .

"Nor does what has been said of the manner in which language enriches itself contradict a prior assertion, that man starts with language as God's perfect gift, which he only impairs and forfeits by sloth and sin, according to the same law that holds good in respect to each other of the gifts of Heaven." (See "The Study of Words," pages 24, 25, 26.)

The distinguished philologist Max Müller, in his "Lectures on the Science of Language," says, —

"What is it that man can do, and of which we find no signs, no rudiments, in the whole brute world? I answer, without hesitation, the one great barrier between the brute and the man is language. Man speaks; no brute has ever uttered a word. Language is our Rubicon, and no brute will ever dare to cross it," &c.

In another portion of his masterly work, Max Müller

3

thus shows how language has gained its greatest triumphs : —

"The idea of mankind as one family, as the children
of one God, is an idea of Christian growth. I date the
real beginning of the science of language from the first
day of Pentecost. After that day of cloven tongues, a
new light is spreading over the world. . . .

"The pioneers of our science were those very apostles
who were commanded to 'Go into all the world, and
preach the gospel to every creature;' and their true
successors the missionaries of the whole Christian Church.
Translations of the Lord's Prayer, or of the Bible, into
every dialect of the world, form even now the most valuable materials for the comparative philologist."

The science of language may seem a difficult study for
our readers; but, in reality, it is only a correct knowledge
of the true meaning of the words we are using every day:
the best manner of using these words will soon follow.

A knowledge of words will not, to be sure, give ideas,
if the power of thought is deficient or uncultivated; but
the study of correctness is a great help to mental activity.
This correctness is among the earliest lessons to be taught
the child; and, as women are the first teachers of every
human being, it follows that women must be well instructed in their own language, or the people will not
speak it correctly.

The great mistake of men, Christian as well as heathen,

when legislating for the benefit of civilization and moral improvement, is, that they have devoted their care and means chiefly for the education of boys and men. So they legislate as if men could be wise while women were left in ignorance!

Never, till woman, in her own home-circle, becomes the accomplished arbitress of the best words for the best thoughts, will our own Anglo-Saxon language become purified and perfected as the *one tongue*, that is, the true Bible expositor of social enjoyment, of moral sentiments, and of religious faith in the Christian world.

. . . .

In the work from which we have quoted (Trench on "The Study of Words"), the following striking ideas are put forth : —

"Is man of a divine birth and stock, coming from God, and, when he fulfils the law and intention of his being, returning to him again? We need no more than his language to prove it.

. . . .

"But has man fallen, and deeply fallen, from the heights of his original creation? We need no more than his language to prove it. Like every thing else about him, it bears at once the stamp of his greatness and of his degradation, of his glory and of his shame. What dark and sombre threads he must have woven into the tissue of his life, before we could trace such dark ones running through his language!

" How else shall we explain the long catalogue of words having all to do with sin or with sorrow or with both?

" It is a melancholy thing to observe how much richer is every vocabulary in words that set forth sins, than in those that set forth graces."

.   .   .   .

In treating of "the distinction of words," the author has some ideas on education that should be heeded : —

" There is no such fruitful source of confusion and mischief as this : two words are tacitly assumed as equivalent, and therefore exchangeable; and then that which may be assumed of one is assumed also of the other, of which it is not true.

" Thus, for instance, it often is with 'instruction' and 'education.'

" Can we not 'instruct' a child? it is asked; can we not teach it geography and arithmetic or grammar quite independently of the catechism, or even the Scriptures?

" No doubt you may; but can you 'educate' without bringing moral and spiritual forces to bear upon the mind and affections of the child? 'Education' must educe, being from 'educare,' which is but another form of 'educere;' and that is 'to draw out,' and not 'to put in.' To draw out what is in the child, the immortal spirit which is there, this is the end of education; and so much the word declares. 'The putting in' is, indeed, most needful; that is, the child must be 'instructed,' as well as 'educated,' — and the word instruction just means furnishing, — but not instructed instead of educated."

.   .   .   .

This use of two words as equivalents, when their meaning is not the same, has had an injurious influence on our language in another instance: the practice of using the term "female" as a synonym for "woman" is vulgarizing our style of writing and our mode of speech.

This serious error it has been our aim, for a number of years, to correct, if possible, by the influences of the "Lady's Book." There is a great improvement already observable in this matter of "restoring" the name of woman to its Eden significance and glory, and there seems no doubt of the result. In some future number, I shall go over the history of this error in our noble language; now I will give the following letter, which came to me as editress of the "Lady's Book."

THE IMPORTANCE OF WORDS.

"My dear Mrs. Hale, — The terms *male* and *female* are best confined to the distinction of sex, as they are used by the translators of the Bible, — men whose English cannot be improved in force, or directness of meaning. When they wish to speak substantively of the feminine half of creation, they say *woman*. When they speak of animated nature as a creation, 'male and female created he them.' That is, male and female of all animals; but, when human beings are spoken of, it is man and woman. If you say, 'I saw a female in the field,' how can we know whether you mean a cow, a hen, a mare, or any other creature of female sex? 'An elegant female' may be a pea-hen, which is certainly very elegant. "A distressed female" may be a cat hunted by boys. What is the use of this obscurity? Why not say hen, if you mean the bird; cat, if you mean the beast; and woman, if you mean your mother, your sister, your friend?

"This vulgarity, like many others, has, through haste or negligence, crept into newspapers; from these, spread into the books and the language of half-educated persons, who have never lived in good company, and who want taste. Everybody knows the slippery ease of a descent into what is wrong. People who ought to know what is right in style, but who are careless, and fond of new diction, allow themselves to adopt slang and erroneous words: they communicate these faults to the atmosphere that surrounds them. Thus the 'pure well of English' is 'defiled' by solecisms and tasteless corruptions, which, if not arrested, take from our literature and our conversation all point, spirit, and propriety."

V.—CLOTHING.

I am the same, without all diff'rence : when
You saw me last, I was as rich, as good;
Have no additions since of name or blood;
Only because I wore a thread-bare suit,
I was not worthy of a poor salute.
A few good clothes, put on with small ado,
Purchase your knowledge and your kindred too.
Heywood's Royal King.

HOW came the art of dress to be considered a silly, trifling matter, when God's word so clearly reveals its high import? Heaven and earth were united in the discovery and application of this art, — the first under the sun.

The merciful Creator acted in concert with his "fallen" children: while Adam and Eve sought to make only a covering for their shame of sin, revealed to them in their nakedness, their heavenly Father made them clothing that typified his pitying love; thus He gave to their race the hope of salvation, through being clothed upon by the righteousness of Christ.

Dress, then, is something more than necessity of climate, something better than condition of comfort, something higher than elegance of civilization. Dress is the index of conscience, the evidence of our emotional nature. It reveals, more clearly than speech expresses, the inner life of heart and soul in a people, and also the tendencies of individual character.

Dress also shows the progress of man in his destiny of subduing the earth; it shows his duty to love and serve God, " from whom cometh every good and perfect gift," not only in material things, but in the invention, taste, and genius of the human mind: thus man has capacities for finding out the hidden treasures of nature, and fashioning these for the use, the enjoyment, and the ornament of humanity.

A popular British writer gives the following remarkable illustrations on " The Importance of Clothing: " —

" A life without clothes, not to mention other inconveniencies, would, we verily believe, be a life without thought. In fact, since the first garment of all, clothes have been knowledge, influence, and expression, and house and home to the wearer. Deep and fanciful minds have speculated on existence, and how they can arrive at the certainty of it in their own person; but they would never have attained to the power of constructing theories, working out problems, reasoning upon their being at all, but for the cultivating, educating, convincing instruction and logic of their clothes.

" It is fundamentally unreasonable, and a mistake in a sculptor of any age, to represent a philosopher as even partially undressed. 'I think, therefore I am,' is the conclusion of adult reason; the baby has leaped to a similar conclusion forty years sooner: 'I have shoes and a red sash, therefore I am.' People will call this infant dis-

covery vanity, because they do not know what else to
call it, *and it seems always safe to attribute human action
to some weak or bad motive;* but our instinct serves us
better than received opinion.

"The chord struck by this smiling, prettily-expressed,
pointedly-enforced argument is one of fellowship; we like
to see the child's pleasure in his movable skin, because
we recognize an act of recognition of himself as a distinct,
separate member and sharer of form, life, and thought.
'Yes, I am here,' he seems to say; 'I have something
which belongs to me.' It is a consciousness of adjuncts,
attributes, belongings, without which no sort of existence
can be understood.

"And not only does dress first awaken to the infant
thought the idea of separate existence and consciousness,
but it continues, with vast numbers, the medium by
which they realize their part and ownership in visible
things. It is this feature of dress, as property, estate,
possession, and, consequently, ambition, which is not recognized by the moralist. With the young, dress is almost
the only thing they can call their own; with the great
majority of women, it includes all to which they can ever,
in strict truth, apply the potent, influential, entrancing
words, 'my' and 'mine.'

. . . .

"All general considerations of dress must, however,
converge towards feminine costume. When we think of
dress in the abstract, we mean woman's dress, whatever

has been in the world's youth, in our time her costume represents the art.

"Weak and trivial as the subject is deemed, and frivolous as many phases of it undoubtedly are, yet fashion has some mysterious connection with thought and intellect, so close and intimate as to render it almost the type of progress.

"Wherever thought is free, there fashion works its changes, and carries out its constant war and its constant victory over habit and custom. Where thought is stagnant and tied down, there fashion finds no place. Where men think in the same groove for centuries, and the son inherits every opinion and prejudice of the father, there the costume of a country remains inexorably the same, and the children succeed to the paternal and the maternal wardrobe, without need to alter a fold or substitute a color. And this must be borne in mind when we hear accounts of the ludicrous sway of fashion under all but impossible circumstances.

.   .   .   .

"When the Kaffir girl, who has only just submitted to the bondage of petticoats, insists on distending her solitary garment with a hoop, we augur better things for the progress and civilization of her countrymen than if she clung with fanatical perseverance to the unchanging blanket of a long line of progenitors. Where we can introduce European fashions, we have a better chance of introducing European modes of thought in all their variety and activity. The sameness of Oriental dress, and the endless change and variety in the West, figure forth all the mighty differences which have set the West above the East.

. . . .

"Uninspired wisdom has always been hard upon fine clothes, and we think, as regarding dress from a narrow and prejudiced point of view, takes a different line towards it than we can detect in Scripture, which surely recognizes attire as the fit natural exponent of rank, condition, and character. It is a case for fair liberty of private judgment.

"There is no necessary connection between a bit of bright color — that delightful scarlet that lightens up the landscape — and vanity. If a woman will mainly seek to please father and mother, brothers, sisters, friends, lover, or husband, she will not be too gay or pleasant to look upon for her own well-being and best interests, however bright, pretty, or charming she may make herself by adorning herself in modest apparel under the teaching of a refined and cultivated taste."

I have given these excellent ideas and opinions to show that *one* masculine mind has looked on the art of dress from the standpoint of a philosopher and a Christian. From my heart I thank the writer, who has, no doubt, unconsciously answered some of a series of questions on this subject of womanly attire, which, as editress of the

"Lady's Book," I put forth in that journal some years ago. Now I will ask my readers, who, I am sure, are my friends, to examine these questions.

1. Are the mothers of men who rule the world found among the *loose-robed* women, or among the women who dress in closer-fitting apparel?

2. Is there not the greatest improvement of the human race where the fashions of dress are most subject to change?

3. Can a people who go naked, or only half-covered, be Christian, or ever become Christianized, unless they clothe themselves?

4. Are not those nations most morally refined in civilization and Christianity where the costume of men and women differs most essentially?

The Bible has lessons of true wisdom on dress: I shall refer to this teaching in some future paper. In the mean time, my readers may find, in the philosophy of the British scholar, some new ideas, that are not to be lightly treated.

Like all the arrangements of a wise Providence, this universal desire to be comely in one another's eyes is, under proper regulation, the source of much that is useful, valuable, and commendable. It prompts ingenuity and promotes industry; comfortable homes are made, families brought up, and public prosperity increased, by this ceaseless ministration to the personal adornment which so thoroughly pervades civilized life, — the art of dress, uniting both as cause and consequence of this civilization.

A home where the decencies and the prettinesses of the toilet are put by as of no account can neither be comfortable nor Christian. The first necessities of outward adornment are cleanliness and neatness, and these are needed for health as well as beauty. To be well dressed does not mean to be expensively arrayed. Form, colors, adaptation are far more important than costliness.

We would have every woman study how she can, in accordance with modesty, discretion, and duty, present the most pleasing personal appearance. Let her discrimination and taste be exercised in the choice of colors that become her, and in styles that best suit her face, her age, and her fortune. A woman who is, either from indolence or indifference, careless about her own personal apparel will not be apt to make her own home pleasant. She must dress for her husband as she would have done for her lover, and be as agreeable as possible in her own house, and with her nearest and dearest friends. The true lady at home is the lady everywhere.

Some good people, sensible and right in most things, have such a desire to crush out all vanities, that they would subvert all taste in dress and decoration.

Have they counted the cost of their reform? Would

it not be somewhat in the style of Dean Swift, who advised the man " to cut off his feet to save the cost of his shoe-leather?"

VI.—RECREATION.

IT is one thing to indulge in playful rest, and another to be devoted to the pursuit of pleasure. Gayety of heart, during the relaxation of labor, and quickened by satisfaction in the accomplished duty or perfected result, is altogether compatible with, nay, even in some sort arises out of, a deep internal seriousness of disposition."

Thus wisely writes the great art-critic of Englishmen, John Ruskin, on the subject of recreation.

Probably most persons will agree in the general scope of these opinions, that recreations or amusements, as we usually term these seasons of innocent enjoyment, are needed in our homes, if we would make them the places of family happiness and domestic confidence and love.

But when we come to the particular modes of expressing this "gayety of heart," which all Christians would tolerate, if not encourage, there arise differences of opinion among good people, — differences so wide in regard to one particular amusement, that the character of our civilization seems to be seriously influenced, and not for the better, by these discordant views.

Is there no way of finding out what sort of recreations and amusements are best suited to the nature of human beings, and, therefore, good for us?

Did the wise Creator, who made all things good, provide for the expression of this "gayety of heart" in his human children? Did He give them any fitting means of or for what we call amusements?

If He did, are not such recreations good and innocent?

In the preceding papers, on love, home, food, language, and clothing, all these things are found to have originated in Eden. What could be lacking, that was needed for human happiness, to the perfected man and woman "made in the image of God"?

"In the cool of the day," they felt the divine presence in the garden, and heard the voice of God. Eden was thus made the open door of heaven to the minds of Adam and Eve, who must have responded to the divine love and goodness. This was their instruction.

For their joys of home and social life, they had always the companionship of each other. They were one in heart and in will, as well as in flesh and bones. Adam says of Eve, she was given "to be with me."

For employments, they had the study of animated nature, and the care of the garden, from which they gathered daily food.

For amusements, there were displayed the perfected

beauties of Nature to please the eye, while the harmonies of creation gave the exquisite pleasures of sound and of motion.

Thus we are taught what care had been taken to provide, not only food to delight the human taste, but excitement and gratification for all the senses in the enjoyments of their Eden home.

These good gifts of the wise Creator were, with one exception, continued to our race, even after the fall.

The loss was the priceless privilege of primeval man in the felt presence of divinity, and the known voice of God; this, forfeited by disobedience, was lost to our fallen nature; neither man nor woman can now know the Father, save through the Christ.

But the other good gifts of the Creator, although shadowed by sin and the cares of the outward world, where the exiles from Eden were doomed to work and weep, were not taken away; all are now in the possession of mankind.

Every married pair, who will obey the divine laws of nature and of revelation, can now rejoice in these blessings, bestowed even through all the losses, sorrows, wants, perversions, and crimes which sin and death have brought into the world.

Still the blessings of love, home, food, language, and clothing are the arrangements of Providence, which God gives us as surely as He gives us air, water, warmth, and light.

And thus, also, He provides for our recreations. The pleasures of sight, of sound, and of motion are everywhere to be enjoyed. But, instead of heavenly harmony, as "when the morning stars sang together," musical instruments, the inventions of men, must be used, and the human voice trained to the harmonies of melody and song.

There are two natural sources of enjoyment or recreation, — one from sound and one from motion, — which seem meant, like language and clothing, to do us good and not evil.

These two enjoyments are named together in the Bible; both are there used as aids in religious ceremonies, and in festivals of innocent joy and rejoicing; neither is, in any way, censured or forbidden; therefore, neither can be evil in its natural tendency, any more than walking or talking is evil.

Both of these recreations might be made of great use in promoting health, cheerfulness, and happiness in the home-circle. Shall we have these as our family amusements? Shall we have music and dancing?

Concerning the first, there will be no question. Music is the art of all arts in its sweet and refining influences on humanity. And although, among our American people, it will never have the political power which Plato affirmed of it in Greece, when he said that "no change can be

4

made in music without affecting the constitution of the
State" (an opinion in which Aristotle acquiesced, and
Cicero afterwards adopted), yet, if wisely cultivated in
our own homes, it would aid much in making good citizens to support and adorn our country.

Let all families in our land consider musical instruction
for their children as one of the "must haves;" and train
them to the practice. The love of song, and the manner
in which this divine gift of discriminating the harmonies
of sound are cultivated or neglected, will have abiding
effect on the happiness of home-life, and the character of
our people.

An able writer has well said, "The infant's eye is aim-
less for a season; but its ear is alert from the beginning.
It enters upon life with a cry; and its first sorrow,
expressed in a sound, is soothed by the first sound of its
mother's voice. One-half of the time of the nurse is
spent in singing; and baby, when not sleeping or drink-
ing, is either making or hearing music.

"Now is it not a thing to be deeply lamented, that the
sensitive ears with which almost every one has been
gifted by God are so little educated, that they might as
well be stuffed with cotton or plugged with lead, for any
good use we make of them?

"To be sure we keep them sufficiently open to hear all
the gossip about us, and can most of us tell when the
cannons are firing; but, as for training them to that
exquisite sense of melody or harmony of which they are
susceptible, how few do it!"

Music forms the universal language which, when all other languages were confounded, the confusion of Babel left unconfounded. The white man and the black man, the red man and the yellow man, can sing together, however difficult they may find it to talk to each other. And both sexes and all ages may thus express their emotions simultaneously; for, in virtue of the power of the ear to distinguish, side by side, those differing but concordant notes which make up harmony, there is not only room but demand for all the qualities of voice which childhood, adolescence, maturity, and old age supply.

If this apply to earthly music, how much more to heavenly! Though every thing else in the future may be dim and dark, and in all respects matter of faith and hope, not of vivid realization, this, at least, can be entered into, that all children of Adam and Eve could unite in the common song of salvation and glory to God.

Of all the organs of the body, therefore, the ear is the one which, though, for its present gratification, it is beholden solely to the passing moments, can, with the greatest confidence, anticipate a wider domain in the hereafter. And the taste for musical cultivation, if wisely improved and made the means of family order, devotion, and cheerfulness, may be a source of moral and spiritual culture and enjoyment, as well as the means of pleasant and healthful recreations in our home-life.

Dancing will be considered in another part.

VII. — THE HOME SUNDAY.

> " Glory to the glorious One,
> Good and great, our God alone:
> He this day hath sanctified,
> First and best of all beside,
> Making it for every clime,
> Of all times the sweetest time."

AND God blessed the seventh day, and sanctified **it**; because that in it He had rested from all his **work** which God created and made. — Gen. ii. 3.

The infinite wisdom and goodness of the Creator are wonderfully displayed in all his works; but the divine love and fatherly care towards the human beings He had formed are most tenderly manifested in the appointment of this day of rest. The poet has rightly described it as the first, the best, and sweetest of all time.

It was made for man. The brute creation have no part in this rest, except as they are subjected to the will and service of men. It is the good gift of God to his human children. This privilege of one-seventh portion of time, free from the tasks of labor, what a boon it is to hard-working people! How they should bless God, who gave this day of rest!

And this law came to us from Eden, and through the testimony of the Bible: all that is good comes from God.

Like all His best blessings, it has a sanctifying influence on the enjoyments of the home-circle. It is a real domestic festival; on this, "the Lord's Day," when the six days of work are over, fathers, husbands, sons, and brothers have the full freedom of home, and its security of a day of rest.

It seems to me that women have never considered, sufficiently, the importance of this day to their own happiness, and to their opportunities of doing good. Moral culture gives to woman her highest intellectual dignity. She never applies her reason to mechanical pursuits. It is the world of human life she should move and model and perfect.

What opportunities these stated days of rest at home present to the wife and mother! The whole family are then brought under the sweet, persuasive feminine influence which, like the power of gravitation, works unseen but irresistibly over the hearts and consciences of men.

How to make the day of rest one of the best blessings of domestic life, I shall discuss in some of these Sunday numbers; now I have a few graphic pictures of its capabilities, from the pen of a distinguished clergyman (Rev. A. II. Vinton, D.D.), which illustrates the good influences it may have on the minds of men, and over the destinies of our Republic.

"In order to illustrate the influence of the Sabbath well kept, let us consider some of its influences of educating the mind. Since we have adopted it as an axiom in our politics, that the prosperity of a free people is dependent upon their intelligence as well as their virtue, the question is invested with first-rate importance, How far the Sabbath is an educator of the intellect.

"Take, for example, that part of education which consists in supplying the mind with facts and suggestions which may be called the mind's furniture, the material of thought, such as comes from reading, and makes what Sir Francis Bacon calls a 'full man.'

"The Sabbath supplies this to the mind, because it is all found in the Bible, and the Sabbath is the Bible's peculiar day. Whatever of instruction, therefore, the Bible can furnish to the intellect of man is part and parcel of the worth of the Sabbath, or Sunday.

"How various that instruction is! There is history, which, so far as it goes, is more authentic than any other ancient records of the race. There are facts and phenomena of nature which are just as truly matters for scientific inquiry as any more recent.

"There is poetry, descriptive, suggestive, and lyrical, grander than Homer, more spiritual than Wordsworth, more tenderly touching than Tennyson; eloquence of every sort, from the grandly vehement to the meltingly pathetic; rhetoric that presents the most apt and striking combinations of human language, and in every form of composition, narrative, didatic, and dramatic.

"There are maxims of life and manners, pithy and sen-

tentious, that cling like burrs to the memory, and are
full of 'the seeds of things;' prudential rules of a wise
life, furnishing every man with a truth just suited to
every chance of his business or behavior. Such is this
many-sided book, as a mere vehicle for instruction to the
mind.

"No man can study its language, fresh from the wells
of English undefiled, without finding his faculties stirred
and refreshed, his understanding informed, his taste
refined, his judgment improved, and his whole mental
stature grown taller and fuller.

.   .   .   .

"Suppose a man, who is destitute of the ordinary facil-
ities of education, to devote the fifty-two Sabbaths of
the year to the studious contemplation of these Sunday
themes, and so for twenty years.

"Does any one doubt that the education of these more
than a thousand days, almost as much as the four years
of a collegiate life, would find this man far in advance of
his associates in all the proofs and fruits of mental culture? Would he not be a first-rate citizen of a free
government, with a riper intelligence than most men,
fitter than most men to cast a ballot, if he were not,
indeed, fitted to govern a commonwealth?

"A great advantage of this Sabbath education is that
it is periodical; not so frequent as to make it a drudgery,
and not so rare as to endanger the permanence of its
impression. It is to every class of men, specially and
peculiarly, a rest and a refreshing.

"To the industrial classes, whose vocations lie among material things, and to the commercial class, whose life is the arithmetic of earthly values and products, the Sunday gives opportunities and incitements to a fresh set of faculties, and opens the windows of their minds to let in the fresh air of thoughts from God and a better life.

"Even to the classes whose business is thought, the Sabbath is still a rest, while it is still an education.

"The lawyer escapes from the perplexities of conflicting precedents, contradictory judgments, and equivocal propensities, into the pure light of truth, and the glorious certainties of righteousness.

"The physician can separate himself a while from the painful study of second causes to familiarize his mind with the workings of the first cause. And the men of science and philosophy would lose nothing, but gain much, by taking God's existence as a standpoint of thought for a while; and God's government and providence as a controlling fact in nature, and the foundation of a system of final causes.

"Such Sabbath thoughts would be no less a rest to them than to the laborious classes. For, to those whose habit of life is thinking, the maxim of Sir William Jones is always true, that 'the change of study is recreation enough.'"

WASHINGTON'S BIRTHDAY.

ON the 22d of February, 1732, a Christian home in Virginia was made joyful by the birth of a "man-child."

The Bible example sanctions the use of this noblest masculine term for infancy: never was the use so justified by after-events connected with the individual (except in one instance, that of the great leader and exemplar of the Hebrews), as in the life of George Washington, the great leader and exemplar of the American people.

When this man-child was first laid in his cradle at Fredericksburg, Virginia was a dependent colony of Great Britain; and this whole continent was under European sovereignty and control. The American colonies then contained perhaps one million of people.

When, in 1799, the hero, George Washington, was laid in his coffin at Mount Vernon, an independent nation, known throughout the world as "The United States of North America," over which he had held the sceptre of chief magistrate eight years, mourned his death as free men mourn the loss of their deliverer, defender, and counsellor.

And, more than this, his coffin was surrounded, in heart and mind, by the whole American people, then numbering over five millions, who, with mingled tears and blessings, showed their reverence for his perfect example of goodness, that draws hearts like tones of love: they were like children that mourn the death of a dear father and wise friend.

The wide world has heard his name; all men who love justice, truth, and freedom, honor his memory; all who are oppressed, or striving to improve, search his history; and, in the hearts and minds of Americans, the celebration of Washington's birthday is like a sacred vow that binds all who call him "our countryman" to be true to the Constitution and the Union.

These patriotic subjects are fittingly discussed in public orations. In this family reminiscence, I shall chiefly refer to incidents of his home-life, and deeds that show his character in his relations with those whose love and confidence he never forfeited, and whose affection and care for him he richly repaid.

In discussing the moralities and amenities of social life, of home, and of the family, no better theme can be found than the life of George Washington.

The influence of a pious and loving mother, of excellent and tender brothers and sisters, and of an elegant and polished selection of friends, formed and unsealed his wonderful character.

It was this model home-life, whose just and noble principles of conduct were made the rule of duty in every day's task, and under all circumstances, that formed his soul to its high standard of self-sacrificing heroism; which not only enabled him to serve and save his country, but also has made him morally and politically the faultless exemplar of self-governed men.

There was certainly the germ of his great qualities in his nature. God had bestowed his best gifts of humanity on that " man-child."

George Washington was, from his cradle, "always a good boy," as his mother said of him, in reply to the eulogies of Lafayette. He was reasonable, conscientious, tractable; loving all those relations, "friends given by God," that surrounded him. And he was pre-eminently endowed with —

> " Good sense, that rarest virtue under heaven,
> And, if no science, fairly worth the seven."

This good sense he showed by never failing to draw profit from all the advantages of his position, and all the circumstances that surrounded him.

Taken notice of, in boyhood, by Lord Fairfax, who had shone among the fashionables of the court of George II, the Virginia lad saw at once the value of polished manners, and of that framework of conventional laws that surrounds society, and preserves it from the raids of egotism and ill-nature.

Politeness is fictitious benevolence: it preserves virtue where she is, and introduces her, or the semblance, where she is not. The boy George Washington was so well aware of this, that he, at the age of fourteen, compiled a code of good manners,* for his own personal advantage.

George was his mother's first-born: her husband died while this son was still a boy, and she cherished him with peculiar tenderness. Those pure magnanimous thoughts, that kept him free from vice, from meanness, and from self-seeking, were first instilled by the daily home precept and daily example of his loved and revered mother: by habits of reflection these strengthened into principles, firm, steady, and enduring, whose fruit was the career of unexampled heroic excellence that is the pride of America, and the earthly hope of mankind.

As a husband and father (for he was truly a father to his step-children), as a master, as a host, Washington was regulated by the habits and ideas learned in that Virginia home, where unsullied character and unclouded conscience were the natural inheritance received by the child, and never lost.

But the home, which conferred all these signal advantages, was itself founded on the authority of God's word. Faith in the Bible, and obedience to God's laws, were the

* This code will be given in another number.

governing ideas of the mother's mind: by this faith she guided her own household, and governed her son.

George was trained to yield implicit obedience to his mother: this habit of duty to her prepared him to command men. He was trained in Bible faith and Christian love, and his uprightness of life testifies his inner purity of spirit.

There have been doubts cast on Washington's faith, because he made no show of religious observances.

He was, by nature and habit, undemonstrative; therefore what he did as a duty has the more importance. A friend of mine has the orders of Washington, when Commander-in-chief in New-York City at the beginning of the war. This lady speaks of the manuscript as "a religious work," from the frequent use of expressions and appeals that none but a devout Christian officer would presume to use in his daily orders to soldiers. It might be well for those who like to search out the matter to examine this manuscript.

The true hero worships God, and honors woman. By this high creed let our hero be tested.

We have seen him in his mother's home-circle and in his country's service. In all these relations and requirements he was — what a Christian knight was pledged to be — brave, loyal, and true. But it was in his own Mount-Vernon home that the noblest qualities of the Christian hero were developed and perfected.

There is an engraving of the Washington Family, that

images their domestic life, and opens the first scene of its history.

"I can never marry again," said a young widow to the noble-looking man who was urging his suit: I must live for my children."

"Be my wife," replied the lover: "*your* children shall be *our* children."

The wife of Washington was worthy of his faithful love and full confidence: these he gave her. His was the true faith in woman as the "help-meet for man;" and he wanted his wife to be with him!

She was with him when he took command of the army at Boston; and with him during every winter when the army was in camp. Her presence was his pleasure, her sympathy his support, next to faith in God. And in this faith the wife set the example as wives should do; softening the man's stern will by ever having on her tongue the "law of kindness."

Thus George and Martha Washington were, in their married life, an example of conjugal faith and domestic enjoyment, which may be truly styled the noblest majesty of human nature,—the twain made one. And this one-ship, devoted to God's service, is the way of righteousness.

How mean beside this moral majesty of manhood, founded on goodness, seems the hero-worship paid the great warriors of history! Take all the names,—Alexander, Cæsar, Napoleon, Peter of Russia and Frederic of Prussia, both styled "the Great."

What example of manly virtue in home-life, of justice to woman, of faith in goodness, have any of these heroes left to guide men in the way of honor and duty and true nobleness?

Washington only, of all the highest heroic names which hold their place through military deeds, has no sorrow in its sound, no sin on its brightness of fame.

It seems but a fitting tribute to the Christian virtues of this husband and wife, that the home where they lived and died, and the tomb where they rest together in the blessed hope of a glorious resurrection, should be watched over by the guardian care of WOMAN.

This sacred charge the women of America have now in trust.

The homestead (two hundred acres), the home, the tomb of Washington and his wife, are made sure as a perpetual inheritance of the people of the United States, because the title-deeds are sure to the women who have purchased and paid for this, the holiest place in uninspired history.

Would this guardianship of woman be fitting over the tomb of any other celebrated hero? Could women sympathize with the warrior's fame of Alexander, Cæsar, Napoleon? or in any greatness won by force, fraud, selfishness, and sin?

Bear in mind, that whatever crushes out moral power destroys the Christian virtues, and that these are chiefly termed *feminine virtues.*

Man's despotic power has always wronged and degraded woman. To honor the tombs of such heroes would seem unnatural and awful, as though we could imagine the women of Bethlehem carrying sweet spices to embalm the body of Herod!

Washington only, among the world's heroes, deserves the homage of women; and to him only has it been given. This is his greatest distinction, and should be held up as the crowning glory of our Great Republic.

In the heart of this free land, there is a domain consecrated to peace, goodness, and Christian love, where war, covetousness, and disunion can never come.

"The Mount-Vernon Ladies' Association of the Union" holds right and rule over this domain. The sacred trust has not been invaded by a hostile footstep during the four long years of the late terrible war. The thunderings of battle have been heard on every side; but the storms have never reached that place of peace, where woman has kept her quiet watch over the dust of Washington.*

PART SECOND.

I. — SHAPING AN AMERICAN HOME.

HOW to make home happy is a question about which there has been much excellent discourse, as we dare say our readers are aware. "How to make our homes comfortable" is another important question, on which much less has been said; and yet there is hardly a subject on which information and advice are more required. There are few men or women in our country, who, at some period of their lives, have not to take part in choosing or erecting a house to live in, and in making a home out of it; and very sad blunders many of them commit in the process. We propose in this article to offer a few hints which some of our readers, who have this duty in prospect, may find useful.

In selecting or constructing a residence, health is, of course, the first consideration. There are localities which are known to be sickly; and no sensible man, unless constrained by some call of duty which cannot be resisted, will set up his homestead in such a place. So long as men can be found to face the cannon's mouth for a shilling a day, there will be plenty to rush into unhealthy regions where money is to be made; but we hope that no reader of these lines will be so reckless as to seek the chance of a fortune with the likelihood of a broken constitution.

There is, however, much room for choice, even in districts which are justly deemed favorable to health. No one will — or at least no one should — fix his house on low and moist ground, when he can secure a high and dry foundation. Every one, we hope, would, by natural instinct, prefer an open, cheerful, picturesque situation to one of an opposite character. But there are points of equal importance which are apt to be slighted. How many, for example, in choosing a place of residence, either in town or country, think of the direction in which it fronts, as a matter of great moment? And yet there are few things on which the health of the residents so much depends. The sun, be it remembered, is to our planet the great source of life and health. We may say of it in a literal sense what is said morally of the Sun of Righteousness, that it rises with healing in its wings. The rooms in which the inmates of a house spend most of their time should enjoy the direct sunlight for the greater part of the day. In the country, with a little contrivance, this can be readily managed. In the city, it is not always so easy; but, as a general rule, if your house is on the north or west side of the street, you should make your chief "living-rooms," as architects call

them, in the front part; if on the south or west side, in
the rear portion; and, if the house is so constructed that
you cannot get a cheerful, sun-lighted sitting-room, it
will be wisdom to look for a habitation more judiciously
arranged. The records of epidemics show that the shady
side of a street usually suffers more than the sunny side.
And we have known several instances in which persons
in declining health have been restored to strength by
simply changing from a dark and gloomy house or room
to a sunny and cheerful one.

The ventilation of a house cannot be too carefully
attended to. Most persons are aware of the importance of
securing a constant supply of fresh air in their dwellings,
but few, except professional architects, know how to manage it. The plans which these propose are often so expensive and complicated as to deter many persons from adopt-
ing them. We find in a very useful little work, entitled
"The Economic Cottage Builder," by Charles P. Dwyer,
a method proposed for warming, ventilating, and (when
desirable) cooling a house, which appears to be simple,
effective, and cheap. Many readers will doubtless be
glad to see the description of it in the author's own
words : —

"By a proper arrangement," he observes, "a pure, soft,
and bland atmosphere can be maintained through the
whole year at a less expense than it would take to heat
a suite of rooms by the old exploded methods of open

fireplaces and close stoves. Ordinarily, no provision is made to cool the rooms in summer, during the hot weather; a thing of quite as much importance as keeping them warm in winter. My plan for warming in winter and cooling in summer may be carried on by the same apparatus, and the most equable temperature secured. The principle I would apply is the well-known philosophical law of temperature, viz., that warm air ascends and cold air descends. For this purpose I would construct a furnace in every cellar, surrounded with an air-chamber, with a current of water circulating through it to prevent its becoming too dry. The air, thus purified and warmed, I would convey to every room in the house it was desirable to warm, by tubes leading to a refrigerator in the attic. These tubes I would close in the middle, opposite each room, with an opening both above and below it. Supposing it is winter; I would unfasten the lower opening, and admit the warm air from the chamber in the cellar till the room was of an agreeable warmth. In summer I would close the lower opening, and open the upper one. In the refrigerator in the garret I would place a quantity of ice, daily, the cool air from which, descending down the tubes, would enter the rooms, and keep them at any requisite temperature. Thus, in the warmest days in summer, a refreshing coolness can be maintained at the daily expense of a little ice; the furnace in the cellar and the refrigerator in the attic reciprocating with each other. The cost of the whole apparatus would not exceed half the amount required to furnish the building with the necessary stoves and fire-places; and the saving of wood, annually, would be an important item in the current expenses of every family."

It would be well if the practice of building houses over cellars, which are usually reservoirs of foul air, could be avoided. In many cases, by a little contrivance, and with no additional expense, the cellars might be so placed (under some back kitchen or other out-building), that the air from it could not enter the house. In any case, no bedroom should be situated over one of these pestilent vaults.

No man ought to build a house without consulting his wife or his intended, in regard to its plan. While he, probably, will only spend a few hours every day in it, he must recollect that it is to be her constant abode, her little realm, which she is to regulate, and adorn, and keep in order. How many weary, useless steps have been caused by a door or a staircase wrongly placed; how much discomfort and waste by the lack of a cupboard or a store-room! We have known a large and expensive building of three stories erected without one closet or cupboard from the kitchen to the attic. The owner was an excellent man of business; but it did not occur to him to show the plan of their future residence to his wife until it was finished: and a more comfortless building was seldom erected.

As to the exterior of a house, it is as easy to make it attractive and elegant as plain and forbidding. In the country, especially, every one should deem it his duty to his neighbors and his family to make his house and its surroundings as tasteful and pleasing as possible. The character speaks in the dwelling as much as in the countenance. A perpetual influence emanates from it upon those who see it and those who inhabit it. A charming homestead may be a constant lesson of improvement for a whole community; and the children who grow up in it will bear through all their lives the impress of its unconscious teachings. A neat porch, a vine-covered trellis, a pretty flower-pot, a few well-chosen trees, will beautify the humblest cottage, and will help to kindle and keep alive that sentiment of ideality, which, next to religious truth, is the great source of human improvement.

HINTS.

1. No one should undertake to build a house without consulting a good architect. The saving which will be made by his advice will always exceed his charges; and his suggestions will certainly add much to the value and convenience of the building.

2. It is well, if possible, to make the contract for building your house in the autumn previous to the spring in which it is to be built. Mechanics will do their work

better and cheaper, if they can take their time for it during the winter; and the materials will be better prepared and seasoned.

3. Never use inferior materials in building because they are cheaper. You will find them in the end the dearest you could use.

4. For the country, the best style of dwellings is the old-fashioned frame-house, "filled in" with brick. Properly constructed and well painted, it is elegant, durable, and comfortable. Such a house should be of two stories, with the sleeping-rooms in the upper story.

5. A house in the country should always be constructed with a view to future enlargement, if necessary. Few persons reside long in any dwelling without finding occasion to make additions to it. The original plan should be so contrived that any future extensions may be made to harmonize with it.

6. In placing a house, regard should always be had to the conditions prescribed by the climate. At the South, where opportunity offers, a dwelling may be placed at a good distance from the road, with an avenue of trees leading to it. In the far North, such an avenue would become obstructed by snow in winter, and cause more discomfort than pleasure.

7. If you are a tenant, be as careful of the house and grounds as if they were your own, and endeavor to leave them in better condition than they were in when you took them. The habit of being thoughtful of the rights

and interests of others is one which brings its own direct
reward in the frame of mind which it creates, and in the
kindness and regard of those with whom we deal.

——

II. — MARRIAGE.

That union where all that in woman is kind,
  With all that in man most ennoblingly towers,
Grow wreathed into one, like the column combined
  Of the *strength* of the shaft and the capital's *flowers.*
                                        Moore.

A S the first man and woman were made to be married, it seems to follow that married life was intended to be the perfect condition of humanity.

This idea is generally held, so far as regards the condition of woman, by all masculine writers. The axiom, as a
self-evident truth, is never called in question, that all women are made to be married.

They believe, too, that woman's noblest virtues of conduct are called forth, and her highest excellences of character perfected, in domestic life; in short, that her destiny
is marriage, and her place of honor and happiness is her
home.

But, when the destiny of men is debated, they do not
reckon marriage as essential to their own well-being, or
home as the best place of their enjoyment and honor.
Yet, if marriage is the best state for woman, it should be

the best for man; or the plan of creation would seem to be in fault.

"Be ye not unequally yoked" was the great apostle's command to Christians; if men are really losers by the union, then marriage is "unequal" for men.

In the history of creation, it seems that Adam was not perfect till Eve was made to be with him. All the works of the Creator were pronounced "good" till we come to man : then the word of God was —

"It is not good that the man should be alone : I will make a help-meet for him."— *Gen.* xl. 7–29.

The happiness and glory of Eden were then perfected. Not that man and woman were then identical or equal in all their faculties and gifts, but the differences were like the tones in music that make up the concord of sweet sounds.

The first married pair were not equals ; they were one : one in flesh and bones; one in the harmony of their wills ; one in the hope of earthly happiness; one in the favor of God. Thus perfect was their union in Eden whilst they were innocent. Yet, as in their corporeal forms woman was the most refined, delicate, and perfect, so her *spirit* (by the term I mean *heart, soul, mind,* including *all* the affections and passions) was purer and holier than man's.

He was formed of the earth, and had in the greatest development those powers of mind which are directed towards objects of sense ; she, formed from his flesh and bones, had in greatest development those powers of mind which seek the affections. But these differences did not hinder their loving union ; such diversities only seemed to enhance the happiness of their home and enlarge the variety of their enjoyments.

It is not disparity of intellect, nor differences in the innocent enjoyments of life, which make the miseries of the married pair. It is disunion of hearts and hopes, the conflicts of passion and will: these mar or destroy domestic bliss. There was nothing to disturb the perfect enjoyment of Eden till sin entered. Then we learn how the sexes differ from each other. While studying the sad history of the fall, we find that the woman's nature never lost its faith in good ; and that to her was intrusted the promise of final triumph, by her seed, over the evils that sin would cause.

And even now, happy homes may be made, if the husband and wife would lovingly work for this sweet enjoyment. Why should all the responsibilities be laid on woman ? Would it not be well to give men a lesson or two on their home-duties ? Why should not the husband be advised to bring home " smiles and sunshine " for the wife, while she is admonished always to " have only smiles and sunshine for the husband when he comes home wearied with his day's labor " ?

It is true that the inner life of home is for woman, and that the wife should reverence and obey her husband.

And it is also true that the hard work of life is laid on men; that, by the law of creation, which keeps the sexes equal in numbers, and by the Eden law, which made man's goodness (or perfection) depend on woman's as the "help-meet for him," it is the duty of every man to marry, if it be the duty of every woman to marry. Moreover, God has expressly laid on every man the duty of "providing for his own household;" of "training his children in the way they should go;" of protecting and cherishing his own wife; he is to "love her as himself"— "honor her as the weaker vessel," which surely means the delicate, appreciating care such as he would take of fine porcelain, in distinction from a common clay vessel; and he is also taught to bear in mind that "the woman is the glory of the man."

Ought not Christian fathers to teach these lessons of tenderness and respect for women to their sons?

In the education of girls, it is thought to be all important that they should be so trained as to become good wives and devoted mothers. Is the lesson of making good husbands and fathers pressed on the minds of boys, or even hinted at in college-classes for young men?

These are important subjects in estimating the future of American homes. Opportunities of domestic happiness are around our people. Every young man who determines to make for his wife and himself a happy home should place her happiness first in the home (as she must pass her whole life in it, while he has duties that will keep him often abroad), and, working bravely for this noble idea, he will realize it. And the wife: there is in the Book of books one perfect picture of happy married life, limned by divine inspiration: it is proof of what the help-meet for man was by her Creator intended to be in her home, and with what exulting joy her husband and children praise her excellence and bless her care.

"Who can find a virtuous woman? for her price is far above rubies.

"The heart of her husband doth safely trust in her, so that he shall have no need of spoil.

"She shall do him good, and not evil, all the days of her life.

"She riseth while it is yet night, and giveth meat to her household, and a portion to her maidens.

"She stretcheth out her hand to the poor; yea, she reacheth forth her hands to the needy.

"She is not afraid of the snow for her household; for all her household are clothed in scarlet.

"She maketh herself coverings of tapestry; her clothing is silk and purple.

"Her husband is known in the gates, when he sitteth among the elders of the land.

"Strength and honor are her clothing; and she shall rejoice in time to come.

"She openeth her mouth with wisdom; and in her tongue is the law of kindness.

" She looketh well to the ways of her household, and eateth not the bread of idleness.

" Her children arise up and call her blessed; her husband also, and he praiseth her.

" Favor is deceitful, and beauty is vain; but a woman that feareth the Lord, she shall be praised.

" Give her of the fruit of her hands; and let her own works praise her in the gates."

This full-length likeness is the representative woman whose married life should be the type and model for her sex.

Who does not see the sweet perfection of character, of manners, and of personal attractions blended in the description? We feel that if she were not gifted with remarkable beauty, still she did possess the natural attractiveness which goodness makes so lovely. All the appointments of her household show the lady of rank, wealth, and influence; and yet how careful is the inspired limner to represent the duties of daily life as under her personal superintendence. And this attention to " small things " does not hinder her mind from acquiring a large and spiritual development. She can " judge righteously; " her conversation is " wisdom: " are not these powers of a high order, proving that her intellectual gifts are suited to sustain the pure moral graces of her feminine nature?

Her husband knows that " his heart may safely trust in

* Read the 31st chapter of Proverbs, from the 10th verse to the close.

her." He can go abroad where his duties as a man require his presence, nor feel any fear that his interest or honor, his happiness or the welfare of his family, will suffer detriment at home. " She will do him good, and not evil, all the days of her life." And even " while he sits in the gates among the elders of the land," he is proud — nay, better — he is thankful that as her husband he.is known; that he has the glory of being the protector of his wife, " whose value is far above rubies."

Do not these two seem one?   And yet, although in mutual confidence, esteem, and love, their hearts and interests are perfectly in unison, they could not exchange duties as equals.

The husband could not be the preserver, inspirer, teacher, and exemplar in his household; the wife could not become the worker and provider, protector and lawgiver, which the man's will and strength, mechanical skill and mental power, " fitted to subdue the earth and rule over it," enable him to be in the outer world, while watching over the welfare and happiness of his own family.

And yet it is the wife in her tender love and hopeful piety, contented in the inner world of home, if her heart is satisfied in its affections, and her soul steadfast in its trust on God, who not only watches over, but makes the best happiness of her husband and children on earth, while leading them, by the aid of divine Grace, up to the bliss of heaven. No wonder her children " call her blessed," and her husband " praiseth her." Moral good-

ness is the same in all ages of the world and in all conditions of life. Moral happiness is eternal in its essence : it
is the elixir of humanity. The happy home life, wherever
found, arises from the same qualities of mind and virtues
of heart which are illustrated in this beautiful picture,
drawn nearly three thousand years ago.

The true marriage and the true obedience to duty
which made this Hebrew household so blessed and glorious must now be found in our American homes, if these
are happy in love and radiant with the honor which entire goodness and true faithfulness in all the relations of
life require. In such a home one influence always predominates; one presence is always felt; one light must
be visible: " a woman that feareth the Lord " makes the
true home.

III. — HOW TO BEAUTIFY OUR HOMES.

A thing of beauty is a joy forever.
Keats.

"KNOWLEDGE is power," always; knowledge used
for good purposes is wisdom. Knowledge, like
gold, must be gained by personal effort; and, usually,
in small quantities and by continued exertions, both wisdom and gold are accumulated.

Personal appearance is important; the art of beautifying a home is important; the knowledge of the ways and

means by which the clothing of a family may be kept in good order, with the least expense of time and money, is important; some knowledge of plants, flowers, gardening, and of domestic animals is of much benefit, especially to those who live in the country. Then there is the very important matter of home-happiness to keep in view; and as one means of procuring, or at least adding to, that happiness, we propose to give a few words upon the art of beautifying our homes in the present article.

Miss Sedgwick has asserted, in some of her useful books, "that the more intelligent a woman becomes, other things being equal, the more judiciously she will manage her domestic concerns."

And we add, that the more knowledge a woman possesses of the great principles of morals, philosophy, and human happiness, the more importance she will attach to her station, and to the name of "a good housekeeper."

It is only the frivolous, and those who have been superficially educated, or only instructed in showy accomplishments, who despise and neglect the ordinary duties of life as beneath their notice.

"The power of littles!" How often has the expression been quoted, and how much it contains! Great things are granted to few; little things to all. But more than this, it is not the great things which give the effect; it is the little things, — the graceful finishing touches: what are termed the trifles are precisely what we most depend upon for forming the harmonious whole.

As home is the place where our best and happiest hours are passed, nothing which will beautify or adorn it can be of trifling importance. Nor let any one suppose that this may be done by wealth alone. Look at rooms so furnished; the costly mirrors, the showy paintings, the elaborately carved furniture: why is it that these so often fail to afford even a transient feeling of pleasure, whilst even a very simple home, filled with the evidences of taste and refinement, pleases and gratifies at once?

It is that the one speaks only of the cabinet-maker or upholsterer; the other tells of the home's mistress, and proves a love which has sought outward expression in bringing brightness and cheerfulness to the dear ones within.

A young bride, first making her own home, should think of this, and remember that much of her future enjoyment may depend upon the halo her hand shall throw around the domestic sanctuary.

Character, it has well been said, is seen through small openings, and certainly is as clearly displayed in the arrangements and adornments of a house as in any other way. Who cannot read grace, delicacy, and refinement in the lady of a house, simply by looking at the little elegances and beauties with which she has surrounded herself in her home? Nor are large means necessary to produce this effect. It is surprising how much may be accomplished by a little ingenuity and judgment where the income is very limited.

A young girl, brought up amidst all the luxuries of a wealthy city home, saw fit to change the conventionalities of life for the lot of a poor man's wife, and the scant comforts of a settler's home. "Give me boards, barrels, hammer, and nails," said she, "and I can furnish a house, and comfortably too." And so she could; and, in case any of our young readers should follow her example in the former particular, we will give them a few hints how they may do so in the latter.

A very comfortable, though somewhat original, chair may be made from a barrel. Saw away half the front, leave the back its full height, and, with the aid of the saw, form the sides into arms. Then fix the seat of wood; place on that a thick, well-filled cushion, with raised sides; pad the back and arms; and cover all with chintz or moreen. Ottomans and settees, of various sizes and shapes, may be made of boxes with cushions on them, and full curtains of furniture chintz hanging round the sides. The interiors of such boxes are very convenient, where the rooms are too small to accommodate wardrobes, or chests of drawers.

A washstand may also be improvised from a cask. Fix a square or octagon-shaped board on the top of a barrel, nail round it a curtain to hang down to the floor, and cut in it a circular hole for the basin. Take away some of the staves of the barrel in front, under the curtain, and fix a shelf half way up, which may be made very useful.

These may seem rough means of securing the necessaries of life, but the daily increasing settlement of our distant territories may render them acceptable to many.

Pretty imitation vases may be made of card, painted, and left without a bottom, so that they may be set over a glass of flowers. Picture-frames are also easily cut from paste-board, covered with pine cones, glued on and varnished. Thus a neat and pretty home may be prepared.

The effect of flowers also should not be overlooked. These have an infinite charm in themselves, either in the graceful grouping of the bouquet and moss-basket, or in the pretty arrangement of trailing vines and growing plants, placed either upon wire or rustic stands.

We are glad to notice an increase of the foreign custom of vines trained over the doors of the vestibules of many of our houses: it has an agreeable and pleasing effect.

Bright autumn leaves, mingled with ferns, pressed and varnished, make also a very pretty decoration for mantle vases, and, with light and careful dusting, will retain their beauty through a whole winter. Dried grasses may also be mixed to add to the effect.

A bouquet of skeleton flowers is a pretty addition to a room, and shows the taste of its occupants, as well as their patience; for it requires neat and careful work.

But those who would thus beautify their houses externally must remember that such adornment can be of little

avail unless accompanied by the gentle courtesies and
amenities of social life, which lend such a sweet charm to
daily intercourse.

Many persons seem to consider that the fact of their
being "at home" absolves them from all necessity of
keeping up the social forms of politeness and good breeding. It cannot be too strongly impressed upon the mind
that mutual respect is the basis of true affection. We
would, therefore, earnestly urge upon every one the importance of avoiding disrespectful titles in the home, as
tending to lesson proper esteem and reverence.

It may seem a light matter in the domestic circle,
whether this or that mode of speech is adopted; but it is
far from being so in reality.

I refer, in the first place, to a custom which some married ladies have of calling their husband by their sur-
names simply, without prefix of any sort. Children and
servants are greatly influenced by outward demeanor;
and the wife who permits herself to address her husband
in a manner unbecoming his high standing as the head
of his house goes far towards lessening him in the opinion of his family.

A habit which is to be even more strongly condemned
is that of children's applying the term, "the old people,"
to their parents, or of boys thinking it manly to call their
father "the governor." All these modes of expression
blunt the fine edge of filial respect and affection, and
should be strictly avoided. They are, moreover, in very

bad taste, and show a lack of the highest breeding. In our country, where the resident of a log-cabin may become the resident of the "White House" at some future day, these matters should be considered on every ground; and a fitness for good society may be as easily learned in a log-hut as in a palace.

Equally undesirable is a custom adopted by some married people of bantering one another before their children. They do not consider the effect which such trifling produces. The husband, who gives a ridiculous name to his wife, and raises a laugh at her expense, lowers himself by so doing, by lessening the respect entertained for him.

The courtesies of life are nowhere of greater importance than in the home-circle. Brothers and sisters should extend, at least an equal share of politeness and consideration to each other with that they bestow upon strangers; yet do we always find such to be the case? Why should they not be as thoughtful to please, and as anxious to avoid what annoys and perplexes, at home as they would be abroad?

If any one's true character is to be ascertained, let us study him in his home. If he stands that test, we may be sure that he will never betray any confidence we may repose in him.

Good-breeding, however, consists in much more than not being ill-bred. To fulfil all the laws of etiquette, to bow gracefully, to have finished manners, will not be sufficient. If you desire to obtain the good-will and affection of your acquaintances, you must seek to render yourself actively agreeable.

Study to give pleasure, by consulting the tastes and inclinations of your friends, and gratifying them, so far as it may be in your power. These little acts of kindness will serve to endear you, and will linger long and lovingly in the memories of those in whose behalf they have been exercised.

IV. — SOCIETY.

Man, in society, is like a flower
Blown in its native bud. 'Tis there alone
His faculties, expanded in full bloom,
Shine out; there only reach their proper use.
Cowper's Task.

GOOD society, in all Christian countries, is the meeting on a footing of equality, and for the purpose of mutual entertainment, of men, or women, or men and women together, of good character, good education, and good breeding.

But what is the real spirit of the observances which this society requires of its frequenters for the preservation of harmony, and the easy intercourse of all of them? Certainly, one may have a spotless reputation, a good education, and good breeding, without being either good in reality, or a Christian.

But if we examine the laws which good society lays down for our guidance and government, we shall find, without a doubt, that they are those which a simple Christian, desiring to regulate the meetings of a number of people who lacked the Christian feeling, would dictate.

I am, of course, quite aware that good society will never make you a good Christian. You may be charming in a party, and every one may pronounce you a perfect and agreeable gentleman; but you may go home, and get privately intoxicated, or ill-treat your wife, or be unkind to your children.

Or, if you be a lady, you may be smiling and attractive abroad, but fretful, peevish, or petulant in your home. If society finds you out, it will punish you: but society has no right to search your house, and intrude upon your hearth; and it may be long before it finds you out. But, *as far as its jurisdiction extends*, good society can compel you, if not to be a Christian, at least, to act like one.

The difference between the laws of God and the laws of men is, that the former address the heart from which the acts proceed; the latter, which can only judge from what they see, determine the acts without regard to the heart.

The laws of society are framed by the unanimous consent of men; and, in all essential points, they differ very little all over the world, with one exception. This one exception is, that *women* are never allowed to appear in heathen society, nor ever mentioned; one-half the race are thus entirely blotted out; their very existence almost utterly ignored.

The Chinese or the Turk * may show his politeness by feeding you with his fingers; the American, by carving your portion for you; but the same spirit dictates both, — the spirit of friendliness and good-will.

Thus, though the laws of society are necessarily imperfect, are moulded by traditional and local custom, and addressed to the outer rather than the inner man, their spirit is invariably the same. The considerations which dictate them are reducible to the same law, and that law proves to be the fundamental one of Christian doctrine. Thus, what the heathen arrives at only by laws framed for the comfort of society, we possess at once in virtue of our religion.

And it is a great glory for a Christian to be able to say, that all refinement and all civilization lead men — as far as their conversation is concerned — to the practice of Christianity. It is a great satisfaction to feel that Christianity is eminently the religion of civilization and society.

The great law which distinguishes Christianity from

* The Chinese holds to the fifth commandment; the Turk, to the first and second; and, although these are held ignorantly, they yet produce, in their lives, a higher morality than is to be found among any other heathen nations without such elements of truth.

every other creed, that of brotherly-love and self-denial, is essentially the law which we find at the basis of all social observances. The first maxim of politeness is to be agreeable to everybody, even at the expense of one's own comfort.

Meekness is the most beautiful virtue of the Christian; modesty the most commendable in well-bred people. Peace is the object of Christian laws; harmony, that of social observances. Self-denial is the exercise of the Christian; forgetfulness of self, that of the well-bred. Trust in one another unites Christian communities; confidence in the good intentions of our neighbors is that which makes society possible.

To be kind to one another is the object of Christian converse; to entertain one another, that of social intercourse. Pride, selfishness, ill-temper, are alike opposed to Christianity and good-breeding.

The one demands an upright life, the other requires the appearance of it. The one bids us make the most of God's gifts, and improve our talents; the other will not admit us till we have done so by education. And, to go a step farther: as a Christian community excludes sinners and unbelievers from its gatherings; so a social community excludes from its meetings those of bad character, and those who do not subscribe to its laws.

But society goes farther, and appears to impose on its members a number of arbitrary rules, which continually restrict them in their actions. It tells them how they must eat and drink and dress, and walk and talk, and so on. We ought to be very thankful to society for taking so much trouble, and saving us so much doubt and confusion. But, if the ordinances of society are examined, it will be found, that, while many of them are merely derived from custom and tradition, and some have no positive value, they all tend to one end, — the preservation of harmony, and the prevention of one person from usurping the rights, or intruding on the province, of another.

If it regulates your dress, it is that there may be an appearance of equality in all, and that the rich may not be able to flaunt their wealth in the eyes of their poor associates. If, for instance, it says that you are not to wear diamonds in the morning, it puts a check upon your vanity. If it says you may wear them on certain occasions, it does not compel those who have none to purchase them.

If society says that you shall eat with a knife and fork, it does so, not because fingers were made before forks, but because it is well known that if you were to use the natural fork with five prongs, instead of the silver one of four, you would want to wash your hands after every dish.

If, again, society forbids you to swing your arms in walking like the sails of a wind-mill, it is not for the purpose of pinioning you, but because beauty is a result of harmony, and society ever studies beauty, — adopts the beautiful and rejects the inelegant. That motion is not lovely; confess it. Society is quite right to object to it.

In short, while society may have many an old law which may need repealing, you will find the greater number of its enactments are founded on very good and very Christian considerations.

You will find also, that, the more religious a man is, the more polite he will spontaneously become, and that, too, in every rank of life; for true religion teaches him to forget himself, to love his neighbor, and to be kindly even to his enemy, and the *appearance* of so being and doing is what society demands as good manners.

How can it ask more? How can it open your heart, and see if, with your bland smile and oily voice, you are a liar and a hypocrite? There is one who has this power — forget it not! — but society must be content with the semblance. By your works, men do and must judge you.

HINTS.

For the Father of the Family.

1. Never raise an impassable barrier between yourself and your children by a mistaken assumption of dignity: invite and encourage their confidence.

2. On the other hand, there is a dignity proper to the head of the household, and necessary to command respect, which, whilst it should avoid stateliness, should scarcely descend to hilarity.

For the Mother.

3. The mother appears more in relation to her children than in any other position; therefore, her mind and

thoughts should be chiefly given to their care and training.

4. Avoid weak fondness, whilst carefully cultivating confidence and love.

The Married Woman.

5. Married women should control society. The present practice of abandoning it almost exclusively to young girls is lowering in its tone, and pernicious in its effects.

6. She should combine dignity with affability, and make her home an attractive and agreeable centre for the young.

The Single Woman.

7. Let her study to make herself useful and agreeable. Her lot bestows more time upon her; therefore let her improve to the utmost the talents God has given her, in order that she may exert the greatest amount of influence for good.

The Young Lady.

8. Let her cultivate quiet and retiring manners. Modesty is the most becoming ornament she can wear.

9. Never omit any mark of respect or deference to age: nothing is more pleasing or graceful in a young person.

The Young Man.

10. If you wish to be agreeable, which is certainly a good aim, you must both study how to be so, and take the trouble to put your studies into constant practice.

11. Cultivate conversational powers. Many men possess much and varied information without the power of imparting it easily and agreeably.

V. — AMUSEMENTS.

He is a noble gentleman; withal
Happy in his endeavors. The general voice
Sounds him for courtesy, behavior, language,
And every fair demeanor, an example:
Titles of honor add not to his worth,
Who is himself an honor to his title.

John Ford.

AMONG the many popular modes of passing time in the social circle, perhaps none are more interesting than the games which stimulate intellectual energy, and call forth quick and ready repartee.

While the plays that children so much enjoy are most valuable as tending to muscular development, we must not forget that children of a larger growth may be mentally and often morally developed by the "blindman's buff" or "hunt the slipper" of the mind. A set of mental gymnasts or intellectual acrobats may thus be trained by the pursuit of what is considered mere amusement.

Under this head may be classed the "game of twenty questions," so popular among the English people, which we may describe in some future number; also "charades," "rebuses," or "capping verses," which latter game, as it may not be familiar to all, may be worth a word of description.

One of the party gives out a line of poetry, which must be instantly responded to by another line beginning with the initial letter of the final word of the last line; this, in its turn, calls forth another, subject to the same rule, and so on. To sustain this game with spirit, there must be no pause; one line must follow another in quick succession; and the effort to call up what is needed from the poetry stored in the mind is a useful and improving exercise.

The following sketch presents a new game, which we should be glad to see introduced among the home enjoyments of American society.

CROWNING THE WISEST.

Some years ago, it happened that a young gentleman from New York visited London. His father being connected with several of the magnates of the British aristocracy, the young American was introduced into the fashionable circles of the metropolis, where, either in consideration of his very fine personal appearance, or that his father was reported to be very rich, or that he was a new figure on the stage, he attracted much attention, and became quite the favorite of the ladies. This was not at all relished by the British beaux; but, as no very fair pretext offered for a rebuff, they were compelled to treat him civilly.

Thus matters stood, when the Hon. Mr. —— (M. P.), and Lady Mary his wife, made a party to accompany them to their country-seat in Cambridgeshire; and the

American was among the invited guests. Numerous
were the devices to which these devotees of pleasure
resorted, in order to kill that stubborn old fellow who
will measure his hours when he ought to know they are
not wanted; and the ingenuity of every one was taxed to
remember or invent something novel.

The Yankees are proverbially ready of invention, and
the American did honor to his character as a man accustomed to freedom of thought. He was frank and gay,
and entered into the sports and amusements with that
unaffected enjoyment which communicated a part of his
fresh feelings to the most worn-out fashionist in the party.
His good nature would have been sneered at by some of
the proud cavaliers, had he not been such a capital shot;
and he might have been quizzed, had not the ladies, won
by his respectful and pleasant civilities, and his constant
attention in drawing-room and saloon, always showed
themselves his friends.

But a combination was at last formed among a trio of
dandies, stanch patrons of the Quarterly, to annihilate
the American. They proposed to vary the eternal evening waltzing and music by the acting of charades, and by
playing various games; and, having interested one of
those indefatigable sinlge ladies who always carry their
point in the scheme, it was voted to be the thing.

After some few charades had been disposed of, one of
the gentlemen begged leave to propose the game called
" Crowning the Wisest."

This is played by selecting a judge of the game, a committee to prepare the examination, and three persons, either ladies or gentlemen, who are to contest for the crown by answering the various questions, never exceeding nine, which the committee propounded. The candidate who is declared to have been the readiest and happiest in his or her answers receives the crown.

Our American, much against his inclination, was chosen among the three candidates. He was aware that his position in the society with which he was mingling required of him the ability to sustain himself. He was, to be sure, treated with distinguished attention by his host and hostess, and generally by the party; but this was a favor to the individual, and not one of the company understood the character of republicans, or appreciated the Republic.

The more certainly to discomfit the Yankee, his three enemies had arranged that their turn for questioning him should fall in succession, and be the last. The first one was a perfect exquisite; and, with an air of most ineffable condescension, he put his question.

"If I understand rightly the government of your country, you acknowledge no distinctions of rank, consequently, you can have no court standard for the manners of a gentleman: will you favor me with information where your best school of politeness is to be found?"

"For your benefit," replied the American, smiling

calmly, "I would recommend the Falls of Niagara, — a contemplation of that stupendous wonder teaches humility to the proudest, and human nothingness to the vainest. It rebukes the trifler, and arouses the most stupid: in short, it turns men from their idols; and, when we acknowledge that God only is the Lord, we feel that men are our equals. A true Christian is always polite."

There was a murmur among the audience; but whether of applause or censure, the American could not determine, as he did not choose to betray any anxiety for the result by a scrutiny of the faces which he knew were bent on him.

The second now proposed his question. He affected to be a great politician, was mustached and whiskered like a diplomatist, which station he had been coveting. His voice was bland; but his emphasis was very significant.

"Should I visit the United States, what subject with which I am conversant would most interest your people, and give me an opportunity of enjoying their conversation?"

"You must maintain, as you do at present, that a monarchy is the wisest, the purest, and best government which the skill of man ever devised, and that a democracy is utterly barbarous. My countrymen are fond of argument: they will meet you on those two points, and, if you choose, argue with you to the end of your life," replied the American.

7

The murmur was renewed, but still without any decided expression of the feeling with which his answer had been received. The third then rose from his seat, and with an assured voice, which seemed to announce a certain triumph, said, —

"I require your decision on a delicate question; but the rules of the pastime warrant it, and also a candid answer. You have seen the American and the English ladies: which are the fairest?"

The young republican glanced around the circle. It was bright with beaming eyes; and the sweet smiles which wreathed many a lovely lip might have won a less determined patriot from his allegiance. He did not hesitate, though he bowed low to the ladies as he answered, —

"The standard of feminine beauty is, I believe, allowed to be the power of exciting admiration and love in our sex; consequently, those ladies who are the most admired and beloved and respected by the gentlemen must be the fairest. Now I assert confidently, that there is not a nation on earth where woman is so truly beloved, so tenderly cherished, so respectfully treated, as in the Republic of the United States; therefore, the American ladies are the fairest. But," and he again bowed low, "if the ladies before whom I have now the honor of expressing my opinion were in my own country, we should think them Americans."

The applause was unanimous, and, for an aristocratic

English drawing-room, quite enthusiastic. After the mirth had so far subsided as to allow the voice of the judge to be heard, he awarded the crown to the young American.

VI.—A PLEA FOR DANCING.

A PLEA for Dancing!" exclaims Mrs. Lovegood, as she opens "The Home Weekly." " Why, Charles, I thought, after reading the article on 'Indecent Dances' in 'The London Review,' that the idea of discussing the subject would be given up."

" There must be something to say in its favor, Mary, or Mrs. Hale would not make a ' Plea for Dancing,'" replied Mr. Lovegood : " we will read this before judging it. There may be more good reasons for this recreation in our homes than we have considered."

" But, if we allow dancing in our homes, we countenance all its bad consequences in society," said Mrs. Lovegood.

" I am not certain on that point," replied her husband. " Some important ideas on this subject have occurred to me since reading that article in ' The London Review.' It is plain that such dances as are there alluded to cannot be allowed in our land."

" How can they be prevented here, if not there ?"

inquired his wife; "and why should we find their consequences worse?"

"Because our Republic is founded on God's truth and the moral virtues of humanity, not on military power and royal prerogative. Woman is the natural guardian of the moral virtues : if she become shameless in her amusements, the inner world of home will soon be corrupted. No republic can be sustained where the moral virtues are dishonored in the social life of a free people."

"The prevention, — how can that be accomplished?"

"By encouraging dances that are innocent, and banishing from our homes and from social life all that are indecent, just as we do with indecent songs in music, or licentious conversation in talking."

"Suppose, Charles, before going further, that you were to read me this article; and then we can discuss it together."

"With pleasure," said he; and, taking up the book, he read aloud: —

A PLEA FOR DANCING.

It appears to me, that it is too much the tendency of many earnest, right-minded, and in the main right-thinking persons, to confound the use with the abuse of various things which are in themselves good and right; and because, owing perhaps to circumstances, perhaps to the natural depravity of man, the abuse has in many cases so overlaid the use as to conceal it almost wholly from view, therefore such persons, seeking and wishing to promote the right, too frequently content themselves with condemning all such things *in toto*, without looking deeper into the question to see whether they are wrong *per se*, or have merely been made so by their abuse.

Foremost among such things, I would place dancing, — a simple, healthy, and useful exercise; a pleasant, social, and innocent amusement; a refined, elegant, and graceful accomplishment; and yet, because dancing has been abused, we find too many of our most conscientious and religious mothers forbidding its use entirely, and thus not only depriving their children of much rational enjoyment, but too often leading them into deceit and future excess in pursuit of a forbidden pleasure.

That it is not my aim to indorse balls, to advocate a career of worldly dissipation, or to defend the demoralizing dances of the present day, I need not say; for that were to defend the abuse, not to separate it from its lawful use!

No: I merely desire to show, that, viewed from the highest stand-point, the simple act of dancing, as a natural and healthy amusement, is not necessarily, and need never be, in any way connected with sin.

No one who is at all familiar with Addison's writings can fail to remember that he considered dancing as, ' not only imparting happiness, but increasing virtue.' He always strongly maintained that ' graceful movements of the body promoted a harmony in the mind;' but, in place of lingering over any such authorities, I prefer to go at once to the fountain head.

Take the Bible, read it from beginning to end, find me one passage where dancing is condemned as sinful, and I will forthwith relinquish my argument. Further than this: from the days of Moses to the present hour, it has been the natural medium which man has sought, unblamed by a higher power, as an expression of enjoyment and rejoicing.

Further still: where, throughout the New Testament, can we find one word of our blessed Lord's, our Great Exemplar, which in any way condemns, or even discountenances, innocent amusement of any nature?

Is it to be conceived that He would at any time have employed, as an illustration, any practice which was in itself sinful?

The thought would be blasphemy; and yet we find an account from His own lips of the return of the Prodigal Son, which was celebrated with music and *dancing*.

But how does it happen that music, which not only may be, but has been, equally perverted, should be allowed to pass comparatively uncondemned, whilst a fierce and constant war is steadily waged against its twin-sister, dancing?

It is true that the former has been consecrated to a higher service, but it has quite as often served the purpose of the Evil One. I, for one, very much question whether he has not found it a far more efficient agent in working out his dark designs than he has found dancing. Be that as it may, one thing is certain, that it is the abuse, not the use, which has caused the evil.

Another source of surprise to me is the singular difference of control which religious and right-minded persons, for I am addressing no others, extend to the different members of the human frame.

Whilst the poor feet commit an unpardonable sin, should they, in obedience to the volition of their owner, keep time in joyful spring to music's stirring sound, the more favored tongue may run riot, uncontrolled, hacking and hewing character, rending and ruining charity, tearing and trampling upon truth; and yet no note of warning sounds forth, no voice is raised to check the fearful wrong, so often caused by such unbridled license. Christian mother! I ask you, in the sight of God, which is the greater wrong?

Again: is it so sinful to gather the home circle in one harmonious group; and let your hand, with all a mother's sweet, self-sacrificing love, weary itself upon the keys, guiding the little feet to time their motion to the tune, your eye, the while, watching their childish happiness, whilst they, thus taught, find home their brightest, dearest spot on earth, — is this so very sinful?

Ask the son, who can look back on such a childhood, whether such teaching ever led wrong. Ask the daughter,

on the other hand, who blushes not to join in wildest
whirl of waltz or polka, if she sought them not because
forbidden in her home all innocent delights and natural
enjoyments of such a kind.

Beware lest a mistaken exercise of power, restraining
what God meant His children to enjoy, shall lead them
into sin which must in future rest upon your own souls!

It may appear to you that I am speaking with a
warmth quite disproportioned to my theme; but I cannot
so think.

Every thing which has in any way to do with the care
or nurture of the young, which tends to make their
home to them the centre of all earthly joy, is, and must
ever be, of infinite importance. Of vital interest is it to
us all, as well as our most bounden duty, to study to at-
tain that golden mean which, whilst thankfully and grate-
fully making use of God's good gifts to men, shall guard,
guide, and restrain such use within its proper bounds.

For these reasons, I think we may safely recommend
dancing, not only as an ornamental, but useful, part of education; as an accomplishment capable of heightening and
refining our innocent amusements; as the means of imparting happiness to our friends, and promoting cheerfulness in our intercourse with society; but, remember,
this approval of dancing gives no countenance to its
abuses.

And remember, too, that to every individual there will
come " a time to mourn " as well as " a time to dance."

"Well," said Mr. Lovegood, as he laid down the paper, "how does this article strike you?"

"I cannot say, Charles, that it has convinced me. I am willing to grant that it may possess some truth, but I cannot see that the main point of the whole question is reached. The writer makes her plea rest principally upon the absence of any condemnation of dancing in the Bible, and upon the added happiness brought to the home by its practice : this leaves the entire subject of the demoralizing effect of it upon the character entirely untouched.

"It strikes me that the very fact brought out and dwelt upon so ably in the article you spoke of in 'The London Review,' of the introduction of the '*ballet*' upon the stage, giving rise, as it does, to such terrible immorality, is sufficient to banish dancing forever from our homes."

" On the contrary," said her husband, "I find in that very fact an argument on my side. It is precisely because Christian parents have (in too many instances) 'banished dancing forever from their homes,' that it has become thus degraded and depraved. Had we given up music in the same way, you would have argued, that, because low, indecent songs were nightly sung upon the stage, therefore it must, as a Christian duty, be 'banished forever from our homes.'

"No. Depend upon it, the duty of those who are placed over the young is to rescue dancing from the depth to which it has now sunk by raising and refining its character; bring it into the Christian home, properly guarded

and exercised; show and teach all men that there is no necessity to make it an agent of evil, but that, on the contrary, properly used, it may and must tend to good: and
I do earnestly believe that the fearful sin, the mass of depravity, now springing from its misuse, would disappear
far more rapidly from such a course than from all the dia-
tribes against dancing that could be uttered while the
world lasts."

"But do you think, Charles, that the course you propose
would put a stop to such things in England?"

"Perhaps not; but I can tell you what would have
the greatest and most powerful effect, — the influence and
presence of the Queen. All these indecent dances have
appeared in their worst form (and it is a point to be specially noted), since the Queen has withdrawn herself from
public life, and from the amusements and entertainments
of her subjects; thereby depriving them of that restraining influence which prevented the excesses into which
they have since fallen.

"No such representations as those of which we have
read would have been permitted, had it been known that
the Queen would be present; and more than this, if she
would discountenance at her court the presence of those
whose lives tend to encourage and increase this evil, a
long step would be taken towards its final eradication."

"Well, then," said his wife, "what do you propose where
we have no Queens?"

"A strange question for you to ask, Mary, when you so

well know my views on that head. Every American woman is a sovereign in her own right in her home: there
she may and must rule in all such matters; and if she orders her household, as I before said, by showing the beautiful effects which may spring from the right use of this
innocent recreation, she will do more than she could in
any other way to abolish the evil influences of its abuse."

"This is such a new view to me, Charles, that I must
have time to think it over seriously, and return to the discussion when I have done so;" and Mrs. Lovegood thoughtfully took up the paper, and once more looked at the
article.

VII. — SUNDAY OUR NATIONAL
DEFENCE.

THE principal agencies for preserving the sacredness of the Christian Sunday in our country are
the pulpit, the press, and personal influences."

Such was the statement made by the New-York Sabbath Committee in 1862. In this personal influence may
not the women of our Republic be efficient helpers?

The following sketch of real incidents may be of some
effect in showing what resulted from an opportunity
improved: —

Some years ago, — it may be nearly a score, — a lady who believed in "the Sabbath day to keep it holy," because God's word and his example had consecrated it a day of rest for mankind, was boarding at the M—— House, then one of the largest and best-appointed of those family homes in Philadelphia.

The lady, whom I will style Mrs. H——, was fond of studying character; and many good opportunities were afforded her in the varieties of the *genus homo* that thronged this pleasant house.

Among the foreign residents were two young gentlemen from the Russian army, belonging, I believe, to the engineer corps, sent hither by the Emperor Nicholas to learn what they could of the coal-mining operations in America. I give these particulars to interest my readers in the reality of my characters.

These young Russians were liberally educated and intelligent; the youngest remarkable for his knowledge of languages and ready conversational talent.

Still it was apparent from their manners and opinions that they had come from different social positions. The elder, Baron V——, represented the nobility: the younger, Mr. P——, had been taken from the people.

The emperors of Russia thus select a certain number of their young candidates for the honors of college and official appointments. Mr. P—— must have been one of these: his broad, massive forehead, with the straight, full, dark eyebrows, that made in their shadows his clear-blue eyes seem always filled with light, gave to his otherwise very plain features a cast of intellectual superiority that no one could mistake.

The talents of Mr. P—— fully justified the imperial selection. Mrs. H—— was soon attracted by his singular *naïveté* and originality of character, so unlike the hurrying business mode in which we live.

He was full of brilliant fancies. His general intelligence rendered his conversation very agreeable; and, while the lady could not agree with many of his opinions, still this served to interest her more deeply in his welfare. She saw how capable he was of doing good if only he would love the work. It thus happened that they became friends: indeed, the young Russian seemed to consider this lady — old enough to be his mother — as his particular friend, and poured into her ear all his new views of life and liberty; for he soon became a real convert to our political institutions, considered Jefferson the great hero of humanity, and all our American laws and customs he would heartily indorse, except one; he could not understand or endure our observance of Sunday.

He never tired of carrying on a crusade against the custom, always in a merry, good-humored way, and calling upon Mrs. H—— to take up the gauntlet in its defence.

"No theatre, no opera, no balls, on Sunday! — how can you live?" he would say. "You call this a *free* country; but where is your freedom if every one may not act as he pleases? You, and those who think with you, need not go to such amusements if they seem to you wrong; but the idea of controlling a whole people, of compelling them to go without what is to them a necessity, is preposterous, horrible, monstrous!"

And then he would go over his first impressions of this "Puritan humbug," as he called it; saying that both were American words, and just fitted each other. Then he described the Sundays in Paris as models for America.

It was difficult to argue with a man whose stand-point was so utterly different as to leave no common ground on which to meet, for the Bible was to him only a work of priestcraft; and therefore it happened, that, after many long conversations, he would return to the subject, apparently entirely unconvinced by any thing which the lady had said. He was always pleasant and good-humored, however, and no excited feeling ever entered into the discussions.

One bright Sunday morning, on returning from church, Mrs. H—— stepped into the parlor to leave a message on her way to her room. Mr. P—— was seated there, reading a French novel: he sprang up, and, placing a chair for her, said, "Ah! do take pity on me. Such a *triste* country as yours I never did see! Tell me, I ask you once more, why are your people such fools as to keep Sunday? What good can ever come of it?"

"It is our national defence, Mr. P——," said she, a sudden thought of his military life suggesting a new idea.

"Your national defence, Mrs. H——! What may that mean?" he inquired.

"How large is your standing army?" she inquired.

He gave its numbers.

"And that of France?"

He named it also.

"And order could not be preserved without such a large army; at least, it would scarcely be considered safe to diminish it?"

"I think not."

"You have, in the way of your profession, Mr. P——, travelled much since you came to this country; tell me, have you seen in our cities, from New Orleans to Boston, or anywhere in our land, any want of order, any need of guards, of military posts or sentinels?"

"So far from it," replied he, "that I have frequently called the attention of the baron to the perfect order which reigns everywhere, and yet without any apparent control."

"That order," said Mrs. H——, "springs from our national defence, — the observance of Sunday."

"You must speak plainer," said he, "before I can perceive your drift."

"I mean," said she, "that all communities, peoples, and nations must be subject to some form of control: it must be either the Bible or the bayonet; moral power or musket power.   Our Government, as you know, has been termed, but most falsely, a paradox, a contradiction in terms, a *free government;* for whilst the word "government" implies, of necessity, control, the word "free" seems to destroy it.   I say seems; for it does not do so in reality: it merely changes the mode of administering it.

"You have admitted to me at various times, that, much as you admire our *free* institutions, you are aware that your people are not fit for them, and that they could not be introduced into Russia.   Why?   Because you, I mean you as a people, have never learned *self-government.*

"You look to be controlled by the sword; we, by the moral power in each man's breast.   A nation is, after all, but an aggregate of individuals; and, in a voluntary government such as ours, each man submits to certain rules and restrictions for the good of the whole.   A republic needs, above all other forms of government, to be guided by reason and conscience: the former, to discover the best mode of harmonizing all antagonistic elements; the latter, to act from the highest motives in carrying out such mode.   Now do you see my drift?   If so, you may work it out for yourself."

"Go on," he said.   "I like your little preachment."

"Well, then, I will only add a few words.   Reason and conscience are only another name for religion: therefore, to insure a nation's success, it must be religious; that is, granting the truth of what I have just affirmed, and, as I said before, as a nation is only an aggregate of individuals, it becomes each man's bounden duty to do his part to promote the right, and not only to do it, but to show to the world that he does it. As God, our Creator, has constituted us, we must have an 'outward and visible sign' of our inward feelings. Sunday, therefore, becomes that 'outward and visible sign,' the expositor, as it were, of our American sentiments.

"You have told me that in Russia you are marched to church by military command, as the Emperor directs; whilst we go voluntarily, to declare in the face of the world our recognition of God's law, and our determination to abide by it. For this reason, also, we carefully abstain on that day from amusements lawful and innocent on other days; and I ask you to tell me candidly, which system seems to you most productive of the real happiness and the best interests of a people."

He rose, and walked rapidly up and down the room, rubbing his hands over each other, as was his way when interested, as though pondering the words of Mrs. H——, but said nothing.

"I had little idea," observed Mrs. H——, "when I entered the room, of preaching you a lay-sermon; but, if it has put a thought into your mind, I shall not regret it."

He still said nothing, apparently lost in reflection; and Mrs. H—— left him to his meditations.

Some weeks later, Mrs. H—— met a mutual friend

8

from the country, with whom Mr. P—— often went to stay from Saturday till Monday. She told her, that, on his last visit, she had been surprised on Sunday morning by his offering to go to church with her. This was so at variance with his usual custom, that she expressed her astonishment.

"Ah!" said he, "I have found out why you keep Sunday in your Republic, and I think there is a good deal in it."

From that time, during the remainder of his visit to this country, Mr. P—— always made a point of attending the morning service; and Mrs. H—— was thus led to hope that her "little preachment" had not been without effect. An incident deepened this impression. One morning, just before Mr. P—— left for Russia, he came to his friend Mrs. H——, saying earnestly, "I have something to show that will make you very glad;" and he took from its morocco case a richly-bound little volume, a copy of the New Testament.

"Indeed! I am glad that you have chosen such a companion for your voyage" said Mrs. H——.

"But I did not choose it myself: it was given me by a young lady as a parting present."

"Then I am sure you will prize it highly and read it."

"Yes," was his emphatic reply, "I will read it."

PART THIRD.

I. — THE HOME CIRCLE.

"My country, sir, is not a single spot,
 Of such a mould, or fixed to such a clime.
 No: 'tis the social circle of my friends,
 The loved community in which I'm linked,
 And in whose welfare all my wishes centre."

Miles's Mahomet.

THESE lines contain a vital truth, and one scarcely enough dwelt upon. What composes our country, and makes its true life? Not its wide prairies, with their billows of undulating green; not its lofty mountains, with their hidden and inexhaustible treasures of ore; not our vast oceans, rolling rivers, nor swelling streams. Grand as each and all of these may be, they are not the country's life, though affecting that life, — not the country's power, though increasing that power: its true life and power must reside in *the Home;* for it is the aggregate of homes which make up the country, and it is from them that all the good must flow which governs and regulates the nation. Hence the importance of making our homes the centre of happiness, usefulness, and intelligence. The higher the home standard, the higher the influence exerted by those who go forth from that home.

The family is God's institution for human happiness as well as for the highest moral culture this life affords. For the sanctuary of a virtuous home, the tender affections are like the sweet May blossoms, that not only shed beauty and hope on the opening year, but from which the best fruits of genius and the sweetest enjoyments of life have their source and culture.

First in the destiny of the home circle, we would place *the mother;* for this is her rightful domain. *The father* goes abroad to toil for his loved ones, and is, of necessity, absent much of his time: but God placed upon the mother the duty and responsibility of tending and training her children; and it has been well said, that, "of all whom the world had honored with the appellation of great, more than one-half might, with the strictest propriety, inscribe on their escutcheons, as the motto of their success, the simple word 'Mother.'"

The relation of brother and sister develops the finest traits of character, calling forth on one side all the most beautiful feminine virtues and the rich treasures of self-sacrificing love, on the other the noblest qualities of man's nature, and the constant exercise of a considerate protecting affection; while from both are required the necessity of mutual concession and forbearance. But, as ever, we find the most accurate and beautiful description of the contrast between "sons and daughters" in the words of Holy Writ: —

"That our sons may be as plants grown up in their youth; that our daughters may be as corner-stones, polished after the similitude of a palace." — Psalms, cxliv. 12.

How carefully the royal Psalmist has, in this burst of sacred song, marked the specific differences in the sexes! Guided by divine inspiration, he has not only delineated the characteristics of man and woman, but he has also, by a flash from the fountain of light, embodied, as in a photograph, their destiny and duties.

"*Our sons*" are "to subdue the earth." Thus intended for the world's work and use, they grow stronger in the storms of life. Springing up, seemingly, by their own volition wherever planted, rough, gnarled, and knotted though they may be, yet struggling heavenward, and ruling over earth, they show bravely in the history of humanity.

And yet they are never able to reach the perfectness of sacred truth, which their *reason* seeks to know, because their worldly wisdom, darkened by the Fall, has its roots, spreading, like the banian, too widely and persistently in the earth, dragging the soul, that should lift its aspirations like the reaching palm on high, downward, to seek

its pleasures in earthly things, and thus buries its strength
in the dust from which man was formed.

" *Our daughters,*" never soiled with the dust of earth
(woman was fashioned from the living substance of the
man, " made in the image of God "), are represented by
" corner-stones, polished after the similitude of a palace."
Is not this description emblematical of moral strength,
and that innate sense of the beauty of goodness conferred on woman by the grace of God, when, after the
Fall, he declared to the old Serpent, or Satan, " *I will put
enmity between thee and the woman*" ?   Also to her was
given the promise of salvation through her " seed."

We are aware that courtesies are not always considered
duties; but we must feel that a very beneficial effect
upon home life would be produced by so considering
them.

Ought we not to exert ourselves, and try to make
home an agreeable as well as a safe place, as it must, after
all, be our stronghold of comfort? Would it not be
well if children were trained to exert their talents, ac-
quirements, and accomplishments, more in the family, and
less for the world? — to enliven and entertain the home
circle, rather than to show off in the ball-room or the
musical entertainment ?

The efforts made to amuse and please " the world,"
which never succeed, would, if as perseveringly made at
home, confer unspeakable delight on those we should
consider first in our love, and who are our best and truest
friends.

In this vast country of ours, with its immense extent of territory, the agricultural population, of necessity, forms a very important feature; and it seems to me that their needs and requirements have not been sufficiently studied.

Dr. Hall, in his "Journal of Health," has some capital suggestions upon the duties of farmers to their families, and the importance of supplying their wives with means to make their homes comfortable as far as their circumstances will permit.

Valuable as his advice is, we would add something further. It is a fact, and one which we have frequently heard commented upon with surprise, that the statistics of all insane asylums prove that the agricultural population uniformly furnishes the largest proportion of patients. Why is this? A cursory view of the matter would lead one to suppose that the "even tenor of their way," the calm, quiet, uneventful character of their lives, would prevent rather than lead to insanity. We are apt to overlook the fact, or, rather, farmers are apt to do so, that the human being is a compound of body and spirit; and, in exercising the former, the latter is too often ignored.

The mind needs something to feed upon: nothing is provided, and it preys upon itself until its balance is lost, and insanity ensues. It will not do to cultivate the acres alone: home pleasures, home enjoyments, and home recreations must come in for their share. We must sow the seed of innocent amusement, and plough the mental field with care, if we would have a harvest of health and happiness in the homes of our agriculturists.

We do not mean to advise a mingling of reading and reaping, meditation and milking, or classics and churning; but we do mean to suggest that each farmer and farmer's wife, or *farmeress*, should endeavor to *happify* his and her home — to coin a word for the occasion — by introducing into it needed and varied recreations. The power of these can scarcely be estimated, save by looking at their beneficial results. The assembling of neighbors and friends for social enjoyment has a good effect in enlivening and cheering. Music should be encouraged. We think it should be taught in all our common schools, forming part of every child's education. Nothing gives more unfailing pleasure in the home circle. Indeed, all the courtesies and amenities of home life have an important influence and bearing upon the character of every one, no matter what his or her station may be, — an influence far stronger and deeper than any one can be aware of who has not given the subject much consideration.

If Nature has not gifted us with great talents, if we are not learned or accomplished, or witty or wise, still there is a charm in kindness that never fails to please. There is a consideration that saves the feelings of others, because it is never guilty of rudeness, never utters a cutting sarcasm nor vulgar epithet to wound the self-respect of another, or inflict a pang on a heart that loves the one who has thus cruelly and carelessly made it suffer.

And all these graces of manner, this charm of giving pleasure, do not require genius or learning or accomplishments; though these will add to the power of those who possess them. But simple goodness will be sufficient — a truly Christian spirit, which obeys always that beautiful injunction of the apostle, "Be courteous!"

Happy the home where the real art of life's courtesies is understood and practised! There selfishness is conquered by the generous desire to promote the general happiness; and thus "the friends whom God has given us," as Mrs. Barbauld prettily calls the family, become the friends of our choice, — one heart in one household.

No. II. — ENGAGEMENTS AND WEDDINGS.

WE have been dwelling upon the attractions of home life; now we come to what, of necessity, precedes them, — courtship and marriage. Especially are these important, as upon the mode in which they are conducted, and the choice made, must much of those very attractions depend.

Perhaps there is no country on the face of the globe where a word of advice is more needed. The youth of

America are permitted a freedom and liberty of choice unequalled in any other land. We may almost say, from earliest infancy, certainly from earliest childhood, boys and girls are permitted to associate together without restraint; and, more than this, youths and maidens are considered eligible for husbands and wives at a much earlier age than abroad.

In many respects, this custom has great advantages. The tastes and pursuits of those marrying early assimilate much more easily than when the connection is formed later in life, when the habits are more fixed. It is also desirable as tending to insure steadiness in a young man. The sense of responsibility, and the consciousness that others are dependent upon him, — often for support, and always for happiness, — cannot be without its effect: his best feelings are constantly called into exercise, and thus his home, the home of his wife and children, has been to many a young man the earthly talisman which has kept him from the gaming-table and haunts of dissipation of every form.

It has been urged, on the other hand, that the choice on both sides would be differently made when the judgment was more matured, and thus more lasting happiness produced; that a boyish or girlish fancy is a thing that will pass, when too late, and the knot is irrevocably tied, and thus results much domestic misery.

But it seems to me that a careful examination of facts, so far as it is possible to ascertain them, proves quite the reverse, — that more happy marriages result from what is termed "mere youthful fancies" than from any other.

The feelings are more keen and sensitive in early years than at any other time. The youthful maiden, as the beloved and honored wife, is even more apt to become the beacon and guiding star of an intellectual man, because she was his "boyish fancy," than a woman of superior attainments, chosen later; whilst she, for her part, ripens and develops daily, by constant association with a vigorous masculine intellect, love stimulating her ambition, and leading her to ever progressing mental effort.

Almost every one must recall some instance where the elevating effect of a congenial union is mutually apparent: on the man, in moral and spiritual growth; on the woman, in intellectual development and power. But it must be remembered that love must be the root, or the plant can never produce either intellectual, moral, or spiritual flowers.

Hence the vast amount of domestic suffering, and the frightful immorality, in those countries where marriage is made an affair of negotiation and business. As one instance, among many, let us look at France, where one of her domestic institutions is the *mariage de convenance*, and where the young girl has her husband selected for her so soon as she quits the school or convent where she has been educated. She is introduced to him, and converses with him in the presence always of one or both parents; the French deeming it most unwise to allow the affections of a girl to be interested before marriage, lest, during the arrangements for the contract, all should be broken off.

The young people are never permitted to be alone together (this would be a terrible breach of etiquette); and they actually stand up to take those solemn vows upon themselves, with a few weeks' acquaintance of this sort — often with less. What possible knowledge can they have of each other's characters? what prospect of future happiness under such circumstances?

There are a few instances where this custom has been departed from in France; but so few as to be only the exceptions proving the rule. Monsieur de Tocqueville married for love, after a five-years' engagement. Guizot, probably from his English affinities, gave his daughters liberty to choose for themselves: they are mentioned as having married for love, as though they stood alone among the daughters of France in such action. Indeed, we find a French countess characterizing the affair as "a very indelicate proceeding."

In England, their views and practice accord much more nearly with our own in this matter, although with far greater restraint in the intercourse permitted; but formerly much the same system prevailed as that of France. We find, from their earlier writers, that a boy of fourteen, before going on his travels, was contracted to a girl of eleven, selected as his future wife by parents and guardians. On his return, he was expected to fulfil his engagement; but, by law, it was imperative that forty days should pass between the contract and the marriage. This period of reflection was never permitted in France, being considered too dangerous; but we do not learn that it was of much service, as the young people still remained subject to the will of their parents, no matter what their private sentiments might be.

We come now to some of the rules of etiquette relating to courtship.

A sufficient knowledge of each other is one of the most important and difficult points to be attained; important, because a prepossessing exterior is not always the reflex of the soul, nor is Lavater's theory infallible; difficult, because, in our present state of social arrangements, a gentleman no sooner seeks the society of a lady by whom he has been attracted, for the sake of discovering her character, than he finds that the world has connected their names, and that he has thus placed the lady in an uncomfortable and embarrassing position. Society does few greater wrongs than this; for not only is much intercourse, mutually agreeable and improving, thus foolishly destroyed, but the necessary knowledge of each other which should precede marriage is almost entirely prevented.

This knowledge can never be calculated by time, since ten years of acquaintance may not effect what certain circumstances may produce in as many months or even weeks.

A gentleman may address a lady by letter, or in words (both modes are open to him); but he will find a few words, spoken in a manly, direct way, far more available in pleading his cause than all the letters that ever were penned. The more care he gives his letter, the more apt it will be to appear studied, and the less likely to reach the heart of her to whom it is addressed; whilst we may venture to say, no true woman ever yet paused to criticise the style of an offer made to her, when feeling gained the mastery over utterance.

The customs recognized on these points vary much in different parts of our country. In the South and West, it is considered a want of delicacy to announce an engagement, whilst at the North and East it is the usual custom. But it may be questioned whether this silence on such an important point always springs from views of delicacy; whether it does not quite as frequently arise from an unwillingness to resign general attention in society. More liberty is permitted to gentlemen, without comment, in the South and West, in their intercourse with ladies; and hence a young lady, especially if she has been much of a belle, is not, as she should be, always ready to give up those attentions to which she has been accustomed: and therefore she conceals her engagement. But surely this is not, in any case, either complimentary or just to her future husband, to whom she is already as much bound by honor as she will hereafter be by law.

And, further, a lady may do a grievous wrong to a susceptible heart, by leaving her position undefined, when one word might have prevented it all. We remember being much struck by an incident at one of our watering-places.

Leaning against the doorway of the drawing-room of one of the principal hotels one evening, might have been seen a young girl, of such exquisite loveliness, both of form and face, as to attract all beholders.

"Who is she?" "Who can she be?" passed from mouth to mouth.

"The beautiful Miss——," was the answer; and a far-famed beauty and belle was named. A moment later, a young man was presented to her; and as he talked, his whole soul in his face, "Love at first sight," whispered one of a group who were watching them.

Chance brought a person, later in the evening, so close to the apparition of loveliness (for this seems the only term to suit her) as to render it impossible not to catch her words, as she said to the lady at her side, in a voice whose rich soft tones consorted admirably with her appearance:—

"Was it indelicate to allude to my engagement to a stranger? I did it on principle."

It so happened that the person heard afterwards, from that stranger's own lips, a warm tribute to the delicacy and beautiful consideration with which this was done, and an expression of the consciousness of how much suffering he had thus been spared. Is not this a proof of where duty lies in this respect?

With regard to marriage, or rather to the wedding ceremony, it is impossible to give rules, as practice must ever vary with circumstances.

Whether one, two, a dozen bridesmaids, or none, must be a matter of private preference or convenience, in no way affecting the social position of the parties. With regard to dress, the same rule exists; therefore no allusion is made to it.

But there is one all-important point, which we should urge upon every one about to be married; and this is that the ceremony be solemnized by a clergyman. This is not necessary to render the marriage legal, and therefore may not be considered vital; but, surely, no one with right views can consent to look upon that great mystery as merely a " civil contract." The Scripture doctrine is, that, as Christ and the Church are one, so the husband and wife are one; and that, " as the Church obeys Christ, so should the wife obey her own husband," — not through compulsion or fear, but with a voluntary obedience, springing from love and reverence. And the husband should " love his own wife as Christ loved the Church; " should protect her, cherish her, honor her, because this is the natural consequence of his position, and " she is his own flesh."

It must be evident, that by thus placing marriage upon its rightful foundation of religious rite, as well as of civil law, our whole social fabric is exalted with it; for the moral tone of a people must depend, humanly speaking, upon their domestic institutions; and therefore, when the true idea of marriage prevails, there will be found the highest and purest tone of moral life and the best models of good society.

III. — FOREIGN TRAVEL.

AMERICANS usually burden themselves with too much luggage. They take huge trunks, which they find themselves obliged to leave in London or Paris; and provide themselves with clothing sufficient for years, without reflecting that they are not going into deserts untrodden by man, but to the very centres of civilization, where any thing they require can be obtained at a moment's notice, ready for instant use.

For a lady, half a dozen of each article of under-clothing would be ample. Wherever you stop, — if but for twenty-four hours, — you can have washing done, which, at any rate, would be necessary to avoid carrying soiled clothing.

The best material for a lady's travelling-dress is black silk or alpacca. The former is preferable: it is easily brushed and smoothed out, and is less liable to be travel-stained. A black silk, of a quality as rich as you please, is also the best adapted for service, while stopping, as an out-door dress. For shopping, sight-seeing, visiting gal-

leries, driving, &c., it is inconspicuous, and the dress of a
gentlewoman everywhere.

The English are always known on the Continent by
some astounding " get up," which they call a travelling-
dress. An American lady's costume is so entirely French,
that she is never conspicuous, unless she takes up the
English idea, and walks about in continental towns with
a grotesque hat, hob-nailed shoes, and flashy underskirts.

For mild weather on the road, a waterproof cloak is
most convenient; if chilly, a Zouave jacket of cloth may
be worn underneath. In cold weather, a heavy cloth
sack will be required.

Never travel without a blanket shawl upon your arm,
ready for instant use. Such a shawl is invaluable, not
only for warmth in sudden changes of weather, but to
use as a cushion, pillow, &c.

A straw bonnet, simply trimmed in the best style, is
the most appropriate head-gear for a lady.

With a little ingenuity, a bonnet may be carried in the
top division of the trunk, and thus avoid another article
of luggage. At all events, the addition of a bonnet-box
may be deferred till Paris is reached, by which time much
experience as to a person's requirements will have been
gained.

A convenient travelling hand-bag is indispensable to
contain many little comforts and conveniences that may
be needed by a lady when separated from her trunk.

The examination of luggage, on landing in England,

is made as little troublesome as possible, especially for ladies, who are not expected to carry tobacco, which is the great bugbear of the English tide-waiters.

In France and Belgium, the custom-house regulations are strictly administered. Large quantities of jewelry are smuggled into France from Switzerland; and it is advisable to carry as few small boxes as possible in your trunk, as they are liable to be rudely broken open in the search.

In Germany, there is but little trouble; but, strange to say, in Spain, in passing from one province to another, the luggage is liable to custom-house search.

The octroi officials abound on the Continent; but a simple declaration will usually suffice for them. In Italy, the custom-house officials are corrupt, more especially in the papal dominions. A small fee, privately adminis-tered, is the method by which the experienced overcome all interference here.

Russia is the only country that presents any difficulty to travellers. They do not encourage foreign travel, and their custom-house and police laws are extremely strin-gent. No books, not even guide-books, can be taken into Russia: they must be left at the frontier until you return.

You move about with the knowledge of the police; and no foreigner can leave Russia without advertising his intention in the newspapers at least a fortnight before his departure, in order that all who have claims upon him may be informed.

All travellers on the Continent of Europe, if able to incur the expense, should employ a courier. The whole anxiety and burden of the arrangements are assumed by him. He speaks all the languages of Europe with sufficient accuracy, understands the usages of the road, understands a thousand little impositions which the unwary foreigner knows nothing of, and shields him from them.

He makes every bargain, pays every bill, writes in advance and engages rooms, sees that they are neat and well-ordered, and, where there are any short-comings, puts every thing right with a strong hand; for the courier is a tyrant in a small way. He brings customers to the hotels; and the landlord, knowing this, is his humble servant. If you have a private table, he is in attendance at meals, carves for you, and sees that you are properly served. He knows the best shops, and all the objects of interest in the towns you may visit; he can conduct you to galleries and museums, and obtain admittance for you to palaces, villas, &c.

A good courier, in short, smooths over every difficulty, and enables you to enjoy, without drawback, your residence in foreign lands.

The objection usually made to couriers is, that they make their percentage out of their employers' money. It is not generally known to Americans that servants in all parts of Europe receive fees from tradespeople, and are thus encouraged to bring their custom. This is no doubt done by those your courier employs, but scarcely more than this.

Couriers may readily be obtained in London or Paris. Salary per month is fifty dollars. He pays his own bill at the hotels (except in Spain), or rather pays *nothing*, as he brings the patronage.

The most luxurious, satisfactory, and also expensive mode of travelling is by post. A carriage may be hired for any number of months; or a new or second-hand one purchased, and, when done with, sold. The posting is regulated by government, according to a settled tariff.

A less expensive mode, which prevails in Italy, is by travelling "vetturino;" that is by hiring a carriage, and placing yourself in the charge of the conductor, or "vetturino." He charges a specified sum by day, and engages to convey you in a given time to your destination. The charge includes all expenses, food, &c. This latter saves the traveller from all imposition of innkeepers, who prey upon foreigners. This mode of travelling is tedious, as, having the same horses, they must rest whenever the vetturino pleases.

Another method is by diligence; but railways and steamboats are now so universal, that, on most of the great routes, the traveller will find these modes of conveyance. To see a country to advantage, however, one must neither make short cuts by sea, or fly through the air by rail.

In crossing the channels to France or Ireland, it is well to go on board the steamers early to secure a sofa or berth. If you dread the sea, choose a calm day, for one is liable to more severe sea-sickness than in crossing the Atlantic, and the boats are usually crowded. Few things are more surprising to an American, accustomed to the floating palaces of his own country, than the small and inconvenient vessels that ply on these important highways.

Railway travelling differs in Europe from our own in some of its arrangements. The term "car" is never applied to their conveyances. They are called " carriages," and are divided into compartments, containing sometimes six, sometimes eight persons.

A party which does not entirely fill a compartment may always secure it to themselves by a judicious application of silver to the palm of the guard.

Shop-keepers in Europe never allow their goods turned over, unless you come to buy. Any lady who enters a shop is expected to purchase something, not merely to look round.

HINTS.

1. As regards passports, it is safer to obtain them in Washington, at headquarters.

2. A sole-leather trunk is the strongest and best for long periods of travel, about sixteen inches high, eighteen wide, and thirty-two long. This size will fit upon any travelling carriage. It should open in the middle, that it may be pushed under the berth on board ship.

3. Trunks may be stored in the luggage-room, if you

sail in a steamer. All the clothing needed for the voyage may be contained in a travelling-bag, twenty-two inches high and thirty wide, made of enamelled cloth, which wears as well and sheds water better than leather. Trunks should have a varnished canvas cover.

4. A gum-elastic bag for hot water is a very desirable article for a traveller who suffers from cold hands or feet, and, when empty, occupies but little space. A light linen or muslin dust-cloth will be found convenient. Soap is never furnished, except in England.

5. A courier generally receives a sum of money on starting, rendering an account of it when it is exhausted. A daily sum, however, may be given, and a nightly account rendered.

6. All travellers should purchase Murray's "Handbooks" of the different countries they intend to visit. They are full of valuable and useful information.

7. In Great Britain, a "Bradshaw" is also indispensable. It is published monthly, and contains all the latest information relative to the departure of trains, steamers, stages, &c.

8. Luggage is not, as with us, always carried in a "baggage-car." That of each person is usually placed on the top of the carriage he is in; the smaller packages and bags being taken inside, and accommodated with nettings above his head.

9. It is not the usage for girls to walk alone in the

streets of the large capitals or towns of Europe. They must be accompanied by a servant or older lady.

10. A little small change of the country you may be in should always be kept in the pocket while on the road, coppers, especially.

IV. — LETTER-WRITING.

PERHAPS there is nothing which marks the lady or gentleman more than the mode in which they write a letter or note. And yet, strange as it may appear, this is a branch of education which is singularly neglected.

It is surprising how many persons of refinement, cultivation, and even of some literary attainment, write in an inelegant and careless manner.

A book has been recently published in England, entitled "The Hand-book of Etiquette," of a somewhat diffuse nature, and purporting to contain every instruction needed to render one thoroughly fitted for the best society; but, with the exception of a few words upon letters of introduction, there is not a single syllable upon the subject of letter or note writing.

A book of this kind surely is quite incomplete without some such notice. It is strange that, as a general rule, parents pay so little attention to their children's education on this point. Let a child be given paper and pencil as an amusement, and encouraged to write notes as a play; a facility both of handwriting and of expression will be obtained, which cannot fail to be of great and lasting advantage in later years.

The power of expressing one's self on paper with ease and grace is no slight accomplishment, avoiding on the one hand all affected or stilted phrases, and, on the other, a careless or slovenly style of writing.

A beautifully written letter, — who has not felt its charm? who has not owned its power? No grand composition, made up of tiresome tirades, vapid verbosity, or provoking platitudes, worrying and wearing the reader; but a true, earnest, simple expression of the writer's feeling, — an utterance of one heart speaking to another. What comes from the heart rarely fails to go to the heart. The plumb-line of love can never touch bottom in another heart, unless it has first sounded the depths of our own.

There seems some mysterious instinct, some magnetic power, which distinguishes between the false and the real article in feeling more certainly than in almost any thing else. The soul instantly detects and rejects a spurious sympathy, though clothed in the most polished periods; whilst, on the other hand, no language can tell the balm poured in by an earnest expression of genuine feeling, no matter how simple the words in which it is offered.

It should also be borne in mind that letters have a power which is often denied to their writer; not only can they reach the most distant points, where, it may be, he can never hope to go; but, more than this, bolts and bars yield before them. Letters can intrude where all other entrance is refused: they can speak for us when we are personally forced to be silent; through their agency we may direct, guide, comfort, and console.

If, then, such power be theirs, does it not become a solemn responsibility to cultivate the power of so expressing ourselves as to enable us to exercise the greatest influence for good?

As this is written for the home circle, a few words must be permitted upon the subject of family letters. It is too common for those who are very fond of corresponding with friends to neglect home letters.

"I never write home when I am away." "They never expect to hear from me, at home, when I am on a journey. "I never can find time to write when I am travelling."

Who has not heard such expressions a hundred times? And yet is not selfishness at the root of all such sayings? You who cannot take time from your own enjoyment to send a loving word to your dear ones at home, to tell them of your happiness, can scarcely put yourself in their place, realize their anxiety on your behalf, or what brightness you may bring to them by an animated, graphic sketch of what you may be passing through at the moment; thus enabling them to become sharers of your pleasure, and to follow you in spirit through your wanderings.

Granted, that, on your arrival at any point, you are weary, worn, and travel-stained, and rest presents itself to you as far more welcome than the effort of writing home; never mind, strive to forget self (a very brief space will be needed), pen a few lines to assure anxious hearts at home of your safety.

Could you follow the letter, and see the pleasure its arrival causes, surely you would think a little added weariness on your part a small self-sacrifice for the happiness produced.

Have you never happened to be the one left at home? and do you not know that this is true? Or, if the wished-for letter failed to arrive, do you not also know how much you suffered, lest the absent ones might not have reached their destination in health and safety?

Some families, when separated, never allow a day to pass without exchanging a chronicle of its events, shorter or longer, as circumstances may require; thus a loving bond, a common interest, is kept up, and family affection is preserved in all its freshness.

HINTS.

1. Strive to write a legible hand: there are few things more annoying than the attempt to decipher an illegible scrawl.

2. Do not cross your letters: it renders them difficult to read, and, in these days of cheap postage, is quite unnecessary.

3. Unless you know that your correspondent is well versed in French, refrain from interlarding your letters with it.

4. Confide to no one the delivery of an important letter. In nine cases out of ten, the mail will prove a far safer conveyance.

5. A letter should never remain unanswered a moment longer than is absolutely unavoidable, particularly if it be upon business. A simple acknowledgment is better than no notice of it at all.

6. Avoid in writing, as in talking, all words that do not express the true meaning: the simpler the form of expression, the better.

7. It is well, in dating every letter, to give the number of your residence, as many mistakes have arisen from the forgetfulness of correspondents on this point.

8. The wording of a letter should be as much like conversation as possible.

9. A lady should always be particular to write a neat note. There can never be any excuse for sending a careless, slovenly one.

10. Do not twist up scraps of paper into curious forms, difficult to open, but use always an envelope. It is much more suitable, and quite as quickly directed.

11. At present, sealing-wax is little used; but, should you put a seal to your letter, make it carefully and exactly: be cautious never to drop the wax upon any other part of the letter.

12. Never give a letter of introduction to a person whom you do not know, nor address one whom you know very slightly.

13. The letter of introduction should always be given unsealed, lest the bearer should incur the fate of the Persian messenger, who unconsciously presented an order to have his own head cut off.

14. It is better, in delivering a letter of introduction, to send it with your card and address, than to deliver it in person. There is an awkwardness on both sides,—in reading it, and having it read, in your presence.

15. Be particular in always putting an accurate direction upon your letter. The name not only of the city or town, but also the county and State, should be given. In this country, we have so many places of the same name, that this should be carefully attended to, to insure safety in the delivery.

16. It is important to remember, that, at the post-office, the name of the State to which the letter is addressed is first looked at, and therefore that should be more clearly and distinctly written than it usually is. Too many persons give such prominence to the name of the individual, that his residence is almost forgotten, — not considering that it is of equal importance. Let the whole direction be clear, legible, and carefully written.

V. — REQUISITES OF GOOD SOCIETY.

THE first indispensable requisite for good society is *education.* By this is not meant the so-called "finished education" of a university or a boarding-school. I think it will be found that these establishments put their "finish" somewhere in the middle of the course. They may possibly finish you as far as teachers can; but the education which is to fit you for good society must be pursued long after you leave them, as it ought to have been begun long before you went to them.

This education should have commenced with developing the mental powers, and especially the *comprehension.*

In order to enter into conversation, one should be able to catch rapidly the meaning of any thing that is advanced; for instance, though you know nothing of science, you should not be obliged to stare and be silent when some one who does understand it is explaining a new discovery or a new theory; though you have not read a word of Blackstone, your comprehensive powers should be sufficiently acute to enable you to take in statements that may be made of a recent legal cause; though you may not have read some particular book, you should be capable of appreciating the criticism which you hear of it.

Without such a power, — simple enough, and easily

attained by reading, attention, and practice, yet too seldom met with in general society, — a conversation which departs from the most ordinary topics cannot be maintained without the risk of lapsing into a lecture; with such a power, society becomes instructive as well as amusing, and you have no remorse at an evening's end at having wasted three or four hours in profitless banter or simpering platitudes.

This facility of comprehension often startles us in some women whose education we know to have been scanty, and whose reading is limited.

Married women are usually more agreeable to men of thought than young ladies, because the married are accustomed to the society of a husband, and the effort to be a companion to his mind has ingrafted the habit of attention and ready reply.

No less important is the cultivation of taste. If it is tiresome and deadening to be with people who cannot understand, and will not even appear to be interested in, your better thoughts, it is almost repulsive to find a man, still more a woman, insensible to all beauty, and immovable by any horror.

In the present day, an acquaintance with art, even if you have no love for it, is a *sine quâ non* of good society. Music and painting are subjects which will be discussed in every direction around you.

Warm arguments should be avoided in good society. A disputation is always dangerous to temper, and tedious to those who cannot feel as eager as the disputants: a discussion, on the other hand, in which everybody has a chance of stating amicably and unobtrusively his or her opinion, must be of frequent occurrence.

But to cultivate the reason, besides its high moral value, has the advantage of enabling one to reply as well as attend to the opinions of others.

Nothing is more tedious or disheartening than a perpetual "Yes," "Just so," and nothing more.

Conversation must never be one-sided. Then, again, the reason enables us to support a fancy or opinion when we are asked *why* we think so and so. To reply, "I don't know, but still I think so," is silly in a man, and tedious in a woman.

But there is a part of our education so important, and so neglected in our schools and colleges, that it cannot be too highly impressed on parents on the one hand, and young people on the other. I mean that which we learn first of all things, yet often have not learned fully when death eases us of the necessity, — the art of speaking our own language. What can Greek and Latin, French and German, be for us in our every-day life, if we have not acquired our own language.

Precision and accuracy must begin in the very outset; and, if we neglect them in grammar, we shall scarcely acquire them in expressing our thoughts. But since there is no society without interchange of thought, and since the best society is that in which the best thoughts are interchanged in the best and most comprehensible manner, it follows that a proper mode of expressing ourselves is indispensable to good society. This art of expressing one's thoughts neatly and suitably is one which, in the neglect of rhetoric as a study, we must practise for ourselves.

The commonest thought well put is more useful in a social point of view than the most brilliant idea jumbled up. What is well expressed is easily seized, and therefore readily responded to. The most poetic fancy may be lost to the hearer if the language which conveys it is obscure.

Speech is the gift which distinguishes man from animals, and makes society possible. He has but a poor appreciation of his high privilege as a human being, who neglects to cultivate " God's great gift of speech."

A knowledge of English literature is also an indispensable part of education. But *how* to read, is, for society, more important than *what* we read.

It is only in bad society that people go to the opera, concerts, and art-exhibitions, merely because it is the fashion, or to say they have been there. For this, too, some book-knowledge is indispensable. You should at least know the names of the more celebrated artists, composers, architects, sculptors, and should be able to appreciate, somewhat, their several schools.

So, too, you should know pretty accurately the pronunciation of celebrated names, or, if not, take care never to use them.

10

Persons who take up nothing but a newspaper, but read it to *think*, to deduce conclusions from its premises, and form a judgment on its opinions, are more fitted for society than those who read volumes without digesting them.

At the same time, an acquaintance with the best current literature is necessary to modern society; and it is not sufficient to have read a book without being able to pass a judgment upon it. Conversation on literature is impossible when your respondent can only say, " Yes, I like the book; but I really don't know why."

A knowledge of old English literature is not, perhaps, always needed; but it gives great advantage in all kinds of society, and in some is indispensable. The same may be said of foreign literature, which, in the present day, is almost as much discussed as our own: on the other hand, an acquaintance with home and foreign politics, with current history, and every subject of passing interest, is absolutely necessary; and a person of sufficient Intelligence to join in good society cannot dispense with the daily newspaper, the literary journal, and principal reviews and magazines.

Respect for *moral character* is also a distinguishing mark of good society. No wealth, no celebrity, no distinction of any kind, should induce a well-bred American lady to admit to her drawing-room a man or woman whose character is known to be bad.

HINTS.

1. Accomplishments are a great charm to society, and a very great assistance to it.

2. The two most indispensable qualities in social meetings are a thinking mind and a ready wit.

3. The most welcome guest in society will ever be the one to whose mind every thing is a suggestion, and whose words suggest something to everybody.

4. Be careful to offer a favor in such a manner as not to offend the delicacy of those whom you wish to serve.

5. The first mark of a well-bred person is a sensitive regard for the feelings of others.

6. In good society, an adherence to etiquette is a mark of respect. If any one be worth knowing, he is surely worth the trouble of approaching properly.

7. The act of "cutting" a person can only be justified by some strong instance of bad conduct. A cold bow, which discourages familiarity without offering insult, is the best mode to adopt.

8. A neglect of, or an adherence to, the forms of society in others towards yourself, is oftentimes the only way in which you are enabled to judge if your acquaintance be *really* considered desirable.

9. In short, harmony and peace are the rules of good society as of Christianity.

VI. — A LIFE OF ETIQUETTE.

IN studying a work recently given to the public, entitled
" Social Life of the Chinese," * one cannot fail to be
struck with the mass of forms and ceremonies with which
their daily life is burdened. On looking closer into the subject, we see that this springs from the fact that their life has
no deeper root than human law. Thus even the one commandment which the Chinese have ever observed, that
of obedience to parents, instead of raising them, as obedience to God's commands, faithfully fulfilled, must ever do,
has but served to rivet their chains by degenerating into
idolatry. The beautiful courtesies, the sweet amenities,
the gracious tendernesses, of the Christian home, are to
them all unknown. We are scarcely aware, till we examine heathen institutions, how much we all owe to
Christianity for even the lower forms of social and domestic enjoyment.

A life of etiquette, unless "rooted and grounded"
on something higher, must ever be, as is clearly shown
here, oppressive and cruel; and only in some such study
as this, do the full force and meaning of our blessed
Lord's words come out: "Take my yoke upon you, and
learn of me; for my yoke is easy and my burden is light."

We find, that, from the birth of a child to its sixteenth

* Harper & Brothers, New York.

year, the unfortunate little heathen is the victim of no less
than *thirteen* distinct ceremonies of the most burdensome
character. We note only four of these, which show the
system: —

1. Washing, the third day after birth, before the
" mother, " or goddess who presides over children, with
appropriate ceremonies.

7. At four months, the second thank-offering to
" mother" is made.

8. Child placed on chair at four months old. This
curious and anomalous ceremony demands a word of explanation. At this age, the maternal grandmother presents the child with a kind of chair, painted red, together
with a quantity of molasses candy. This soft candy is
placed in the seat of the chair: the child is then seated
upon it, and sticks to the chair for the time being. The
object is said to be to teach it to sit up, and not require
to be carried: whether the symbolism of teaching it thus
early to *stick* to its duty through life be also intended,
we are unable to say.

9. Anniversary of birth observed, with many ceremonies. The third thank-offering to "mother" then takes
place. This thank-offering is continued on the birthday
of children, every year, until they are sixteen.

There is much that is curious, and more that is sadden-
ing, in these ceremonies, as also in those connected with
death, mourning, and burial, which occupy a large portion
of the volume; but the limits of this article forbid any

more extended notice. We must refer our readers for
any further explanation to the work itself.

Its title, as we have said, is "Social Life of the Chinese;" but the term is scarcely an appropriate one, for
such a thing can hardly be said to have an existence in
the one-sided life of that nation.

Social enjoyment of every kind is there confined exclusively to men, women never joining in it in any way
except at the time of their marriage. The ceremonies
incident to this time, although of the most elaborate
character, are not here dwelt upon, because more familiar
to most readers.

In taking a comprehensive view of the Chinese, as a
people, it is impossible not to perceive that the cause
which has ever prevented their advancement and improvement is the manner in which they have treated their
women, without consideration, appreciation, or respect.
Their crime in this matter has re-acted, as it must ever
do, upon themselves; for man can never be rightly educated, or elevated in moral tone, where woman's influence
is unknown.

It is worthy of note, that, whilst reams of paper have
been filled with denunciations of the iniquities of the
opium-trade, a few quires would suffice for all that has
ever been said upon the subject of that far more deadly
drug, that moral narcotic, whose stupefying influence
has paralyzed the energies of the whole nation, — the
wrongs of woman among the Chinese.

We find many interesting facts also in another work, by the celebrated traveller, M. Huc, whose perfect knowledge of the language, and opportunities for observation of the manners and customs of the Chinese nation, entitle his opinions to much weight.

He only confirms all the previous accounts of other writers as to the condition of woman; showing that she is always the slave or victim of the man, never protected or even recognized by the law: if, by chance, allusion be made to her in any legal proceeding, it is merely to remind her of her inferiority, and that she is only in this world to obey and to suffer.

More than this, in all China, which may be termed a literary republic, where the highest honors come to men from literary distinction, can it be believed that women are not even *taught to read?* The girl is never educated in any manner.

M. Huc says, "Privations of every kind, and of every day; invectives; curses from time to time; also blows, — these are her heritage, which she must endure with patience."

He mentions one scene, of which he was an eye-witness, where, on seeing a crowd assembled round a young woman, bruised and bleeding, he inquired the cause, and found her husband had beaten her for the simple reason that "people were laughing at him because he had never beaten his wife;" the elevated standard of morality amongst this people deeming a negligence on this point a forfeiture of marital dignity.

The woman, whom he admitted had never in any way offended him, died two days afterwards from the effects of his treatment.

In many places, the women of the Chinese Empire are so miserable, that their sufferings in this life have suggested to them the hope of a future one, and, for want of a knowledge of Christianity, they have accepted the extravagance of Metempsychosis.

They have formed a sect called the "Abstinents," by obedience to whose rules they trust to secure the migration of their souls into another body, when they hope to have the happiness to return to life as men.

This hope supports them under their daily mortifications, and enables them to endure the troubles and hardships they have to suffer from the other sex, promising themselves, doubtless, ample compensation, should their husbands be transformed into women.

There is something truly sorrowful and pathetic in seeing the whole nature of woman thus perverted by a long continuance of ill-treatment, exaction, and tyranny of every kind. A nation composed of three hundred millions of people, about half of whom must be women, can never take a high rank amongst civilized nations whilst that half are persistently kept in a state of degradation.

The results of such a system are, if possible, more painfully evident in the men than in the women; their whole character being debased by the loss of the elevating influence which woman was intended by her Creator to exercise over man.

There is not opportunity in this article to point out many other bad customs; but enough has surely been said to prove that a "life of etiquette," unless the rules are drawn from Christianity, can never, in any way, exalt the character of a people.

Their ceremonies and polite manners are merely the results of human law: they govern entirely by brute force, never appealing to the moral sense, which, indeed, they seem to want entirely. Their punishments are of the most terrible and cruel nature, showing that they lack pity and mercy for men as much as they lack justice and respect for women.

There is something frightful in the immorality which exists amongst the Chinese as a nation. They have been termed an orderly, respectable people; but any study of the works of Europeans upon the subject will prove that this order proceeds from physical causes, not from love of righteousness.

Infanticide is of every-day occurrence. Thousands of girls perish in the waters of the rivers, or in the jaws of beasts. Boys are saved, because they carry on the business of life, ahd sustain the parental worship; but, with a girl, there is never the slightest hesitation in murdering her, if inclination or convenience prompts, as women are not supposed to possess souls.

In short, we might as reasonably expect, that, if one-half of the sun were covered with a pall of black, we should still enjoy the full brightness, beauty, and bounteousness of earth, as to look for happy homes and good society, where womanhood, in its social, moral, and intellectual influences, is totally blotted out.

VII.—SHAKSPEARE'S SUNDAY BOOK.

SHAKSPEARE and his Bible! How lovingly Will Shakspeare must have read his Bible when he was a boy! And he must have continued to read it when he was a man; but the fountain of its truths seem to have been unsealed to him at an early age, judging from the manner in which he has wrought their divine wisdom into his dramatic writings.

Dr. Johnson, in his grand way, thus describes the scope of those writings:—

"This, therefore, is the praise of Shakspeare, that his drama is the mirror of life; that he who has mazed his imagination in following the phantoms which other writers raise up before him may here be cured of his delirious ecstasies by reading human sentiments in human language; by scenes from which a hermit may estimate the transactions of the world, and a confessor predict the progress of the passions."

Dr. Johnson had a vast fund of learning, and talents

of great power; but his genius, in comparison with Shakspeare's, was as the north star to the moon: both draw their light from the sun; but the star is only a guide for the few travellers and voyagers, or for those who need its light for some particular knowledge, while the moon is queen of heaven to everybody, and brightens nature and gladdens the human heart with her night-lamp throughout the whole world.

A volume * has lately been republished here, containing a collection of extracts from Shakspeare's plays, intended to show the moral and religious tendencies of this master of the drama. The attempt is not very well executed; but, every time that we are drawn to his wonderful genius, something beyond other men presents itself, something new and of real worth is discovered.

The familiarity with Scripture which pervades the writings of Shakspeare has never been sufficiently noted: it is the most remarkable characteristic of his dramatic works.

It should be remembered that King James's translation of the Bible did not appear till Shakspeare's youth had passed, and his poems had been written. It must therefore have been a love for the Word of God, which had made him so diligently search for it in the partial and rare translations to be obtained in his younger days.

If his works be compared with those of the dramatists

* " Religious and Moral Sentences, culled from the works of Shakspeare," with an Introduction by Frederic D. Huntington, D.D.

of his time, his will shine in their delicacy, morality, and piety, with a lustre that could only have its pure and holy source in a believing mind and a God-fearing heart. And then remember that he left the stage in the very noonday of his fame; he broke his wand of power when his hand was the strongest to subdue men; and he buried his genius, that now enlightens the world, in the quiet shades of a humble village, before middle age had set the "signet sage" upon his brow.

Is it imaginative to suppose that the unworldliness of a Christian spirit urged him to leave the scenes of gayety, if not of dissipation, for "a life more sweet than that of painted pomp?" In our times, and especially in our land, where every man, from his childhood upwards, has the Holy Scriptures before him, where do we find an author of eminence from whom scriptural thoughts and scriptural words flow as they did from Shakspeare's pen, as we may read them now in those immortal productions of this great English poet? The volume to which allusion has been made contains over eight hundred quotations.

Here are a few of its sentences: —

> He that of greatest works is finisher
> Oft does them by the weakest minister;
> So Holy Writ in babes hath judgment shown,
> When judges have been babes.
>
> > Henry V., i. 2 ; Isaiah, iii. 4.

> With Cain, go wander through the shade of night,
> And never show thy head by day nor light.
>
> > Richard II., v. 6 ; Genesis, iv. 14.

It is as hard to come, as for a camel
To thread the postern of a needle's eye.
> Richard II., v. 5 ; Matthew, xix. 24.

God saw him when he was hid in the garden.
> Much Ado about Nothing, v. 1 ; Genesis, iii. 8.

To say the truth, so Judas kissed his Master,
And cried All hail! whereas he meant all harm.
> 3 Henry VI., v. 7 ; Matthew, xxvi. 48, 49.

Whiles the mad mothers with their howls confused,
Do break the clouds, as did the wives of Jewry
At Herod's bloody-hunting slaughtermen.
> Henry V., iii. 3 ; Matthew, ii. 18.

In the Book of Numbers is it writ,
When the son dies, let the inheritance
Descend unto the daughter.
> Henry V., i. 2 ; Numbers, xxvii. 8.

To keep that oath were more impiety
Than Jephthah's when he sacrificed his daughter.
> 3 Henry VI., v. 1 ; Judges, xi. 31.

God forbid that I should wish them severed
Whom God hath joined together.
> 3 Henry VI., iv. 1 ; Matthew, xix. 6.

The great King of kings
Hath in the table of his law commanded
That thou shalt do no murder.
> Richard III., i. 4 ; Exodus, xx. 13.

A virtuous and a Christian-like conclusion,
To pray for them that hath done scath to us.
> Richard III., i. 3 ; Matthew, v. 44.

Blessed are the peace-makers on earth.
> 2 Henry VI., ii. 1 ; Matthew, v. 9.

There is a special providence in the fall of a sparrow.
> Hamlet, v. 2 ; Matthew, x. 29.

He that doth the ravens feed,
Yea, providently caters for the sparrow,
Be comfort to my age.

> As You Like It, ii. 3 ; Psalms, cxlvii. 9.

I never see thy face, but I think on hell-fire, and
Dives that lived in purple.

> 1 Henry IV., iii. 3 ; Luke, xvi. 19-23.

Where then, alas ! may I complain myself ? —
To Heaven, the widow's champion and defence.

> Richard II., i. 2 ; Exodus, xxii. 22

Wisdom cries out in the streets, and no man regards it.

> 1 Henry IV., 1. 2 ; Proverbs, i. 20.

The cloud-capt towers, the gorgeous palaces,
The solemn temples, the great globe itself,
Yea, all which it inherit, shall dissolve.

> Tempest, iv. i ; 2 Peter, iii. 10, 11.

Heaven.

Shall we serve heaven
With less respect than we do minister
To our gross selves ?

> Measure for Measure, ii. 2.

The will of Heaven
Be done in this and all things.

> Henry VIII., i. 1.

This sorrow's heavenly :
It strikes where it doth love.

> Othello, v. 2.

So much my conscience whispers in your ear :
Which none but Heaven, and you, and I, shall hear.

> King John, i. 1.

Heaven's bounty towards him might be used more thankfully.

> Cymbeline, i. 7.

When I am in Heaven I shall desire
To see what this child does, and praise my Maker.

Henry VIII., v. 4.

My words fly up, my thoughts remain below:
Words, without thoughts, never to Heaven go.

Hamlet, iii. 3.

Soul.

Heaven's above all; and there be souls that must be saved,
And there be souls must not be saved.

Othello, ii. 3.

Now God be praised, that to believing souls
Gives light in darkness, comfort in despair.

2 Henry VI., ii. 1.

God have mercy on his soul;
And on all Christian souls, I pray God.

Hamlet, iv. 5.

Prayer.

We, ignorant of ourselves,
Beg often our own harms, which the wise powers
Deny us for our good; so find we profit
By losing of our prayers.

Antony and Cleopatra, ii. 1.

We do pray for mercy;
And that same prayer doth teach us all to render
The deeds of mercy.

Merchant of Venice, iv. 1.

Piety and Devotion.

Let never day nor night unhallowed pass,
But still remember what the Lord hath done.

2 Henry VI., ii. 1.

O Lord! that lends me life,
Lend me a heart replete with thankfulness!

2 Henry VI., i. 1.

I have hope to live, and am prepared to die.
                              Measure for Measure, iii. 1.

To Thee do I commend my watchful soul,
Ere I let fall the window of mine eyes :
Sleeping and waking, oh, defend me still !
                              Richard III., v. 3.

Lord, we know what we are, but know not what we may be.
                              Hamlet, iv. 5.

These quotations are merely a few gleanings, and doubtless a closer examination of Shakspeare would furnish us with many more. These, however, may suffice to lead the reader to pursue the study for himself. The aim in presenting them is not to offer the plays of Shakspeare as a book for Sunday reading; but, on the contrary, to induce men to study the Book which he studied, and from which he derived the marvellous power to interpret human nature for all generations.

We can find no account anywhere of his obtaining more than the rudiments of education; and yet where is the author to whom the whole world so willingly agrees to turn for example and imitation?

Dryden says, "In Shakspeare we find all arts and sciences, all moral and natural philosophy, without knowing that he ever studied them;" and Dr. Johnson seems much at a loss to know how, when, or where Shakspeare got his education. He knew little of languages, save his own; nor of sciences; nor of life, except in a small village and among players.

Where, then, could he have obtained that clear insight into character, that keen perception, that close analysis, that wonderful power of description, save from a faithful and constant study of the Book of books?

It is well known that the Bible was a rare treasure in those days, and much accounted of. Can it be that the blessing of having it more freely in our midst has diminished its usefulness? If this be so, how comes it that a careful study of its pages is one of the last requisites to the formation of the scholar of these days? And may we not question whether the rarity of modern Shakspeares may not, in some measure, arise from the rarity of those who follow his practice in this matter?

All Shakspeare's biographers unite in a tribute to the sweetness and amiability of his disposition: the utter absence of any facts against his character is surely the strongest negative proof of its purity. He was a Christian man, as both life and writings show; and this is the more surprising when we look at the temptations with which his profession and occupation of necessity surrounded him.

It is a curious fact, that but one single record, and that an unnoted one, can be found of Shakspeare's consciousness of his own greatness. He never appeared to set any value upon his own works, made no collections of his writings, nor any effort to rescue those that had been already published from the errors that obscured them.

11

The record to which we allude is his epitaph, written by himself: —

> " Good friend, for Jesus' sake, forbear
> To dig the dust enclosed here:
> Blest be the man that spares these stones,
> And curst be he that moves my bones."

Does not a careful consideration of these four lines betray a foreshadowing of what has already occurred — that his tomb would become, not only one of the " Meccas of the mind," but of the body also, — the shrine where loving hearts repair and eager feet still hasten after such a lapse of years? Have not those simple words stood sentinel through all this time above his grave, guarding from irreverent touch, with a power beyond all bolts and bars, — the power of moral force?

PART FOURTH.

I.—THE GLORIOUS FOURTH; OR, THE HOME
LIFE OF THE NATION.

THE national birthday brings with it, as is meet,
not only general rejoicing, but much eloquent
speaking and writing about the past glories and future
greatness of the country. Without pretending to enter
a field which is already so well occupied, we may take
the opportunity of saying a few words concerning what
may be called the domestic view of the subject; and perhaps it will be seen that this view is, in reality, the most
important of all.

Our nation is usually termed a federative republic, and
so it is in more than one sense. If it is a people made up
of federal States, it is also a community composed of
united households. It is important to bear in mind, that,
in our nation, the unit is not the individual, but the
family. Every household is a little republic in itself.
The husband and wife are the heads, dividing the departments between them, after the mode prescribed by nature
itself. The children take their proper parts in the little

community, according to their ages and characters, from the wee citizen of three years old, whose whole duty is to be as obedient and happy as possible, to the sprightly and busy maiden or youth of eighteen or twenty, who is an influential member of the household cabinet. And how truly do all together constitute a genuine " commonwealth "!

Of all the plain, sound, hearty Saxon words which enrich our language, there is none more expressive and pleasing than this. True, the Latin word "republic" (*respublica*) meant originally the same thing; but that primitive meaning is not apparent to an English ear. The word " commonwealth " carries with it at once a description and a lesson. It describes a community united together for the common good of all its members; and it reminds us, that, in such a community, no individual should be excluded from a share in the general weal. The true type and germ of such a community in every free and Christian country is to be found, as has been already observed, in the family. Six millions of such domestic commonwealths possess our land from ocean to ocean, and make up the American people; and on the virtue and intelligence of these six millions of families depend the welfare, happiness, and liberty of the nation.

Let us consider this point for a moment. A nation may exist in which the institution of the family, in the sense in which we understand it, is unknown. In Sparta, for example, under the laws of Lycurgus, private households could hardly be said to exist. The men lived in public, and took their meals together at common tables. The children were considered to belong to the State, which withdrew them from their parents at an early age, and educated them under a rigid system for the public service. The domestic affections were contemned, and purposely smothered.

We are told in history, that after the famous battle of Leuctra, which was so fatal to the Spartans, and which they had fought not for the defence of their country, but from motives of ambition and revenge, "the parents of those who died in the action congratulated one another upon it, and went to the temples to thank the gods that their children had done their duty; whereas the relatives of those who survived the defeat were inconsolable." The whole object of Spartan laws was to convert their community into an army of trained soldiers, not merely in order to protect their country, but for the ambitious purpose of making it the ruling power in Greece. For this object, — to make their sons accomplished manslayers, — all natural affection was stifled, all family ties were broken, and all the restraints of morality disregarded. The Spartans had their reward. History records, that, for a few centuries, they were known as a race of famous soldiers, the terror of Greece. But history further declares that art, science, and virtue withered and died in that ungenial soil. Not one great philosopher, statesman, orator, artist, or author is known in the annals of that country. Even in their own special calling of warfare, their leaders were not among the greatest generals of Greece. No Spartan commander ranks with Miltiades, Themistocles, and Epaminondas. The whole history of that remarkable people shows, that, when the institution of the household is destroyed, there may remain a community of unhumanized men and unsexed women; but the elements of goodness and greatness are lost, and the seeds of progress and improvement perish.

The Mahometan nations afford another striking example of this truth. The founder of their religion, by sanctioning polygamy, made the existence of the true household impossible. For a few generations, the frantic fanaticism of his followers gave success to their arms, and extended their sway over many countries. But the lack of the domestic virtues soon began to sap their power. For centuries past, all the Mahometan nations have been wasting away, and gradually giving place to nations whose children are trained in Christian households.

In short, if we survey all the nations of the earth, "from China to Peru," we shall find that the happiness and prosperity of every people will be in exact proportion to the degree in which the institution of the family is esteemed, protected, and cherished among them. We have no doubt that all our readers will concur in this view, and that they will further agree with us in the opinion that the central figure in this institution, the one on whom its essential excellence depends, is the wife and mother. She is the teacher and exemplar, from whom the future citizens of the Republic derive their first lessons in knowledge, manners, and morals. In this view, it seems to follow that the chief duty of American politicians and legislators is somewhat different from that which is usually assigned to them. The great object of our laws should be to insure that our nation shall be composed of well-ordered, intelligent, and virtuous families, and none other. When this object is achieved, all other desirable ends are attained with it. Freedom, wealth, art, science, the social charities, all that refines and exalts a nation, will flourish as flowers and fruits natural to such a soil.

And this brings us to the direct and logical conclusion, that the education of American women — such an education as will fit them to be the centres of our household commonwealths, and the trainers of the nation's children — is the most important object to which our statesmen can give their attention. If we could only convince our lawgivers of this fact, and persuade them that the subjects which ordinarily engross their minds, questions of the currency, the tariff, protection, free-trade, and the like, however important, are insignificant compared with that of the proper education of the future wives and mothers of our nation, we should feel that we have achieved a great national gain. It is well that public lands should be given to found agricultural colleges in every State; but if our national legislature would set an example to the

States, by furnishing, in the same manner, the means of establishing in each of them a model school for girls, and a seminary for young women, it would confer a more important benefit upon the nation than has resulted from any act ever before passed by any Congress.

Such, gentle reader, is our Fourth-of-July oration. If not as eloquent as some productions of the sort to which you have had the happiness of listening, we may at least affirm that it is dictated by a no less sincere love of our common country. May peace and safety, and that brotherly concord which springs from an enlightened love of liberty, law, and virtue, bless our land, and unite all its households, from ocean to ocean, in the bonds of charity and good will forever!

SONG OF THE FLOWER ANGELS.

For the Fourth of July.

We tend the flowers of every hue,
But love the red and white and blue:
 Red and white and blue!
The red is love's sweet blushing hue,
And white is fair as faith to view,
And hope is imaged in the blue;
 Red and white and blue!
Where faith is free, and love is true,
We sow the red and white and blue.

In Eastern lands the seeds we cast;
But weeds would choke, or drought would blast,
 Red and white and blue!

Sweet Love was lost in Passion's fires,
From idol worship, Faith retires,
And Hope by despots' frown expires:
 Red and white and blue !
All wilted, withered where they grew,
The flowers of red and white and blue !

Then to the Western World we came,
And sowed the flowers of holy name,
 Red and white and blue !
Faith and hope and love were sown,
And, oh, how strong the plants have grown !
And through the earth the flowers are known,
 Red and white and blue !
For freedom, eagle-pinioned, flew,
And bore the red and white and blue.

Now in *one* Banner fair to see,
We twine the hues in trinity :
 Red and white and blue !
The red and white are leaves of light,
And stars as flowers the blue bedight;
And o'er the world this banner bright,
 Red and white and blue,
Has guardian angels,* strong and true,
Who love the red and white and blue.

* "Angels that excel in strength."—Ps. ciii. 20.

II.—ACCOMPLISHMENTS OF MEN.

WE Americans are too grave a people; we laugh too little; we amuse ourselves too little; we make business the "be-all and the end-all" of life. Work is both better done, and more thoroughly done, when varied and intermingled with recreation. There are many amusements and accomplishments which should form part of the training of every young man. This is far better understood across the water than with us, and we should be glad to see the games of the universities of Oxford and Cambridge introduced amongst us.

Boxing, fencing, boating, riding, and dancing are all both useful and desirable amusements, which should be cultivated, as tending to muscular development and personal health; and, to those who are aware how much mental effort is aided and stimulated by a sound condition of body, nothing which can produce such condition will seem of slight importance.

Thus for the amusements; for the accomplishments, we would place first a knowledge of music, which, by some strange freak of fashion or custom, has, until lately, been considered more for women, and beneath the dignity of men. Surely, whatever brings out and cultivates man's softer qualities, whatever refines the home and home enjoyments, should never be so considered.

An English writer says, and with much truth, "I believe that there is a taste for music in every child born, and that, if it disappears in after-life, it is for want of cultivation. Was there ever yet a baby which could not be sung to sleep?"

However this may be, to play on some one instrument is of more value to a man than at first sight appears. To the character it is a refiner. Music is the medicine of the soul: it soothes the wrinkles of a hard life of business, and lifts us from thoughts of money, intrigue, enterprises, hatred, and disgust, to a calmer, more heavenly frame of mind.

To a man himself, therefore, the power to play is of use. He may not always have a sister, wife, or daughter, to sing and play to him; he may not always be within reach of the opera or concert-rooms; and then, too, half the enjoyment of music is gone when you cannot enjoy it as you list, and of what kind you need, gay or grave, as your fancy lies. It is an indulgence to a pure mind, and it is one of those few indulgences which are free from harm.

A knowledge of languages is perhaps the most useful accomplishment one can possess. Independent of the wide field of literature thus opened, it makes one at home in whatever quarter of the globe he may chance to be thrown, and enlarges greatly the sphere of enjoyment.

It seems scarcely necessary to add, that every young man should possess a knowledge of current literature and passing affairs. In this country, our boys are only too apt to think for themselves, and assert their opinions with a dogmatism worthy of the Seven Wise Men. But the knowledge we refer to is such as should enable them to look at a question on every side, and exercise the judgment so as to decide without being swayed by popular clamor or party prejudice.

With regard to a man's opinions, it has been well said, "Whatever his views, he should be able, as a man of sense, and in order to be agreeable, to look upon them independently, to support them reasonably, or abandon them gracefully."

It may possibly be thought too trifling to allude here to the *art of carving*, or to apply to it the term "accomplishment;" and yet, were a little more attention given to education upon this point, many awkward scenes might be avoided.

We must all at some time have had our appetite destroyed by the mangling process carried on by our host on an unfortunate fowl, in defiance of every law of anatomy or even common sense. We have often felt thankful, when receiving some nondescript piece, *haggled* off, and triumphantly presented, as though the carver were proud of his successful effort of detaching some portion, no matter in what condition, that the bird had been subjected to the process of fire, lest it should have flown at its torturer, and picked out his eyes in revenge.

Awkwardness in small things suggests awkwardness in

great ones; and there is much to be mentally overcome before one could connect such *fowl cutting* with *fair dealing*, or expect to find a wise counsellor in a clumsy carver.

" Ceremony is the phantom of friendliness." We should not forget, nevertheless, that free and easy familiarity is in as bad taste as ceremony is pretentious. It is far removed from exquisite politeness and good taste, and should be banished from society.

We may define the character of politeness. We cannot fix its practice; it follows usage and received customs; it is bound to times, to places, to people; it is not the same in the two sexes, nor under different conditions; the mind alone cannot divine it; we must pursue it by imitation, and improve ourselves in it.

But it is, above all, in conversation, that a man of society ought to shine, and it is for that he must cultivate his mind; for there he is exposed to the encounter of reefs against which he may go to pieces.

La Bruyère says, " Very slight resources are necessary for politeness of manner; very abundant resources, for politeness of spirit."

This thought is confirmed by the following from Chateaubriand : —

" Conversation of superior minds is unintelligible to mediocre wits, because there is a great part of the discussion which is understood and taken for granted."

" Indeed, we often compare Napoleon to Cromwell, and

how can he who does not know what Cromwell was understand what we intend to say in comparing Napoleon with him?"

HINTS.

1. Never nod to a lady in the street, neither be satisfied with touching your hat; but *take it off:* it is a courtesy her sex requires.

2. Remember that all your guests are equal for the time being, and have a similar claim to your courtesies; or, if there be a difference shown, those of the lesser rank require a *little more attention* than the rest, that they may not be made to *feel* their inferiority.

3. Nothing more clearly indicates the true gentleman than a desire evinced to oblige or *accommodate*, whenever it is possible or *reasonable:* it forms the broad distinction between the well-bred man of society, and the coarse and brutal crowd, the irreclaimably vulgar, — vulgar, not from their inferiority of station, but because *they are coarse and brutal.*

4. A perfect freedom from affectation, and an observance of the feelings of others, will always exempt a person from the charge of vulgarity.

5. In round games, which are patronized by people who have not the accomplishments to supply their place, or the wit to do without them, the main fault to be avoided is *eagerness.*

6. Of single games, you should know as many as pos-

sible. The finest of them is chess, which is worthy of any man, and a splendid mental exercise.

7. A man should never permit himself to lose his temper in society, nor *show* that he has taken offence at any supposed slight: it places him in a disadvantageous position, betraying an absence of self-respect, or, at the least, of self-possession.

8. In meeting a lady of your acquaintance in the street, it is *her part* to notice *you first*, unless, indeed, you are very intimate. The reason is, if *you* bow to the lady first, she may not choose to acknowledge you, and there is no remedy ; but, if *she* bow to *you*, you, *as a gentleman, cannot cut her.*

9. No man may stop to speak to a lady until she stops to speak to him. The lady, in short, has the right in all cases to be friendly or distant.

10. Do not shake hands unless the lady puts out hers, which you may take as a sign of particular good will. In this case, you must not stop long; but the lady has again the right to prolong the interview at pleasure. It is she, not you, who must make the move onwards. If she does this in the middle of a conversation, it is a proof that she is willing you should join her; and, if you have no absolute call to go your way, you ought to do so. But, if she does so with a slight inclination, it is to dismiss you; and you must then again bow, and raise your hat.

11. Do not take upon yourself to do the honors in another man's house, or constitute yourself master of the

ceremonies, as you will thereby offend the host and
hostess.

12. Gentility is neither in birth, manner, nor fashion,
but in the MIND. A high sense of honor, a determination
never to take a mean advantage of another; an adherence to truth, delicacy, and politeness towards those with
whom you may have dealings, are the essential and distinguishing characteristics of A GENTLEMAN.

———

III. — ACCOMPLISHMENTS OF WOMEN.

THERE is certainly no lack of amusements or accomplishments for women and girls; but, in these
days of ours, we have come to consider too many healthy,
innocent sports as *unladylike.*

In the training of young girls, it has become far too
much the custom to forbid any thing which may lead to
rough play or rudeness in any shape; and thus, in avoiding the Scylla of hoydenism, we have fallen upon the
Charybdis of premature young ladyism, a thing to be far
more seriously deprecated.

Contrast for a moment the children of the present day
— little men and women, in velvet and fine lace, sent
forth for a promenade, with directions not to spoil their
clothes — with the youngsters of the day of our grand-

parents, who were turned out of school at noonday for a hearty game of romps, — boys and girls together, having no thought or fear for their costume, laughing, playing, leaping, running, to their hearts' content, — and say which system must, of necessity, produce the stronger, more vigorous race of men and women?

It is not my wish or aim to make a woman other than feminine; but there is little danger that healthy, active play can ever have such effect.

Whilst a few words with regard to the instruction of boys in music seemed necessary, no such advice is required in the case of girls. They are taught it almost as a matter of course, and too often merely consider it as a bait to lure a lover. The lover being lured, the bait is detached from the hook, and looked upon as useless for the rest of existence.

This is oftener the fault of the trainer than the trained.

Let the mother or the teacher instil into the young girl's mind that she is learning not merely a showy accomplishment, useful only in society as a means to gain an end, but what may and should be used, to the end of her life, as a means of brightening and enlivening her home, — let her be taught this, and we shall cease to find music and matrimony so fatally opposed as they appear to be at present.

The use of the pencil could be cultivated with advantage much more than it is amongst us.

Many women have a taste for drawing, which, had it

been cultivated in early life, would have been to them a source of great and lasting pleasure.

There are many hours in life when the spirit is not in tune for music of any sort; when the mind has lost, for the time, all power of concentration, and reading is well-nigh impossible: at such times, the pencil often affords a salutary relaxation, occupying the attention without straining the mind.

This, also, is one of the many arguments in favor of fancy-work, or even plain sewing. A crusade has been waged against fancy-work, as wasting time, leading to extravagance, &c.; but it seems to me that there is no good foundation for such an attack. Unless such amusement be carried to excess, there are far more arguments for than against: the *pros* have it decidedly over the *cons.*

In many, indeed most kinds of fancy-work, there is scope for invention, originality, neatness, precision, despatch, a cultivation of the taste, a study of the harmony of colors, and of the effects of light and shade. Can that which calls forth all these be mere waste time?

In Germany, plain sewing has been carried into society, very gracefully, as a charity. At Munich, during Lent, the court circle give working parties, the proceeds to be distributed among the poor. At one of these re-unions, the queen made a baby's shirt, the king picked lint for the hospitals, whilst every lady of the court had some useful article before her: little dresses were made, stockings knitted, and warm shawls made with the crochet-needle.

Little tables were set about, and the assemblage was broken up into small parties, each table holding a lady or two, with a gentleman near her. The example thus set by the court and nobility cannot fail to have a happy influence upon the whole nation.

Among outdoor amusements, we would name riding on horseback, skating, and archery, according to the different seasons. All these are healthy, elegant, and appropriate exercises for women: they tend to fine muscular development, and also to the strengthening and bracing of the whole system. Games in the open air should also be encouraged. Croquet, a new and graceful one, has lately become quite popular. It can be played equally well by ladies or gentlemen, and offers a pleasing and healthful variety in the amusements of watering-place or country-seat life.

The game consists in sending balls, struck by wooden cues, through a succession of iron hoops, placed in the ground at intervals, and according to a fixed rule. The players (for the game is usually divided into opposing sides) who can reach the goal first win the game. To defeat this object, or retard it as much as possible, is the constant aim of the adversary; and the effort to guard against or prevent such action on his part gives excitement and spirit to the game.

Amusements of this sort will do more to restore the

roses to the cheeks of our young girls, faded by a campaign in a winter's ball-rooms, than all the doses which the materia medica can suggest.

HINTS.

1. "In good society, a tacit understanding exists, that whatsoever conversation may take place shall be, to a certain degree, sacred, and may not honorably be carried out of it, and repeated to the prejudice of the utterer." This axiom cannot be too strongly inculcated; as, if such practices were allowed, all confidence would be destroyed, and there would be no end to the mischief caused by silly or malignant people.

2. There cannot be a custom more vulgar or offensive than that of taking a person aside to whisper, in a room with company; yet this rudeness is of too frequent occurrence.

3. Slight inaccuracies in statements of facts or opinions should rarely be remarked upon in conversation.

4. Nothing is more rude than to converse whilst people are singing. If you do not like music sufficiently to listen to it, you should remember that others may do so, and that not only do you interrupt their enjoyment of it, but you offer an offence to the singers.

5. Lounging on sofas, or reclining in chairs, as if in the privacy of one's own dressing-room, is always considered indecorous, and should be carefully avoided.

6. Mothers should be on their guard not to repeat

nursery anecdotes or *bon mots*, as, however interesting to themselves, they are seldom so to others.

7. Long stories should always be avoided in society, as, however well told, they interrupt general conversation.

8. Study neatness at all times. A true lady should be as careful of her toilette at her own breakfast table as in the most crowded ball-room.

9. Ladies of good taste seldom wear jewelry in the morning, and, when they do, confine themselves to trinkets of gold, or those in which opaque stones only are introduced. Ornaments with brilliant stones are unsuited for a morning costume.

10. When asked to sing, if you do not intend to do so, refuse so decidedly that you cannot be compelled; but, the more decided the refusal, the gentler should the manner be. There is a style of saying "No" that never offends.

11. If you intend to sing, accept at once. Do not hurry up to the piano, as if glad of an opportunity to show off, but go gently. If, by request, you have brought your music, leave it down stairs : it can be sent for.

12. In the choice of songs, variety is to be adopted. German music pleases generally ; but let no one not conversant with the right pronunciation of any foreign language sing in it: there is nothing so unpleasant as broad French, mincing German, or lisping Italian.

13. In manner be perfectly natural and simple. Avoid every form of affectation. The first rule for manner is self-respect.

14. Always show a respect and deference to age. This is too apt to be neglected at the present day.

15. Do not imagine little ceremonies to be insignificant, and beneath your attention. They are the customs of society; and, if you do not conform to them, you will gain the unenviable distinction of being pointed out as an ignorant, ill-bred person.

16. Avoid a loud tone of voice in conversation, or a "horse laugh;" both are exceedingly vulgar and un-feminine.

IV. — LITERATURE. — NEW NOVELS.

THERE are evils under the sun that Solomon never dreamed of. In our land, one of these evils is a deluge of books. Works of fiction, perhaps from being "light reading," are floating on the top waves, filling our homes with an ever-flowing stream of the "last new novels," and threatening to wash away from the minds of the young all love for works of truth and soberness.

I am not intending now to discuss the evils of this mania for fiction. That there are injurious effects from this habit of indiscriminate novel-devouring, everybody will allow.

How to prevent it, is the question. This involves the whole system of home-life.

It is easy enough to describe how not to do it. As an

illustration of one important failure in doing it, I will give
you the following sketch: —

DOCTOR NORTON'S STORY.

"It is a long time ago," said Dr. Norton, "over thirty
years, since I made my first visit to Boston.

"I was then a young man. Men will grow old," he
added (as in a parenthesis), turning to the ladies, Miss
Barker and her sister Maria, who were listening earnestly; "but women may keep their youth as long as they
keep their hearts warm with the love of truth and goodness. I believed in women when I was young."

"Do you doubt them now?" said Maria, smiling. She
was a very lovely girl.

"I will tell you when I have finished my story," he
replied gravely. "It happened that I had letters to some
of the most distinguished families in Boston, and was
introduced into what is called, by courtesy, 'the first
circle.'

"I passed my time very pleasantly, in a round of dinner-parties, balls, and the usual fashionable amusements;
and had been nearly three weeks in the city before I
found leisure to return the early call one of my father's
friends had made me.

"Mr. Tuttle was a very rich man, and highly respected
on 'Change, as *rich men* are; but his strictly religious
character, which he was very scrupulous to sustain, prevented his associating much in fashionable parties.

"He had been liberally educated, and designed to become a clergyman; but, when he had completed his theological studies, the state of his health was such, that he was obliged to go on a voyage at sea, and finally he entered business as a merchant. He had been very successful, was a millionnaire, and his daughters were great matches.

"I sent up my name. Mr. Tuttle was out; but his wife met and welcomed me with all a woman's cordiality and grace when she wishes to please; very different, indeed, from the formal reception I had anticipated. She assured me that they had been expecting my visit; that she felt quite acquainted with me, because she had entertained so high an opinion of my father; and so on. Compliments cost nothing: would that railroads were as easily made!

"Mrs. Tuttle led the way to her private parlor, observing that she wished to introduce me to her daughers as they *were*. In this, she showed a managing mother's tact; for her daughters really needed no foreign aid of ornament.

"They were lovely enough in their neat, morning-dresses; indeed, so very beautiful were the two eldest, that it surprised me I had not seen them at the parties I had attended. I soon found it was not from want of interest in such amusements, for they overwhelmed me with inquiries respecting how I had enjoyed them: and then came a sigh, and those portentous words, 'Papa does not approve of balls!'

"I endeavored to change the conversation by alluding to the book which had so claimed their attention when I entered, remarking, that I supposed they enjoyed their leisure more than the trifling did society. As I ended, I looked at the volume: it was 'Eugene Aram,' then just published.

"I have serious objections to the Bulwer novels, though they have some high merits; and I should never recommend 'Eugene Aram' for a young lady's reading.

"However, I found they had no scruples on the subject. They began, and poured out their eulogiums on Bulwer and his 'charming novels.' 'Pelham' 'was so interesting, so witty, and full of such delightful descriptions of high life,' and 'Paul Clifford' was 'such a fascinating hero, — so brave and generous!'

"What signified his robberies? Adelaide, the second daughter, declared she should have 'doted on him.'

"And then 'The Disowned,' — what lofty sentiments, what deep, powerful pathos!' &c. Thus they went on, while their delighted mother told me, though how she edged in the words no one could tell, that 'Susan and Adelaide were so fond of Bulwer's works they had read through "Eugene Aram," since the preceding afternoon.'

"I tried hard to make them praise one of my favorite writers, Miss Austen ; but it would not do. She was too natural, and only seemed to know the middle classes: no lords or ladies of any note figured in her volumes.

"'We want pictures of fashionable manners, of the *beau monde* in Europe,' said Miss Tuttle.

"'There is not any spirit or originality in the works of Miss Austen,' said Miss Adelaide. 'One might as well read a tract or a sermon.'

"In the midst of these discussions on novels and fashionable life, Mr. Tuttle entered, unexpectedly, I presume.

"The conversation ceased instantly. I observed that Susan dexterously threw her handkerchief over the 'charming book,' and, gathering it up, placed it behind her on the sofa, and then, hastily reaching her work from the table, seemed wholly absorbed in the progress of her needle.

"After the usual salutations, inquiries, and welcomes to me, Mr. Tuttle, who appeared very fond of his children, told Adelaide that her eyes looked heavy, and he feared she confined herself to her work too closely (she was knitting a bead purse); and inquired if she had been out that morning.

"'No, papa: I have been so engaged!'

"'To finish that purse, I presume. I wish, my dear,' turning to his wife, 'you would be more particular, and see that these girls walk or drive out every pleasant morning. I do not wish to have them so constantly engaged at their work.'

"'You know, my love, their work is designed for *charity*. How can they be better employed?' And Mrs. Tuttle looked so innocently in her husband's face.

"I thought of 'Eugene Aram,' and determined to

probe the matter a little. Perhaps I was wrong; but I wished to learn the father's opinion of his daughters' studies.

"So I asked him if there were any new books worth reading in the 'Literary Emporium.'

"He replied that he really did not know. He found little time for reading, except the newspapers; but his daughters could tell me.

"'Oh!' said I with a very grave face, 'I was not alluding to the new novels.'

"'Novels!' he repeated, with a solemnity of accent that was almost severe. 'My daughters never read novels: I never permit them to be brought into my house.' Here the young ladies looked at each other, and their mother grew fidgety.

"'But you do not utterly discard novels?' said I inquiringly.

"'Indeed I do, sir. I know exceptions are often made by Christians, nor will I say that all novels are bad. But the habit of novel-reading *is* bad, most pernicious to young ladies; and my girls, as they never have been indulged in this exciting and dangerous mode of killing time, find, as you see, their amusements in useful employments. They never read novels, Mrs. Tuttle being entirely of my way of thinking.'"

"Were not the ladies utterly confounded?" said Miss Barker.

"Not in the least," replied the doctor. "They wore an

air of the greatest *nonchalance.* It was quite a scene for a drama."

" Whom do you think most to blame in this matter?" inquired Miss Barker.

"The mother. Mr. Tuttle was wrong, very wrong, in devoting his whole time, as he did, to the acquisition of wealth. No doubt that this laid the foundation of the mischief, — the want of sympathy and confidence between the husband and wife. He had made *business* the *duty* of his life till he had no taste for any other worldly pursuit.

" It was easy for him to renounce all pleasures but the one of money-getting. So he called all others sinful, forgetting that the Word of God has declared the *love of money is the root of all evil.* It was this bitter root which was destroying his family. His riches had given them leisure and the means of luxury, and they felt the want of amusements. He could not spare time to regulate these, or to teach them the true principles of self-government.

" He was proud, indeed, to bestow on them every means of self-indulgence. And this led the mother, a vain woman, whose object of ambition it was to get her daughters into the most fashionable society, to a series of falsehoods and dissimulations in order to give them those accomplishments considered most fashionable. Novel-reading was one of these : she foolishly supposed it would teach them the *beau ideal* of European manners.

To obtain these graces, she was willing to sacrifice *truth,* that pearl of the soul, the reverence for which, when once lost, is rarely restored."

"Did you become much acquainted with them?" inquired Miss Maria.

"No, I never saw them afterwards. But their history might serve for a warning to many of the would-be-fashionables.

"Mr. Tuttle failed, and removed with his family to the 'Far West,' to build up some new settlement with the backwoodsmen. I doubt not that he was a much better man for the reverse; but his wife and daughters must have had hard lessons to learn. I hope one of these was sincerity. And now, in reply to your question, I do doubt an untruthful woman. There cannot, in the home under her guidance, be either rest or peace."

V. — THE IMPORTANCE OF NEEDLEWORK.

SHE was knowing in all needlework, and shone in dairy and in kitchen too, as in the parlor."

By this term we mean not only the immense variety of elegant fancy-work which now engages the delicate fingers of the daughters of our land, but every sort of plain sewing; a knowledge of which must, after all, underlie needle-work as an accomplishment.

While urging attention to mental culture, let us never

forget the importance of ingenious handiworks and useful accomplishments in domestic knowledge. The only mechanical invention of Eden was the sewing-needle: it will be the indispensable handmaid of fallen humanity till the advent of the New Jerusalem.

It is exceedingly difficult to give habits of domestic industry to those who have no need of labor; yet on such habits depends the physical health of woman, and also much of that cheerfulness of mind which makes her useful and agreeable at home. We regret to see that, in a lady's education, needlework has of late been so sadly undervalued.

The old-fashioned accomplishments of embroidery and cross-stitch were preposterous, when they demanded all the time of woman; and so would be music or drawing, or any accomplishment we term literary. A young lady should be trained to vary her employments, and display in every department of womanly knowledge good sense and refined taste; and she may as truly exhibit sense and taste, and elegance of fancy, in her needlework, as in reciting philosophy, quoting poetry, or playing the harp.

But she must also be taught, from earliest childhood, that there is nothing degrading or dishonoring to the highest social position in a thorough and complete knowledge of plain sewing. No woman should grow up in ignorance of this most important art. Who can tell, in the various changes and chances of life, at what moment such information may be of the greatest value to her? And, because a woman knows how to sew, does it follow that she must give up literary pursuits, if time and circumstances permit her to follow them?

Knowledge of any kind is valuable, and never to be despised. It is therefore with regret that we have often listened to the announcement from the lips of some young girls, uttered as a boast, that they "didn't know how to sew, " never had stuck a stitch in their life," &c. There seems something unfeminine in such a statement; but, usually, the fault is a remove farther back, and does not rest with the speaker, but with the mother, who should have trained the little fingers to sew, and to find a pleasure in sewing. Much may be done in this way, by encouraging children to make clothes for their dolls; or little presents of their own work for members of the family, as Christmas presents, or offerings for a birthday. By thus connecting pleasant associations with sewing, a girl will soon learn to love it, and acquire a skill and dexterity in the use of the " ONE-EYED SERVANT," which may be of incalculable advantage in later life.

We presume many if not most of our readers are already familiar with Miss Ingelow's pretty little tale, "ONE-EYED SERVANT," in which she contrasts two homes: in one, poverty, carelessness, neglect; in the other, contentment, neatness, and comfort — the result, respectively, of the absence and the presence of the "one-eyed servant," as the needle is well termed, and knowing how to

make use of it. This sketch of Miss Ingelow should be
read.

Children always enjoy making patchwork, and may
more easily be taught to sew neatly, by saving bright-
colored pieces, and arranging them with taste, than by
the weary monotony of a long seam. Skill and neatness
may be combined in this way; and this reminds us of a
very beautiful idea of the highest form of this work,
which we have received an account of from a young lady
in Rhode Island.

THE AUTOGRAPH BEDQUILT.

This bedquilt is formed by a curious and valuable collection of autographs, in an original and very womanly
way: the design is to insert the names in the counterpane or bedquilt. Each autograph is written, with common black ink, on a diamond-shaped piece of white silk
(placed over a diagram of white paper, and basted at the
edges); each piece the centre of a group of colored
diamonds, formed in many instances from "storied" frag-
ments of dresses which were worn in the olden days of
our country. For instance, there are pieces of a pink
satin dress which flaunted at one of President Washington's dinner-parties, with other relics of those rich silks
and stiff brocades, so fashionable in the last century.

The whole number of pieces required is 2,780 ; of these,
556 are to contain autographs. The novel idea of the
quilt has found such warm favor in the hearts of those

whom this ingenious *needle-artiste* has addressed, that, two years ago, she had obtained *three hundred and fifty autographs* (when we last heard from her), many of them from men highly distinguished in the literary, political, scientific, and military history of the present century.

We will name a few of these renowned contributors: Humboldt, Bunsen, Walter Savage Landor, Louis Blanc, Kossuth, Washington Irving, Prescott, Benton, Choate; six American presidents, viz., Van Buren, Tyler, Fillmore, Pierce, Buchanan, Lincoln; while many have contributed upon the little white silk diagram characteristic sentiments or verses. To give a specimen, one poet has written this comforting distich: —

> " Dream what thou wilt
> Beneath this quilt,
> My blessing still is — Yours,"   *N. P. Willis.*

In short, we think this autograph bedquilt may be called a very wonderful invention in the way of needlework. The mere mechanical part — the number of small pieces, stitches neatly taken, and accurately ordered; the arranging properly, and joining nicely, 2,780 delicate bits of various beautiful and costly fabrics — is a task that would require no small share of resolution, patience, firmness, and perseverance.

Then comes the intellectual part, the taste to assort colors, and to make the appearance what it ought to be, where so many hundreds of shades are to be matched and suited to each other. After that, we rise to the moral, when human deeds are to live in names; the consideration of the celebrities, who are to be placed each the centre of his or her own circle. To do this well, requires a knowledge of books and life, and an instinctive sense of the fitness of things, so as to assign each name its suitable place in this galaxy of stars or diamonds.

Notwithstanding the comprehensive design we are attempting to describe, we have no doubt of its successful termination The letter of the young lady bears such internal evidence of her capability, that we feel certain she has the power to complete her work, if her life is spared.

And when we say that she has been nearly ten years engaged on this quilt, and seems to feel now all the enthusiasm of a poetical temperament working out a grand invention, that is to be a new pleasure and blessing to the world, we are sure all our readers will wish her success. Who knows but that, in future ages, her work may be looked at, like the Bayeux Tapestry, not only as a marvel of woman's ingenious and intellectual industry, but as affording an idea of the civilization of our times, and also giving a notion of the persons as estimated in history?

In the days of Queen Matilda, the great men could not write even their names; and all that we can bring of these old warriors to our minds is the style of their armor and the shape of their lances. Now, when brain predominates, in the estimation of the world, over thrusts and blows, a more fitting idea of carrying the illustrious **to** posterity is a specimen of their handwriting, particularly when this is used to perpetuate any of their thoughts, and devoted to the service of a lady.

We think our readers who have not time for such a great undertaking as this autograph counterpane might make some interesting collections in a smaller way. A young lady might, by limiting her plan to scores, instead of hundreds, of names, soon obtain enough of these lettered diamonds to make a sofa-cushion, a cover for a small table, or some other ornamental design. The size of the diamond is a little over two inches each way. We have not room on this page to give a diagram ; but we trust that, with these directions, any lady who has a love for the needle and the pen may achieve success.

We cannot conclude without a few words on the importance of knitting and crochet work. Every little girl should be taught to knit, as a pastime and a pleasure ; and she will thus make use of her knowledge when she has left the nursery far behind.

It would be difficult to compute the number of *hours* saved by keeping a piece of knitting or crochet on hand to fill up the odd minutes, otherwise wasted, throughout the day. If a lady makes it a rule to have something of this sort at hand, ready to take up when opportunity offers, she will be amazed to discover, in a short time, how much she has accomplished.

We know a lady of large means, and surrounded with

every luxury, who always kept a pair of woollen stockings on hand, knitting them whilst waiting for meals and at vacant moments, for poor pensioners. In this manner, she managed to give comfort to several poor old women who were entirely unable to supply themselves.

We all remember how much was done in this way, during the war, for our soldiers. The advantage of having learned to knit easily and rapidly in childhood was never more strikingly displayed than at that time.

The contrast between the facility with which those familiar with knitting made use of their knowledge, and the weary, blundering efforts of those who were striving to learn the art for the first time, anxious to do good, and to be useful, proved most conclusively the truth of our words.

If "the boy is father of the man," make the *girl the mother of the woman* in all useful arts and accomplishments, and she will thank you throughout her life.

VI.—YOUNG AMERICA.

THE real worth of a diamond is never known till it is cut and polished. In a rough state, it seems hardly worth being set in a kingly crown, or having the place of honor among bridal ornaments.

Thus with childhood, the diamond of humanity. The boy, especially, needs to be rightly trained and taught, if the lustrous worth of manhood is to be developed and perfected for the noblest duties, and made capable of enjoying the best happiness of his nature.

Rules of courtesy are necessary in every family and for all stations of life in our country, because here all have a chance of improvement. Those who profess Christianity should be particular to form these habits of good breeding. The missionary of the South-Sea Islands would tell you that savages need to be taught the rules of courtesy, or their religion would never be civilization.

The true spirit of good manners and of good morals is so closely identical, that it is not possible to teach the faith of the Bible without thereby improving the manners of men.

The precepts of Jesus Christ are patterns on which to form the character of a perfect gentleman. What a lesson in politeness is His rebuke of the forward manner of those who press eagerly on to get the upper seats at banquets! The apostles also left us many injunctions to gentleness and courteousness of manner, which should form the basis of every manual of good behavior.

The wisest among the heathen philosophers saw the importance of this spirit of courtesy in social life. An English writer says, that "the greater part of Aristotle's 'Ethics' might be turned into 'A Guide to the Complete Gentleman.'"

Among the British philosophers, the greatest — Lord Bacon — has devoted an essay to the subject of "Manners," in which he intimates, that, "as a precious stone must be of a very high value to do without setting, a man must be very great indeed to dispense with social observances."

Many more opinions of celebrated writers might be given in favor of the study and practice of politeness; but the one authority to be set forth and quoted at length is worth more than all other secular writings for Young America; because the words of the boy who thus pictured what he hoped to be, were realized in his own example.

George Washington conquered where Aristotle and Bacon both failed. Our American hero conquered himself. He was a hero in home life as well as on the battlefield. This is the example needed for our fast people. All American boys want to be heroes. Every one should be encouraged to hope, that, if he strives well, he may reach, by the age of fourteen, as Washington did, the place of a brave soldier in the army of "Good Behavior,"

To aid each one in this struggle, the careful study of the "Washington Code of Good Manners" is a very important part of education for Young America. It should be cherished with his "Farewell Address," as twin "legacies" to the American people, of honor in national character, and union in national life.

WORDS OF WASHINGTON.

["Rules of Civility and Decent Behavior in Company and Conversation. Written by George Washington aged 14."]

Every action in company ought to be with some sign of respect to those present.

Be no flatterer; neither play with any one that delights not to be played with.

Read no letters, books, or papers in company: when there is a necessity for doing it, you must leave. Come not near the books or writings of any one so as to read them unless desired nor give your opinion of them unasked; also look not nigh when another is writing a letter.

Let your countenance be pleasant, but in serious matters somewhat grave.

Show not yourself glad at the misfortunes of another, though he were your enemy.

When you meet with one of greater quality than yourself, stop and retire, especially if it be at a door or any straight place, to give way for him to pass.

They that are in dignity or in office have in all places precedency; but, whilst they are young, they ought to respect those that are their equals in birth or other qualities, though they have no public charge.

It is good manners to prefer those to whom we speak

before ourselves, especially if they be above us, with whom in no sort we ought to begin.

Let your discourse with men of business be short and comprehensive.

In visiting the sick, do not presently play the physician, if you be not knowing therein.

In writing or speaking, give to every person his due title, according to his degree, and the custom of the place.

Strive not with your superiors in argument; but always submit your judgment to others with modesty.

Take all admonitions thankfully, in what time or place soever given; but afterward, not being culpable, take a place or time convenient to let him know it who gave them.

Mock not nor jest at any thing of importance; break no jests that are sharp-biting; and, if you deliver any thing witty and pleasant, abstain from laughing thereat yourself.

Be not hasty to believe flying reports to the disparagement of any.

In your apparel be modest, and endeavor to accommodate nature rather than to procure admiration. Keep to the fashion of your equals, such as are civil and orderly with respect to times and places.

Associate yourself with men of good quality, if you esteem your own reputation; for it is better to be alone than in bad company.

Speak not of doleful things in time of mirth; nor at the table speak of melancholy things, as death and wounds; and, if others mention them, change, if you can, the discourse. Tell not your dreams but to your intimate friend.

Break not a jest where none takes pleasure in the mirth. Laugh not aloud, nor at all, without occasion. Deride no man's misfortune, though there seem to be some cause.

If two contend together, take not the part of either unconstrained, and be not obstinate in your own opinion. In things indifferent, be of the major side.

Think before you speak. Pronounce not imperfectly, nor bring your words out too hastily, but orderly and distinctly.

When another speaks, be attentive yourself, and disturb not the audience. If any hesitate in his words, help him not, nor prompt him, without being desired; interrupt him not, nor answer him till his speech be ended.

In disputes, be not so desirous to overcome as not to give liberty to each one to deliver his opinion, and to submit to the judgment of the major part, especially if they are judges of the dispute.

Speak not evil of the absent; for it is unjust.

Be not angry at table, whatever happens, and, if you have reason to be so, show it not. Put on a cheerful countenance, especially if there be strangers; for good humor makes one dish of meat a feast.

When you speak of God, or of his attributes, let it be seriously and in reverence.   Honor and obey your parents, though they be poor.

Let your recreations be manful, not sinful.

Labor to keep alive in your breast that little spark of celestial fire called conscience.

VII.—THE BOOK, AND HOW TO READ IT.

THERE is but one Book, was the death-bed testimony of Sir Walter Scott; and he had ransacked the world's literature, and made himself master of its best stores of wisdom and knowledge.

"Viewed merely as a human or literary production, the Bible is a marvellous book, and without a rival.   All the libraries of theology, philosophy, history, antiquities, poetry, law, and policy, would not furnish material enough for so rich a treasure of the choicest gems of human genius, wisdom, and experience.   It embraces works of about forty authors, representing the extremes of society, from the throne of the king to the boat of the fisherman. It was written during a long period of sixteen centuries; on the banks of the Nile, in the desert of Arabia, in the Land of Promise, in Asia Minor, in classical Greece, and in imperial Rome.   It commences with the creation, and ends with the final glorification, after describing all the interesting stages in the revelation of God and spiritual development of man. It uses all forms of literary composition; it rises to the highest heights, and descends to the lowest depths, of humanity; it measures all states and conditions of life; it is acquainted with every grief and every woe; it touches every chord of sympathy; it contains the spiritual biography of every heart; it is suited to every class of society, and can be read with the same interest and profit by the king and the beggar, by the philosopher and the child; it is as universal as the race, and reaches beyond the limits of time into the boundless regions of eternity."

So says the learned Dr. Schaff; and yet how few of the millions who now have the Bible in their homes think of it as a continuous history of the human race from the creation to the final judgment-day! Is not the unity of the narrative overlooked, owing to the variety of means employed for the same end, and also to the many changes of agents by whom God was carrying onward his great design of salvation?

As this is the paper for our Sunday series, perhaps we cannot do better than examine into the mode in which the Bible should be read. Many of us have seen, and all of us have read, accounts of the pictures of mosaic-work in other lands, marvellous in their beauty, and wonderful in their execution.

For the formation of these pictures, unity of design, harmony of coloring, and correct blending of the shades, are the principal requisites. The artist must keep before

him the end he has in view throughout the work; viz.,
to form a perfect and complete whole. As each separate
piece of glass or precious stone, as it may be, is of the
same color throughout, the gradation of tints, the melt-
ing-off of any one color from its highest light to its
darkest shadow, can be obtained only by an immense
number of small pieces, arranged with a view to the
general effect. It is said that forty thousand different
tints, all of which must be kept methodically sorted and
arranged, are requisite for this kind of mosaic-work.

So is it with the Bible. It is a uniform whole, composed of various parts, smaller or larger; but each, in its
appointed place and sphere, going to make up the one
design, which is to show how man is to be saved. The
one idea running throughout the whole volume may be
found in the words of the Lord God to the Tempter: "I
will put enmity between thee and the woman, and between thy seed and her seed: it shall bruise thy head,
and thou shalt bruise his heel." — Gen. iii. 15.

To show the manner of the fulfilment of this promise
is the purpose of the Book.

All the inspired writers, each in his own manner, and
with the impression of his own times, have set forth the
same truths. They never conflict in their testimony to
the holiness of God, and to his requirement of holiness
in men. They all testify of human wickedness, and all
teach of a Mediator.

In the Old Testament he is promised. In the New
Testament he is come.

The history of man's redemption is the golden thread of divine revelation: its light shines out most clearly in the miracles, the parables, and the preceptive teachings of our Saviour.

Is it not usually the case that children, and even adults, lose the connecting thread of God's Word, that is, the history of man's salvation, by the manner in which they read, and the delays they are obliged to make?

But let the *idea* of this continuity be once firmly fixed in the mind, and then all the other portions of Scripture will be found to harmonize with the history, and also contribute to the development and elucidation of the same idea.

This is no new thought, originated for these articles. It has been the result of the study and the conviction of years. This may be seen by a reference to the "Bible-Reading-Book," which we selected and arranged some years since with this precise view. The plan of our work — one never before attempted — was to abridge the sacred volume in such a way as to retain portions most essential to the understanding of "the ways of God to man," while avoiding the numerous repetitions, and omitting the long lists of names, the obsolete laws (of the Jews), and such collateral histories, — that of Ishmael for instance, — as were not absolutely essential in understanding the scope of the divine purpose.

We would by no means be understood to say that the whole Bible is not indispensable as it stands; but just as the deserts and waste places of the earth have their uses, and yet may not be personally profitable to us, so with the portions here omitted. It is not that they are not equally inspired; but they may not be as *personally profitable* for our study, or for our use in family instruction.

To mothers and teachers who would like to know this short-hand way of Bible reading, so as to grasp the idea of consecutive history, we say, study the first three chapters of Genesis; then read the story of the Flood; of Babel; of the three patriarchs; of Joseph and Moses; also the Book of Exodus, so as to remember all the miracles of God's mercy to the Hebrew people, and his divine laws of the Decalogue for all mankind; then the 28th chapter of Deuteronomy, with the 33d and 34th chapters: and you will be furnished with such an outline of the plan and purpose of the Old-Testament history, as will enable you to discern the correspondence of all other portions in this same plan.

Take, for instance, all the prophets, sixteen in number, from Isaiah to Malachi, whose writings fill over one-fourth of the Old Testament.

What is the burden of their books? There are but three grand themes: all agree in these, and all teach substantially the same ideas and the same results, —

1st. Of the Jews, as God's chosen people.

2d. Of the Messiah, and his kingdom on earth.

3d. Of the punishments of the heathen nations, who oppress and hate God's people.

We have not room here to enter into this subject more at length; but a careful study will make this clear. Such study should be given in view of the important position which the Jewish people hold at present in the world. Their preservation to this day is a standing proof of the truth of the prophecies. Who can enter a Jewish synagogue, and not find tangible evidence that such a person as Abraham did indeed live when we see before us his descendants?

Another proof of the truth of the Scriptures may be found in the perfect adaptation of their teachings to the supernatural element in the mind of a child, so early developed in the imagination.

Where is there a more beautiful lesson for all ages than the trusting faith with which these little ones receive the most wonderful truths from the lips of a parent? Where is the child who ever listened to the marvellous story of Jonah, and doubted?

Children will naturally, if permitted to follow the bent of their own inclinations, select for their reading, in opening the Bible, the Old-Testament stories, the miracles, and the parables. These attract them, and they should be encouraged to become familiar with them as children. Their faculties are more receptive, their minds more easily impressed, their imagination more vivid, and their feelings more sensitive, than in later years; and truths stamped upon heart and brain at that time remain indelibly fixed there, requiring a serious effort to efface those early impressions.

The Bible is pre-eminently the book for Sunday; and no Sunday-school teaching should ever be allowed to take the place of the parents' reading it themselves with their children.

Sunday-school teaching may often be most valuable; but, too frequently, it is disjointed and fragmentary. A lesson is given and recited without any question of what interest it may excite in, or what benefit it may be to, the mind of a child. A case in point occurs to us. A little boy, in answer to the question, —

"What did you learn, to-day, at Sunday school?" replied, "I learned a text."

"Can you repeat it?"

"And Mary arose in those days, and went into the hill country with haste, into a city of Judæa!"

This was the child's teaching for the day, and surely is beyond comment.

Instead of such instruction, if parents will only follow a child's lead, and make it familiar with what it naturally prefers, benefit will result to parent as well as child; for they will thus both become interested in following what we have called the golden thread of the story of man's redemption, which runs throughout the whole volume, and is most clearly seen exactly in the portions which we have already referred to as the child's own choice.

Besides the spiritual influence of the Scriptures, their effect upon character, in elevating and refining it, should never be forgotten. We need most specially to remem-

ber this in our country, where we have no court standard
of manners, and the Bible precepts, "Be courteous," &c.,
are the rules which, as a people, we must depend upon.

The effect of these teachings may be best shown by
the following anecdote : —

About the year 1232, when Henry the Third was on
the throne of England, the Bishop of Lincoln was distinguished for the elegance of his manners. The king
one day remarked that it was strange that a man who
was only a student, and of low birth, should have all the
graces of a refined gentleman.

The bishop replied, that "he had been educated among
the brightest exemplars and the principal characters of
the world."

The king demanding an explanation, the bishop said,
that, "in reading the Scriptures, he had found those who
were able to instruct him no less than if he had seen and
conversed with them; and that he had endeavored to
imitate those models of behavior."

One of the highest departments of human genius, the
art of poetry, has its most perfect models in the Bible, and
in those uninspired compositions which are most imbued
with its morals and philosophy ; as we find in the works
of Shakspeare, Dante, and Milton. In this poetry of religion, woman, whenever she shall be allowed the advantages of mental culture equally with her brother man, will
excel. Professor Wilson (Christopher North) thus describes the characteristics of her poetry : —

14

"Women are privileged from on high to write poetry — yes, the highest poetry; for innocence and purity are of the highest hierarchies; and the thoughts and feelings they inspire, though breathed in words and tones gentle and low, (an excellent thing in woman), are yet lofty as the stars, and humble, too, as the flowers beneath our feet."

Piety is essential to the cultivation of poetic genius in a woman. She cannot but look upward; for her heart and imagination crave that which is nobler, lovelier, purer, than actual life supplies. Hence it is that so much of her poetry is religious: those who consider religion and sermonizing synonymous may call it monotonous; but the subject of poetry always receives the impress of the mind through which it passes, as light takes a hue from stained glass. No person can truly estimate the highest genius of woman who has not moral delicacy of taste, and a reverence for things holy and good.

The poetry of Mrs. Browning is an excellent illustration. No one doubts her title to the first poetic place among women; and observe, that much of her writings is directly religious, and all is penetrated with the spirit and power of Christianity. The same is true of lesser lights, Miss Ingelow, Miss Rossetti, Miss Procter. No English poetess, we think, can be named, whose works do not bear witness to the influence of religious feeling.

PART FIFTH.

———◆———

I. — HEATHEN HOMES.

THE qualities of things are best understood by their opposites. Night and day make us realize darkness in contrast with light. Thus, too, the conditions of life are most truly apprehended, when we place the good in contrast with the evil, — love with hatred, mirth with grief, joy with sorrow, happiness with misery.

This mode of illustration is indispensable to a right appreciation of the social advantages and domestic blessings which the home-circle enjoys in our country; and yet how few among us ever reflect to what cause we are indebted for these advantages and blessings.

The aim of this, and a former article upon the "Social Life of the Chinese," is to reach precisely this point, and to show that our present condition of life, and all the enjoyments resulting from that condition, are due to our Lord and Saviour, and to the blessings flowing from the light of God's holy Word.

This can be proved in no clearer manner than by force of contrast, — by looking at the results of heathen rule.

We have therefore set forth the state in which the Chinese women are kept, to show how their debasement acts, and must ever act, upon the whole nation, — man suffering equally with the woman whom he seeks to degrade; for he must ever feel the loss of the moral power given to woman by her Creator, to influence mankind. And, in looking over the heathen world, we shall find, that, just in proportion as woman is lowered, just in the same proportion must man ever sink. The world shows no solitary instance of the highest form of national greatness, socially, politically, and morally, where woman's influence is ignored or systematically destroyed.

We have, as yet, only looked at a portion of heathendom. We propose, at present, to go a little further into the matter, and show that the same state of things exists, with the same results, throughout the Pagan world.

And first of the Hindoos and Burmese.

Rev. Dr. H. M. Scudder has truly portrayed the actual condition of the women of India, by quoting from the Hindoo Shasters, or sacred law, written eight hundred years before Christ, the following unalterable statutes concerning women : —

"Women have no business with the texts of the Veda, or Sacred Book; thus is the law fully settled. Having, therefore, no evidence of law, and no knowledge of expiatory texts, sinful women must be as foul as falsehood itself; and this is a fixed rule."

"By a girl, or by a young woman, or by a woman advanced in years, nothing must be done, even in her own dwelling-place, according to her mere pleasure."

"No sacrifice is allowed to women apart from their husbands, no religious rite, no fasting: as far only as a wife honors her lord, so far is she exalted in Heaven."

"A husband, however devoid of good qualities, must constantly be revered as a God by a virtuous wife. She who slights not her lord, but keeps her mind, body, and speech devoted to him, attains his heavenly mansion."

These extracts contain the very letter of the law with regard to the women of India. As explained by Dr. Scudder, they declare that woman has no individuality; but in childhood she exists in her father, and in later years through her husband. There is, consequently, no occasion for her being taught any thing, or receiving any ideas. Her husband must think, read, believe for her. At his death her existence ceases; or, if she has any hopes for the future, they are based upon her husband.

It is this belief that has so long caused the suttee, or the practice of burning wives upon the funeral pile of their husbands; and it is the explanation of the present terrible condition of widows in India, where millions, married in childhood by the act of their parents, are widowed in their youth, and denied the suttee by the power of British military authority, live a wretched existence of shame, reproach, and persecution on earth, with no brighter hope for the future, than that after death they must continue upon the earth in the form of some vile animal.

The high-caste women of India are entirely secluded from the society of men. At the age of two or three years they are married by their parents to children of their own rank in society. On arriving at thirteen or fourteen, they are claimed by their husband, and removed to his house, where confinement is their lot for the rest of their lives. No social intercourse is ever permitted; nor are they even looked upon by their husbands as companions, nor informed of an eternal state. No wonder, therefore, that they consider feminine existence as a curse, and seek to destroy the lives of their daughters.

We come next to the Mohammedan theology, as existing among the Arab races.

The term heathen will scarcely apply in the strictest sense to the nations that hold this faith; for, amidst much error, they worship, not idols, but the one God: yet we find that woman is, in some things, even more degraded than among the Hindoos and Burmese; for she is never allowed to enter a Mohammedan mosque, or participate in any religious rite whatever, whilst, among the Burmese, she often takes a place of importance in their sacred ceremonies.

In a recent work upon Central and Eastern Arabia, by an Englishman, W. G. Palgrave, which has met with much favor from the British critics, we find this view very fully confirmed. Mr. Palgrave had widely extended opportunities of informing himself upon the subjects of which he treats, and his statements are entitled to the fullest confidence. Speaking of the social condition of the people of Arabia, where he travelled, he remarks : —

"The daughters of a family are something to be ashamed of, and are never mentioned."

As the result of this system of degrading women, and keeping them in seclusion, he further mentions, that "in the social gatherings of the Arab men, where he was present, the conversation was often so lascivious and shamefully indecent, that it could not be recorded or even described." Wherever men have debased the moral influence of woman, by keeping her in ignorance, there the men are shameless; and, when they banish women from their social gatherings, their own hearts soon become foul with all evil and sensual propensities.

We have merely alluded to a few of these evils. Did space permit us to pursue the inquiry, it would be easy to show that the habits and customs of all Oriental nations would but serve further to establish our theory, that, where woman is degraded, the moral power of man is destroyed, and the progress of humanity is seen to be dwarfed or turned to wickedness. The Japanese, Tartars, and all the swarming millions of Africa, and the inhabitants of the islands, would tell the same tale of corrupt society. An examination of the statistics of the population of the world shows that only about one-fourth of the whole are nominally Christians; thus leaving hundreds of millions of women in this sad and degraded condition.

In all Pagan countries, we should remember also that polygamy is permitted by law; and this, of necessity, is utterly subversive of domestic harmony and destructive of domestic happiness.

Our object in pursuing this inquiry will not have been attained, unless we can persuade our readers to think upon this subject for themselves, and, by looking at the horrors of existence for women under heathen rule, form some appreciation, by contrast, of the infinite blessings which have been bestowed upon those more favored ones whose privilege it is to have been born in a Christian land, and in the full enjoyment of Christian opportunities.

Where women have the benefit of this moral culture, they intuitively use their influence for the promotion of goodness or the Christian civilization. From this wealth of purity and loveliness is developed, besides the moral graces of character, all the best and most refining influences of good society.

The moral sense is the highest natural faculty or element of the human soul: girls have this moral sense — the intuitive feeling of disgust for selfishness, false-hood, and sensuality; the intuitive feeling of love for the beautiful, the true, and the tender — earlier developed and more active than is found in boys. It follows, that, wherever women are degraded and debased, there the race of mankind must necessarily become ignorant, corrupt, barbarian, brutish, and without power of recovery from this degradation. That the true life of moral, intellectual, and social development depends on the character and condition of women has been acknowledged by many eminent statesmen and scholars who were not particularly led by Christian sentiment to this result.

Sheridan says, " On the cultivation of the minds of women depends the wisdom of men." Thackeray has left his testimony that "women are pure, but not men; women are unselfish, but not men." Napoleon acknowledged that " The future destiny of the child is always the work of the mother."

While we consider the condition of heathen homes, as contrasted with our own, shall we not thank God for this crowning mercy to our land, the position which, through his grace, has been accorded to American women ?

II. — PRIVATE VISITS AND SOCIAL PARTIES.

THERE are many great men who go unrewarded for the services they render to humanity: even their names are lost, while we daily bless their inventions. One of these is he (if it was not a lady) who introduced the use of visiting cards. In days of yore a slate or a book was kept, and you wrote your name upon it. But then that could only be done when your acquaintance was "not at home." To the French is due the practice of making the delivery of a card serve the purpose of a personal appearance; and this custom has been eagerly adopted by other countries, who recognize its necessity in large communities.

The visit, or call, however, is a much better institution than is generally supposed. It has its drawbacks. It wastes much time; it demands much small talk; it obliges one to dress upon the chance of finding a friend at home; but, for all this, it is almost the only means of making an acquaintance ripen into friendship.

In this visit, all the strain which general society somehow requires is thrown off. A gentleman receives you in his rooms cordially, and makes you welcome, not to a stiff dinner, but to an easy chair and conversation. A lady, who, in the ball-room or party, has been compelled to limit her conversation, can here speak more freely. The talk can descend from generalities to personal inquiries; and, if any one wish to know a young lady truly, she must be seen at home, and by daylight, in what is well termed her "undress uniform."

The main points to be observed about visits are the proper occasions and the proper hours. A friendly visit may be made at any time on any occasion. Among gentlemen, one is more welcome when the business of the day is over, in the afternoon rather than the morning;

and you should, even as a friend, avoid calling at meal times. Visits, however, are also frequently made in the evening, another French custom, and we think a very good one.

A well-bred person always receives visitors at whatever time they may call, or whoever they may be.; but, if you should be too much occupied to be interrupted, instruct your servant to that effect beforehand, so as to prevent the awkwardness of admitting persons, and then declining to receive them.

In good society, a visitor, unless he is a complete stranger, does not wait to be invited to sit down, but takes a seat at once easily.

A gentleman should never take the principal place in the room, nor sit at an inconvenient distance from the lady of the house. A well-bred lady, who is receiving two or three visitors at a time, pays equal attention to all, and attempts, as much as possible, to generalize the conversation. The last arrival naturally receives a little more attention ; and the first comers, in such cases, should leave as soon as convenient. People who outsit two or three visitors are usually voted "bores," who do not know when you have had enough of their company.

In regard to visits at country houses, a general invitation should never be acted on. It is often given, without any intention of following it up, but, if given, should be turned into a special one, sooner or later. An invitation should specify the persons whom it includes, and the person invited should never presume to take with him or her any one not specified.

It is in equally bad taste to take too many trunks, as that appears like a hint that you mean to stay a long time. The English custom of specifying the length of a country visit in the invitation is an excellent one, as saving all doubt upon the subject.

SOCIAL PARTIES.

People will make a party for any thing, — a party to see a sunset, a party to take a walk, a party to go to church, or a party to do nothing at all. There are people who cannot even read their Bible without a party; and the very persons who object to balls and gayeties of that sort are usually foremost in originating the same style of thing for religious or charitable purposes, such as Sunday-school excursions, picnics for missionary pur poses, fairs for churches; and every one is aware, during the war, how much was done by social gatherings and social amusements of every kind.

We are not naming this to condemn it, but merely to point out the gregarious tendency in human nature. We were so created; and, if this tendency be properly reg- ulated, there is nothing of necessity wrong in it.

The system of gathering a little assembly to join in every pleasure, as long as it is free from ostentation and scandal, only shows what sociable and sympathetic beings we are; for, in most cases, the real object of these parties is not the sunset, the walk, or the professed aim, but the pleasure of being in one another's society.

The main difference in all kinds of parties lies in the selection of the guests, the dress they wear, and the amusement of the evening. Another great distinction lies, too, between town and country parties.

Town parties consist in tea-parties, matinées, private concerts, or private theatricals, and what are known as " Receptions," or " At homes." These last have for their chief object conversation only; so that, in the selection of guests, youth and beauty are less considered than talent, distinction, and fashion.

For such entertainments, two or three rooms should be thrown open : curiosities, choice engravings, rare books, old china, photographs, stereoscopes, &c., placed upon the tables ; and there should be a liberal supply of seats.

The lady of the house must take care to create circulation, and the guests should never pinion themselves to one spot or chair.

The tea-party should always be a sociable affair, and must vary in the number of its guests : they should, if possible be all of one set, and known to each other, but, if not, should be generally introduced. The amusement usually consists in music, vocal or instrumental ; and round games are sometimes introduced, as serving to destroy stiffness.

Private concerts and amateur theatricals ought to be very good to be successful. Professionals alone should be engaged for the former, and none but real amateurs for the latter. Refreshments should always be handed round between the acts, as they are generally fatiguing.

Very different is the character of country parties. These consist chiefly in small dances (not balls), private *fêtes*, and picnics. Sociability and easy mirth are the main features in all of them. You are expected to make yourself generally agreeable, to be merry, humorous, and ready for any thing that may be proposed.

Country hours are much earlier than those in town; and you are expected to be punctual, and not an hour or more after date.

Picnics have a special enjoyment of their own; and we cannot but regret, that, with the advance of civilization, this good old custom bids fair to be lost, of each one's furnishing a *quantum* to the entertainment. The opening of the baskets, the droll mistakes, the arranging of provisions, all give birth to hilarity and death to formality. The barriers of society were for the time broken down, and every one was at his ease.

Have we gained in true real enjoyment by increasing elegance, and requiring no one at present to bring any thing but their best dress, their best looks, and their best spirits? We think not, and plead for the good old-fashioned picnic of other days.

HINTS FOR VISITS.

1. Ceremonial visits must be made the week after a ball. A card will suffice for these. A day or two after a din-

ner-party, and a week after a small party, these calls must be made in person.

2. Visits of condolence and congratulation must be made about a week after the event.

3. On marriage, cards are sent round to such people as you wish to keep among your acquaintance; and it is their part to call first.

4. When a stranger comes to stay at the house of a friend, she should be called upon as soon after her arrival as possible.

5. A lady never calls upon a gentleman unless professionally or officially.

6. In paying a country visit, give as little trouble as possible, conform to the habits of your entertainers, and never be in the way.

7. Retire for a time after breakfast to your own occupations, unless your host or hostess form plans for your morning.

8. Be punctual at meals; never keep your friends waiting from your delay.

9. A host should provide amusement for his guests, and give up as much of his time as possible to them.

10. A guest must not, however, interfere with business engagements, or the domestic routine of the house.

HINTS FOR SOCIAL PARTIES.

11. At a musical party, nothing shows worse breeding than to talk incessantly. In good society, people know when to use their tongues and when their ears.

12. In giving receptions, the simplest form of invitation is to put the name of your day upon the card, which, once left, answers for the winter.

13. For private theatricals, the audience-room must be filled with chairs and benches in rows; and, if possible, the back rows raised higher than the others.

14. In receiving guests, no matter what the size of the party, the hostess must be perfectly self-possessed; never bustling in her welcome, or flustered in her manner.

15. For *fêtes* or country parties of any description, a light, airy, and graceful style of dress is most fitting: the hat trimmed with either feather or flower is generally worn.

16. The collation for a *fête* or picnic should be of a more solid and substantial character than that of a town supper, as appetites are usually increased by the country air and exercise.

17. In your demeanor at a country party, steer between the Scylla of dulness and the Charybdis of romping.

18. In planning a picnic, create an interest, if possible, by proposing something to see in the neighborhood, — a lake, a waterfall, or picturesque spot or building.

III. — CHARACTER.

D R. JOHNSON, the great moralist, says of the great
dramatist, "Shakspeare is above all writers, at
least above all modern writers, the Poet of Nature. His
characters are not modified by the customs of particular
places. His persons act and speak by the influence of
those general passions and principles by which all minds
are agitated and the whole system of life is continued in
motion. In the writings of other poets, a character is
too often an individual; in those of Shakspeare it is
commonly a species." — *Preface to the Life of Shakspeare.*

The reading world, as well as the critics, are agreed
upon this point: all believe that Shakspeare has delineated man's characteristics more truly than any other
uninspired writer; only in the Bible can be found a
clearer impress of the inner nature, the inherent qualities, of men. If this be so, then the characteristics of
women must, in Shakspeare, be truly set forth. His
creative genius is here in the same unison with Bible
truth as in his delineations of men.

Shakspeare's women, in all moral qualities, excel his
men; and this peculiarity of character has never appeared
to move any of his learned critics or eulogists even to
notice.

15

At length the morning of hope for woman is breaking, the horizon of truth is clearing. One of England's remarkable men, the distinguished art-critic, John Ruskin, has written on this subject. His ideas are worth the earnest study of Americans.

Our national life is founded on moral qualities in human nature. As Shakspeare, in his mimic life-pictures, has delineated the characteristics of women, it would seem important that their moral qualities should be cherished and honored if our republic is to be distinguished by its power for good over the nations of the Old World. . . .

THE WOMANLY AND THE MANLY.

" *The relations of the womanly to the manly nature,* their different capacities of intellect or of virtue, seem never to have been measured with entire consent. We hear of the mission and the rights of woman, as if these could ever be separate from the mission and the rights of man; as if she and he were creatures of independent kind and of irreconcilable claim. This, at least, is wrong. And not less wrong, perhaps even more foolishly wrong, — for I will anticipate thus far what I hope to prove, — is the idea that woman is only the shadow and attendant image of the man; owing him a thoughtless and servile obedience, and supported altogether in her weakness by the pre-eminence of his fortitude.

" This, I say, is the most foolish of all errors respecting

her who was made to be 'the help-meet for man.' As if he could be helped effectively by a shadow, or worthily by a slave !

"Let us try, then, whether we cannot get at some clear and harmonious idea — it must be harmonious if it is true — of what womanly mind and virtue are, in power and office, with respect to man's; and how their relations, rightly accepted, aid and increase the vigor and honor and authority of both.

"Let us see whether the greatest, the wisest, the purest-hearted of all ages are agreed in any wise on this point. Let us hear the testimony they have left respecting what they held to be the true dignity of woman, and her mode of help to man.

" And, first, let us take Shakspeare.

" Note broadly in the outset, Shakspeare has no heroes: he has only heroines. There is not one entirely heroic figure in all his plays, except the slight sketch of Henry the Fifth, exaggerated for the purposes of the stage, and the still slighter Valentine in the 'Two Gentlemen of Verona.' In his labored and perfect plays, you have no hero. Othello would have been one, if his simplicity had not been so great as to leave him the prey of every base practice round him ; but he is the only example, even approximating to the heroic type. Coriolanus, Cæsar, Antony, stand in flawed strength, and fall by their vanities ; Hamlet is indolent and drowsily speculative; Romeo an impatient boy; the Merchant of Venice languidly submissive to adverse fortune; Kent, in King Lear, is entirely noble at heart, but too rough and unpolished to be of use at the critical time, and he sinks into the office of a servant only. Orlando, no less noble, is yet the despairing toy of chance, followed, comforted, saved, by Rosalind. Whereas there is hardly a play that has not a perfect woman in it, steadfast in grave hope and errorless purpose; Cordelia, Desdemona, Isabella, Hermione, Imogen, Queen Katherine, Perdita, Sylvia, Viola, Rosalind, Helena, and last, and perhaps loveliest, Virgilia, are all faultless, — conceived in the highest heroic type of humanity.

" Then observe, secondly, —

" The catastrophe of every play is caused always by the folly or fault of man; the redemption, if there be any, is by the wisdom and virtue of a woman, and, failing that, there is none. The catastrophe of King Lear is owing to his own want of judgment, his impatient vanity, his misunderstanding of his children: the virtue of his one true daughter would have saved him from all the injuries of the others, if he had not cast her away from him; as it is, she all but saves him.

" Of Othello I need not trace the tale, nor the one weakness of his so mighty love; nor the inferiority of his perceptive intellect to that even of the second woman character in the play, the Emilia who dies in wild testimony against his error: 'O murderous coxcomb! What should such a fool do with so good a wife?'

"In Romeo and Juliet, the wise and entirely brave stratagem of the wife is brought to ruinous issue by the reckless impatience of her husband. In Winter's Tale and in Cymbeline, the happiness and existence of two princely households, lost through long years, and imperilled to the death by the folly and obstinacy of the husbands, are redeemed at last by the queenly patience and wisdom of the wives. In Measure for Measure, the injustice of the judges, and the corrupt cowardice of the brother, are opposed to the victorious truth and adamantine purity of a woman. In Coriolanus, the mother's counsel, acted upon in time, would have saved her son from all evil; his momentary forgetfulness of it is his ruin; her prayer, at last granted, saves him, not, indeed, from death, but from the curse of living as the destroyer of his country.

"And what shall I say of Julia, constant against the fickleness of a lover who is a mere wicked child; of Helena, against the petulance and insult of a careless youth; of the patience of Hero; the passion of Beatrice; and the calmly devoted wisdom of the 'unlessoned girl,' who appears among the helplessness, the blindness, and the vindictive passions of men, as a gentle angel, to save merely by her presence, and defeat the worst intensities of crime by her smile?

"Observe, further, among all the principal figures in Shakspeare's plays, there is only one weak woman,— Ophelia; and it is because she fails Hamlet at the critical

moment, and is not, and cannot in her nature be, a guide
to him when he needs her most, that all the bitter catastrophe follows. Finally, though there are three wicked
women among the principal figures, — Lady Macbeth,
Regan, and Goneril, — they are felt at once to be frightful
exceptions to the ordinary laws of life; fatal in their
influence also in proportion to the power for good which
they have abandoned.

"Such, in broad light, is Shakspeare's testimony to the
position and character of woman in human life. He
represents them as infallibly faithful and wise counsellors,
incorruptibly just and pure examples, strong always to
sanctify, even when they cannot save."

Some readers may say the judgment of Mr. Ruskin is
in fault, as he finds so little to censure in the feminine
character. They may call his pictures ideal, because they
seem so unlike the plain, prosaic sketches of life in our
homes, and say that his heroines are no examples.

This is the mistake which spoils much innocent enjoyment, and hinders much good, — that we do not enough
prize the present, nor take advantage of our own opportunities. Every one has a part to perform in the "Drama
of Life:" the aim should be to do it in the best manner.
Every example of a "perfect woman" is a lamp to our feet.

American ladies have advantages of education, social
position, and home life, which should make them excel
even the heroines of Shakspeare, as Mr. Ruskin has
interpreted their characters.

IV.— CONVERSATION.

MUCH has been said and written upon conversation: still it seems to me that its true nature is too little understood; that forgetting the double character it should possess, and which the very etymology of the word suggests to us, we are all too apt to make it a one-sided affair, a sort of monologue, instead of a *turning over* of subjects *with another.*

Conversation, in the strictest sense, must ever be the interchange of thought and feeling; not the assertion or declaration of opinion on one side, without the permission of corresponding expression on the other.

This is not unfrequently the case with persons who are said to possess "great conversational powers;" but that term is certainly misapplied. Great talkers they may be; and, more than this, they may have a vast fund of information; but they can never be agreeable companions, or popular in society, from their unwillingness to permit any sort of dissent from their opinion, indeed scarcely an expression of any opinion at all from anyone else.

In M. Boitard's book, a French work of some little note, entitled " *Guide-Manuel de la Bonne Compagnie, du Bon Ton, et de la Politesse,*" there are some valuable hints on this subject. Here is one.

In speaking of the habit just alluded to, he cites a case in point.

A young widow, with all the graces of youth, beauty, and intellect, in place of charming every one in the *beau monde*, as she should have done with such combined attractions, wearied them with her incessant flow of words, scarcely allowing an instant's pause between her stories and *bon mots*.

Much as she was beloved by her friends, they could not fail to perceive this defect; and, at length, one of them resolved to give her what he trusted might prove a salutary lesson. He laid his plan accordingly, and lost no opportunity of speaking to her, with the warmest enthusiasm, of the brilliant talents and intellectual attainments of a young man whose acquaintance he had just made.

Her curiosity and interest became at length so much excited, that she begged her friend, Mons. T——, to bring that literary paragon to see her. Her request was readily accepted, and the next morning she greeted them warmly. The young man was singularly pleasing, modest, and quiet in his deportment, but with much easy grace of manner. He saluted her politely, and seated himself silently, she thought almost with an air of diffidence.

The lady, to set him at ease, as well as according to custom, opened and continued the conversation. An hour soon slipped away, when the gentlemen rose and retired.

The same evening, meeting Madame L—— at a party, Mons. T—— inquired her opinion of his friend.

"Charming!" said she. "I have just been praising him to these ladies, — so full of mind, such brilliancy, his whole conversation sparkles with wit. We talked for an hour, and it seemed but a moment. You really must make Mons. T——— present him to you," said she, turning to her hostess.

"I will most willingly do so," replied Mons. T———; "but perhaps I should first mention that my young friend labors under an infirmity which perhaps every one might not pardon so readily as Madame."

"An infirmity, did you say? I perceived none," said Madame L———.

"Yes, madame: he is *deaf and dumb!*"

The surprise and confusion of the lady may be conceived. As her habit was, she had talked so unceasingly as never to have been conscious of his defect.

La Bruyère has said, "The spirit of conversation consists less in displaying your own powers than in developing those of others: he who leaves your presence satisfied with himself and his own gifts is sure to be at the same time thoroughly satisfied with you. Men do not care to admire you; they prefer to please; they seek less to be instructed or even gratified, than to be appreciated and applauded; and the most exquisite pleasure is ever to make that of others."

With regard to this, M. Boitard remarks, "We must conclude from these words that the highest merit in conversation must consist, not in knowing how to *talk* well, but in knowing how to *listen* well;" with interest, without impatience or any sign of weariness.

To know how to listen, he considers almost as indispensable as to know how to talk; and he says, "It is especially in this particular that we recognize the man of the world and one accustomed to good society."

A habit to be carefully avoided also is that of constant interruption when another is speaking. Some persons make a point of always correcting the slightest inaccuracy in the statement of another, such as a wrong date, one day substituted for another, or even one hour for another, — something which cannot materially effect the story: this is always annoying and unwelcome to the narrator, and far oftener productive of harm than the correction can ever be of benefit.

Connected with this, and equally objectionable, is the custom which too often prevails in the home-circle, when one of its members takes up a story which another has begun, and finishes it according to his or her own view! It may very possibly be, that a consciousness of the power of repeating it in a more graphic manner, and an unwillingness to see a good story spoiled in the telling, may have given rise to this habit; but this is not sufficient to excuse it.

The implied superiority cannot fail to give pain; and if it comes to the question which shall be spoiled, the story, or the temper of one of your family, surely there can be little doubt which should take the precedence.

This may seem trifling; but nothing should ever be so considered which may have an influence to increase or destroy home happiness.

1. In general conversation, beware of engrossing the whole attention: afford others the same opportunity for an expression of opinion as they have yielded to you.

2. Let your words be simple, clear, and forcible, without any affectation of superiority.

3. In conversation, never rise above the comprehension of your listeners. Never speak upon subjects which it is not probable they could comprehend.

4. The first rule for a good talker should be, to speak his own language with purity and precision.

5. Assert your own opinions firmly, but gently. Nothing is more offensive or irritating than a manner which implies that of necessity you are right, and the rest of the world in error.

6. Be as brief as possible in your recitals. Long stories are wearisome to your auditors, especially if upon subjects of trifling importance.

7. Listen with deference to persons older than yourself; and, if compelled to differ, do so with modesty and diffidence.·

8. Never be ashamed, in listening to the conversation of those wiser than yourself, to ask explanations of what

you do not understand. A few well-put questions will often vastly increase your fund of knowledge.

9. Do not continue an argument, when you find either your own temper or that of your opponent giving way. It is better to drop the subject than to quarrel over it.

10. Speak of self as little as possible in general conversation. What will be a subject of interest to your friends cannot be so to mere acquaintances; and we should strive to keep this in mind, lest we become wearisome.

11. Never doubt any one's word: even if the story appear improbable, it is better to think that it *may* be true.

12. Above all, never forget that you are responsible for your words. Surely, if we more firmly believed this solemn truth, there would be more silence on the earth than there is at present.

V.—A LADY'S DRESS.

IN one of the earlier parts of this volume, we gave an article about clothing; but, as this was merely upon the general subject, some practical hints are needed about dress, in its details and in its requirements for good society.

Every woman should habitually make the best of herself. We ornament our receiving-room with flowers:

are their inmates to look inconsistent with the drawing-room over which they preside? We make our tables elegant with silver, glass, and china: should our women be less attractive than all around them?

Amongst the rich and great, the love of dress promotes some degree of exertion and display of taste in themselves, and fosters ingenuity and industry in inferiors: it also engenders contrivance, diligence, and neatness of hand.

An attention to dress is almost requisite in the present state of society, a due influence in which cannot be attained without it. It is useful, too, as retaining, even in the minds of sensible men, that pride in a wife's appearance which is so agreeable to her, and which, for his sake, she should endeavor to preserve as long as possible.

But, whilst a properly regulated taste for dress is desirable, we must not forget the dangers arising from such a taste, when uncontrolled, and stimulated by coquetry and personal vanity. It not only produces great evils in the way of example, excites envy, unduly enriches that extortionate class of persons, milliners and dressmakers; but it also leads to selfishness and vanity, and not unfrequently causes domestic unhappiness, by calling forth remonstrances, and often reproaches, from the one who suffers most from a wife's extravagances, — her husband.

Indulgence in personal luxury, in women, has also an injurious effect on the moral tone. A woman of simple habits, accompanied with nicety and good taste, rarely goes wrong. Luxury in dress, at first an indulgence, soon becomes a necessity; and, if the power to gratify such taste be withdrawn, discontent, a sense of humiliation, and a yearning for what cannot be had, are sure to follow.

America used to be looked upon as the country where excessive dress was a reproach. The magnificent silks, the foreign lace, and expensive evening dresses, have often been the theme of comment. But Paris at present stands pre-eminent for extravagance. The Empress Eugenie has been the originator of extreme richness and variety in dress; and her example has been only too closely followed, not alone in France, but even in England, where French customs are rarely adopted, and also in America.

The expenses of the smaller items of a lady's dress, such as cuffs, under-sleeves, collars, pocket-handkerchiefs, and dress-trimmings, are in themselves at present enough to ruin any one of moderate means. The cost of dress depends so much on the prudence as well as the discrimination of a lady, — for she should know how to choose her dress, — that it is impossible to lay down any rule of expenditure. English women have had their dress-expenses defined by high authority. Lord Eldon laid down as a maxim, that forty pounds a year ($200) was enough for any girl not of age, even if she had large expectations; and that was all he allotted to a ward of Chancery, who was heiress to five thousand a year. In a trial in which a celebrated barrister in England, who had an expensive wife, was sued for her dressmaker's bills, the judge decided that sixty pounds a year ($300) was an ample allowance for the wife of a professional man; and, beyond that, bills could not be recovered. *That* was essential; more was extravagance.

"The London Times," in an amusing "leader," made a remark to the effect, that a tasteful, careful lady, with the start of a moderately good *trousseau*, ought (and many do) to make twenty pounds a year ($100) suffice for the dress of herself and children during the first few years of married life, and this without any compromise of respectability!

What would be thought of these views in a land of such lavish expenditure as ours? Much of the expense of dress depends upon management, and also upon the care taken of it. In these respects, both English and French are greatly our superiors. We discard half-worn dresses and articles which they remodel and use again.

On entering the rooms of a *modiste* in Paris, an American lady remarked upon the elegance of a ribbon trimming on a court-train, and was not a little surprised to be shown the old dress from which the unsoiled ribbon had been taken, and arranged to do duty the next night at the Tuileries, where the lady saw it on the sister of a duke and marshal of France, who was herself a countess.

The due care of dress is also a great point towards reasonable economy. Here also the French are far more particular than we are. "I once followed," said an American lady, "a French lady in her carriage, as we both went to the same party. She stood up in her carriage the whole way, for fear of crushing her dress, which was an exquisite one of tulle, with puffings of the same."

It is one of the minor virtues to make a good appearance on small means. "A man's appearance," says "The Spectator," "falls within the censure of every one that sees him; his parts and learning very few are judges of." The same is true in regard to women. No stranger knows the heart that beats beneath an ill-made gown, or the qualities of head that lie hidden beneath a peculiar, old-fashioned, or hideous cap. A woman may be an angel of goodness, a Minerva in wisdom, a Diana in morals, a Sappho in genius, yet, if she wears a soiled dress where all around are fresh, or has an antiquated head-dress or bonnet, esteem, and even affection, will not resist a smile or a sigh, and mere acquaintance will ridicule her ignorance of the habits of good society.

The modern custom of wearing crinoline, in spite of the crusade waged against it, has many advantages. It is to be regretted that it should have been carried to such an extreme; but it cannot be denied that it shows off a dress, and preserves it from trailing on the floor, whilst it supports and lightens the weight of other clothing; thus possessing that rare virtue with any fashion, that it is in many cases a sanitary measure. Ladies should endeavor to wear smaller hoops, when going into cars, or in walking, than for evening dresses, and thus prevent much inconvenience to their fellow-travellers: we cannot desire that the practice should be entirely abolished, but simply that it be rightly regulated.

In short, the principle of all that relates to dress should be delicacy, consistency, and suitableness. If these are once lost sight of; if fifty apes fifteen; if the lady dresses worse than her own housekeeper, or the maid vies with her mistress; if good taste and good sense cease to be the foundation of the important whole, — then all special directions will be unavailing.

HINTS.

1. Adopt the prevailing fashion, but do not carry it to excess. A lady is less conspicuous in this way, no matter what her age, than by persistently ignoring the customs of the day.

2. Study harmony of colors in dress. Nothing is more painful to the eye than the mingling of ill-assorted shades.

The difference between morning and evening costume should be distinctly marked. The morning dress should always be tasteful, but simple, and made to fit and show off the figure perfectly.

4. The perfection of a lady's dress consists in the completeness of all its details: nothing is to be considered too trifling to produce entire harmony.

5. Avoid wearing too much jewelry. There is a want

of refinement about it, and a true lady is very particular upon this point.

6. The walking-dress should be quiet in color, and simply elegant; never showy, and, above all, harmonizing with bonnet, gloves, etc.

7. Carriage or visiting dresses should be gayer in color and richer in style than is desirable in a walking-dress.

8. Ordinary evening-dress admits of much taste. A low-necked dress may then be worn with advantage; but, in the daytime, a thin dress with high neck is preferable for dinners, unless, where, as in England, the custom is the reverse.

9. Natural flowers, worn as ornaments for young girls, are by far more appropriate and becoming than any thing else.

For the country, the attire should be plain and strong, yet taste should always be consulted. The hat, now so universally adopted, should be trimmed with a feather, in preference to flowers. A cloak of a light material for summer and stout in winter, the balmoral skirt, and thick leather walking-boots.

11. For outer coverings in city life, the cashmere shawl, velvet cloak, or richly-trimmed mantilla, are the most desirable; but the fashion of the day must settle that point.

12. The parasol or sunshade has come to be an important appendage to a lady's toilette. These vary also with the fashion. At present, white silk, with a covering of

black lace and coral finishings on handle and tips, are the most elegant.

13. A riding-dress should be made of cloth of a dark shade, fitting perfectly to the figure, and never more than half a yard longer than an ordinary dress: nothing increases the risk to a lady on horseback more than a long skirt.

14. A plain linen collar and cuffs should be worn with the habit; gauntlet gloves of thick leather; but no ornaments of any sort, save the riding-whip, which may have a handle of agate, carnelian, or some appropriate stone.

15. The riding-hat must suit the style of the day. The most becoming is the low, round hat with graceful, sweeping feather. The stiff hat, to resemble a man's, is trying to a woman's face, and should only be worn when fashion forbids any other.

VI. — PETS AND THEIR USES.

THE Rev. Daniel Wilkie, "one of the most kindly Christian men that lived to do good," strongly advised that all boys should be trained to love pets: it was such a great preventive against the thoughtless cruelty and tyranny they are so apt to exercise towards all dependent beings!

If boys are to be thus humanized, girls must also be trained how to care for pet animals; because, as sisters and mothers, they must help and teach boys in whatever things are good, tender, and lovely.

Home-life is the place for all innocent loves; and, when the love of pet animals can be judiciously cultivated, it leads to the love of natural history and intellectual improvement, as well as to thoughtful tenderness and moral sensibility.

The family circle is made better, wiser, and happier, by having its amusements of pets, which naturally bring all the household into some kind of participation and enjoyment in its innocent recreations.

As grandmother to a happy little set of children, I have, for the past eight or nine years, enjoyed their delight in a zoölogical collection, including creatures from each class of " Animated Nature," — beast, bird, reptile, fishes, mollusca, and insects.

Our May has been hitherto queen of our petdom, but is now quietly resigning in favor of sister Fay and brother Carolus (Latin seems appropriate for boys: it sounds collegiate; and grandmammas have wonderfully bright pictures in the future for their little men) who loves all living things, but forgets sometimes that to be loved in his fashion is not so pleasant for his pets.

The small wood-tortoise will be found to be one of the best, safest, and most convenient pets for little boys. Children always long to handle a pet; and they can do so here, without risk either to themselves or the object of their affections. We shall have more to say on this point later.

Our aquarium has had a large population; but, as in the world of humanity, few individuals have risen to particular distinction. Fishes are monotonous pets; still it is pleasant to see an aquarium, with its variety of life, and very little care is needed to make the pets comfortable. The chief pleasure to the owners of this "water-colony" is in replenishing it; and one might well envy the happiness of our May, when she comes home with her wealth of snails, bugs, tadpoles, and dragon-flies.

The glory of our aquarium has departed. Only fishes, gold and silver, remain, with one eel and two lizards. During the past winter, this eel lay concealed under the pebbles and gravel at the bottom of the aquarium; but at the call, or rather whistle, of *pater familias* or May, this "water-snake" would wriggle itself up and out, eager to get the little rolls of meat held in the hands of its friends, even thrusting its long head above water to seize its food.

We have had a large collection also of birds, canaries, paroquets, ring-doves, and a mocking-bird. The paroquets were a novelty at first, and made a grand sensation at the end of their career. May had set her heart upon a parrot, and *pater familias* promised to bring her one from Brazil; but the fleet was ordered home suddenly while lying at Monte Video, where only the larger kind of paroquets abound, and the result was that May had two paroquets instead of one parrot. We all tried to love and praise these birds, and to persuade May that they were beauties.

Their color was beautiful, — green all over, in different tints, from the softest spring green of grass and opening leaves, to the dark shade of the closing summer foliage; and then their brotherly love (they seemed like brothers) was more beautiful than their colors. Nestled closely side by side, as their habit was, with their necks crossed together, like green ribbons to be tied in a knot, they were indeed lovely.

At first they were very quiet; but, as time went on, their vocal powers developed. They did not talk; but oh, when they opened their beaks, what a volume of strange sounds those green throats could pour forth!

Unfortunately for our peace, a piano in full practice was within hearing of our paroquets. They listened and learned, and, after some time, began, on their own resources, a performance which none who heard can ever forget. It was as if every chord in music had broken loose, every quaver gone distracted, every semi-tone become a grand crash. This caused laughter at first; but, as the unearthly din went on day by day, even our steadfast patience with pets gave way, and we hailed the escape of one of them from the window, and exchanged the other for a pair of ring-doves; and thus ended the farce of the paroquets. May has never since coveted a parrot.

The ring-doves proved stupid as dunces, rarely opening their beaks except to eat, and then sitting with stuffed
crops, seemingly asleep. Nobody thought these would
fly away, but they did. Dunces are usually discontented;
neither birds nor people are happy who have no resources
within themselves.

Our mocking-bird was a female, and therefore could
not be expected to sing; but, as it was a present from
May's uncle, General ——, who was among the early
magnates of the war at the South, and brought the bird
from Port Royal, we all prized it exceedingly. Mocking-
birds, however, should never be confined pets. Their
nature requires space and freedom. Poor Dixie! Every
feather in its plumage seemed to quiver with its longings
for liberty. One of her tricks excited much amusement.
When we said, " Hurrah for General ——!" teaching her
to know, by a particular motion of the hand, she would
fly round and round the cage, like a whirligig, always
watching our hand, and ceasing when we ceased to cheer
and wave.

One bitter cold night the furnace went out, and Dixie's
little life went out with it. She was buried in the garden,
beneath frozen turf, but May's warm heart gave her a
" *Hic jacet.*"

Of the beast kind, our *guinea-pigs* were a nuisance,
the *mice* pests, and the *gray rabbits* not much better.
But Bunny, our white rabbit, was Fay's particular treasure. Bunny was well trained, and would stand on his

hind legs, and hold up his paws for food. He would come
at call, and lick your hand, — "kissing" Fay calls it, —
and be very innocently winning.

In appearance and habits, this Angora species of rabbit
seems to unite the distinctive qualities of several animal
tribes, — laps milk like a kitten, nibbles grass like a sheep,
browses like a goat, and loves sweets like a bear; he
plays like a lamb, leaps like a kangaroo, and has, like that
strange animal, long hind legs and strong tail to assist his
bounds; whiskers like a cat, ears like a donkey, fur white
and soft as the ermine, and eyes that, in some gleams of
light, shine like rubies.

In short, we cannot but wonder where the rationalistic
philosophy would place the "development" of our
Bunny, and from what class of animal life he can claim
to have been "evolved." Probably the learned Herbert
Spencer would himself rank these queries among "The
unknowable."

Among our domestic favorites the most distinguished
is a very small *English terrier*, black and tan color, pure
blooded and thorough bred, one of the most perfect
specimens of doghood to be found in petdom. *Mio*
belongs to May; but we all feel that "Mio" means
mine, and so all claim a share in loving him. Mio's
reverence as well as affection is certainly given to the
pater familias, who — softly be it said — is as fond of
pets as any of *us* children, old or young, can be. So Mio
is pampered and petted, and leads a useless life, except

that he gives much pleasure to the household. His own happiness would be complete, but for one fault; he will bark when gentlemen come in, and then he is scolded. This wounds his feelings, especially if the reproof comes from his master. Then tears gather in Mio's eyes, — veritable tears, tears that sometimes fall; and his whole manner is so humble and pleading, that you could not but forgive him had he bitten you. We should add that he admires ladies more than gentlemen, and rarely barks at a lady dressed in black.

Our sketch is growing long; but we cannot close without a notice of Tip, the only reptile we ever petted. This little turtle was given to May, as one of the water-species, for her aquarium: it was kept three years among the fishes. While there it was only known as the "snapping turtle," and deserved its name. It snapped up and ate or killed bugs, snails, the insects of all kinds, and even the little fishes. It was the ogre of the aquarium: though its shell was not larger than might have been covered by a silver dollar, it seemed so fierce we were all afraid to touch it lest it should bite.

At length it was discovered accidentally, that this turtle could live out of water, — indeed, seemed to like the change, and became more gentle in its nature. May was glad to be freed from such a destructive in her aquarium, and gave it to little Carolus who had been longing for a pet of his own; but, as he could not take care of it, both boy and pet came under grandmamma's protection; and so we had a reptile to instruct.

The first thing was to give it a name; and *Tippecanoe,* shortened to *Tip,* was chosen. The first lesson was to teach this name. We have been often asked about the process; the best illustration may be gathered from "Molly Dumpling's" way of "calling spirits from the vasty deep;" that is, calling for her drowned lover and his drowned dog: —

> "Oh! tearfully she trod the hall,
> And ' Thomas!' cried, with many a sob;
> And thrice on Bobtail did she call,
> *Repeating sweetly, ' Bob! Bob! Bob!'*"

There's the secret; *repetition,* "*sweetly.*" Fix your eye ("sweetly") on your pet's eye, and thus chain his attention; then repeat the name ("sweetly") till the lesson is learned. This will be much sooner, probably, than you expect.

"Tip" soon knew his own name, and we then went further. We placed him upon our hand, extending the arm, saying, repeatedly, "Come, 'Tip,' come, if you love me;" and the little creature would run up the extended arm, and nestle at our throat. This feat he refused to perform with any other member of the family, although always ready to come to them when they called his name. But, alas! "Tip" proved himself unworthy the confidence reposed in him, and grieved us all by wandering away and getting lost. His place was then supplied by two little turtles, named "Tip" and "Tina," to which they responded when called, but never developed the intelligence shown by our old favorite.

Carolus has now a wood-turtle named "Terry," who seems to enjoy its new life upon carpeted floors and amidst the luxuries of civilization. We know little of his powers as yet, but trust much the effect of the two great tamers and civilizers, — kindness and love. We find our opinion in this matter confirmed in a charming little work which has lately appeared, "The Chronicles of a Garden, its Pets and its Pleasures," by Miss Wilson, niece of Dr. Wilson, who seems to have a large experience in pet-life. She says, —

"The great secret of training and attaching animals seems to be kindness and quietness, and a certain sort of friendly intercourse with them, which, perhaps, is only understood by those to the manner born. All teasing them, even in fun, should be avoided, if you wish them to trust you and be gentle. There are individual exceptions in every species; but there are few exceptions, either among quadrupeds or birds, that will not soon get attached to the person who feeds them; but they are frequently far more attached to the individual who understands them, and keeps up a quiet, friendly intercourse with them.

"Unless this sort of 'rapport' is established between us and our pets, they are (to my mind) hardly worthy of the name: they degenerate into 'captive animals,' and can neither give pleasure to others nor be made happy themselves."

THE SILK-WORM.

We find, in every living form
  That bears the mighty Maker's seal,
There lies some worth or lives some charm,
  If we have hearts to feel.

I saw a fair young girl, her face
  As lilies pure, as roses sweet,
Just at the age when childhood grace
  And maiden beauty meet.

She raised her silk-worm to her cheek,
  And let it rest and revel there.
Oh! why for outward beauty seek?
  Love makes the loved one fair!

That worm! I should have shrunk, in truth,
  To feel its crawlings o'er me move;
But, loved by innocence and youth,
  I felt 'twas worth the love.

And then I thought that if we would
  Love all God trusts to us for care,
Oh, we might have a world as good
  As God has made it fair!

And we should see, in every form
  That bears the loving Maker's seal,
Some latent worth, some living charm,
  That our own hearts could feel.

VII.—HAPPY SUNDAYS FOR CHILDREN.

EVERY first thing continues forever with a child. The first color, the first music, the first flower, paint the foreground of life. Every new educator effects less than his predecessor, until at last, if we record *all life* as an educational institution, a circumnavigator of the globe is less influenced by all the nations he has seen than by his nurse.

So says Richter; but he does not add the most important point of all,—the nurse should always be *the mother*; and perhaps there is no one circumstance connected with our childish days, which leaves so powerful an impression, or lingers so long, upon the memory, as the manner in which our Sundays have been passed. Has the day been to us a stern tyrant, dark-browed, sombre-visaged, compelling us to relinquish every childish joy, and substituting wearying, burdensome rules in their place, making us hate its coming and hail its going? or has it come like some bright angel from a better land, with gentle footstep and love-laden looks, bringing ever in its train a brightness, happiness, and enjoyment of its own,—peculiarly its own?

Accordingly as we have considered the day in one or other of these aspects in childhood,—as we have taken the tyrant or the angel view of it,—so shall we usually find ourselves looking upon it later in life. We have seen the evil results of false training upon this point affect a whole life; leading children to connect religion and restraint, and cheerfulness and carelessness, in a way which they seemed unable to separate as they attained maturer years.

We have seen unhappy little creatures, victims to a mistaken sense of duty on the part of rightly-meaning parents, and pitied them from our heart as we watched every treasured toy torn from their baby-grasp, with nothing to take its place, — nothing to amuse, nothing to please; and, to the infant pleadings for some enjoyment, the only response is, "No! no! it is *Sunday!*"

We feel confident that this could not have been the course pursued by Dr. Livingstone when training the natives of Africa, who are little else than children. He tells us, in his recent interesting work, that many of them came to him when he was instructing his class, begging that they might be " *Sundayed* too." We find much in the expression to prove that he had managed to connect something pleasing to their minds with the very name of the day. Surely, had they been deprived of every enjoyment, and made to submit to stern and rigid rules, we should not have found them thus seeking to be "Sundayed."

There is something monstrous in thus linking Sunday and sadness in the brain of a child; and be very sure any one so taught will conclude, by a process of induction which begins in children's minds far earlier than we are aware, that the Creator of such a Sunday cannot be the loving, tender Father which he is represented to be. Children are active observers, and often settle difficult points for themselves long before parents or friends realize that they have any power to do this.

We are far from meaning that the day should not be marked to children as something distinct from other days; but let it be by linking holiness and happiness, by changing their amusements, not annihilating them. We may please them by showing and explaining to them some coveted volume of sacred pictures, and provide for them pencil and paper, should inclination prompt their copying what they see; grant them privileges on that day given on no other. Tell them, in winning phrase, those Bible stories, which, so learned, they never will forget; and, above all, you who are fathers, talk to them, and lead them to talk to you. The business of the week necessarily engrosses and separates you; but, upon Sunday, let your children feel that you give yourself to them. Study their characters, — guide, teach, and lead them.

It is wonderful how a child's mind will unfold under your explanations, and how curious it is to watch its working! Some years since, we were struck by this fact in the case of a little boy, to whom a whip, with sounding cracker, was a recent acquisition and great treasure. The thoughts of the new toy could not be laid aside with the article when Sunday came, and Sunday pleasures were substituted. To his father, explaining to him the wonderful power of God, he said, "Can He do every thing? Could he snap a whip without taking hold of the handle?"

This to him was, at that moment, the highest reach of power which his opening mind could grasp, and probably conveyed all the more to him from having been his own thought.

Even in very trifling ways, or what seems so to us, — but we should remember they are not so to the little ones, — it is well to mark the *day* with some pleasure or gratification. We know of a lady who always gives preserves or sweetmeats to her children on Sunday, simply that they may have the remembrance of something agreeable connected with the day. It is well, on the same ground, to reserve the appearance of a new dress, new bonnet, new coat, or those treasures to children, new shoes, for Sunday. This has a double advantage, — the one we have just mentioned, of forming a pleasant connection in the mind of the child, and also making him feel that Sunday is a day upon which the best of every thing is to be used.

Strict cleanliness, both of person and dress, and also of all the arrangements of chamber or play-room, should be insisted upon. This rule is quite as important for grown persons as for children. It may not be in the power of many to afford fine or expensive clothing, but it is most certainly so for every one in our country to be neat and clean; taking care to provide a nicely-washed dress, even of the plainest calico (if the means permit nothing else), for the Sunday's wear. There is a moral effect in this. We are all aware how much we are under the influence of our surroundings; and, if every thing about us on that day is suggestive of purity, one step is gained towards the purity of heart which we should ever be seeking.

We all teach our children, and hold for ourselves, that Sunday is a "day of rest." So it is. But, upon this subject, it seems to me that there is a mistaken view. The word "rest" implies not idleness or tedious vacuity of thought, but a rest from the wearying secular cares of earth, from physical toil, in order to allow the mind and spirit to mount up towards its God, and dwell upon His perfections.

We are bound and chained to earth and its engrossing cares for the six days; but, on the "day of days," we may rest from those employments, and not turn from thought, but change its channel, and exercise the powers which are God's best gift to man, in studying our duty to Him and his wonderful goodness to us. By educating our children to this view, we shall find that we are at the same time teaching ourselves.

While it is most important, as we have said, that the father should instruct his children upon religious subjects as far as possible, we must never forget that it is from the

17

mother that children receive their chief lessons on this
subject. The Bible, history, experience, all show the
mighty influence of the mother's teachings: the religion
of the household and of society is mainly woman's.

Our thoughts were turned to the noble manner in
which John Bunyan, that Shakspeare of Christianity,
illustrates this by the simple words of a child.

"Grandmamma, which character do you like best in
'Pilgrim's Progress?'"

"Christian, of course: he is the hero of the book."

The child hesitated: he evidently had formed a different conclusion.

"And which did you like best, my darling?"

"I liked Christiana best."

"Why so?"

"Because, grandmamma, when Christian set out on his
pilgrimage, he went all alone; but, when Christiana went,
she took the children with her."

There was a deep truth underlying the child's simple
words: the great mission of woman was contained. in
that one sentence. She must, through life, "take the
children with her;" and to her moulding and guiding
hand they have been intrusted.

There are some other points of importance. The character of the reading should be changed. Let the week-
day story-books be laid aside, and others substituted. Far
from there being any penance in this, if the right kind
are supplied, greater enjoyment will be secured, more

especially if the father will read them with or to his children; as every one knows how this increases a child's pleasure. The habit also is a good one; and children so trained will never, or very rarely, select novel-reading, in later years, as a Sunday amusement.

Good habits are great helps in the right way of life. Children should be taken to church as early as they can be trained to sit still, and not disturb the services. This is matter of some difficulty, — not that children wish to do wrong; but their natural love of action makes them restless and mischievous when they have nothing to do. We must find some motive for their minds while under constraint of body, which shall seem to them like action. A happy illustration of this mode has been given in

THE LITTLE GIRL THAT HELPED HER MINISTER.— Nellie was but three years old when her mother took her to church, telling her she must help the minister.

"How can I help him?" was the child's question.

"A little girl about as old as you are was taken to church one Sunday by her mamma; and she sat very still, looking straight at the minister while he was preaching. Some children, and some grown people too, I am sorry to say, do not behave so well, but are restless and inattentive, looking about, and even whispering sometimes; all of which must be very unpleasant and distressing to the minister who is talking to them."

"Was that all?" said Nellie, as her mother stopped.

"That was all. The little girl helped the minister by sitting still and listening. He said, when people sat still and listened, it was a great deal easier for him to preach; and, when he saw her eyes fixed on him through all the sermon, it helped him to forget the inattention of others."

"I'll be very good and listen," said Nellie earnestly; and she kept her word.*

It is much to be wished that every family who can afford it should possess a melodeon, and give their children the pleasure of sacred music on Sunday evenings. The practice of assembling the family at that time, to sing hymns has a happy influence on each of its members; giving them a common interest and pleasure, to which, through all the changes of life, they will look back with loving and longing remembrance. The joys of music are more nearly connected with heaven than any other manner of recreation. These pleasures are not only innocent, but really elevating to the mind; and every household that is ordered wisely will find the art of singing one of its essential aids in the ways of peace and pleasantness with children on Sundays.

* We have taken this extract from a little Magazine edited by T. S. Arthur, called " The Children's Hour."

PART SIXTH.

—◆—

I. — GERMAN HOME-LIFE.

WE Americans owe a tribute of respect to our old Teutonic ancestry for their domestic virtues. The German tribes had, according to Tacitus, kept the Eden idea of marriage and the sanctity of home-life, as Christians now understand God's law, while all other Gentile peoples had become corrupt and licentious. And from the customs and manners of these Germans, styled "Barbarians" by their Roman conquerors, "the original institution of chivalry has often been traced," says Sir Walter Scott. So surely does the purity of the home-circle and the honor paid to woman elevate the minds and exalt the characters of men.

It is too much the custom, at the present day, to ridicule the Age of Chivalry; but the effect of the institution upon man was certainly beneficial. Its tendency was to raise the moral tone, and to increase veneration and reverence, by calling forth sentiments of honor and devotion to woman, which reacted on the manly character, beautifying and adorning it. Perhaps no people

261

of modern times have preserved the habits and feelings of those days more than the Americans. No country on the face of the globe has so beautifully accorded to woman her true place, and so faithfully and truly cherished, protected, and shielded her, the result telling (as it must ever do), in its turn, upon the masculine nature, trained and elevated by her moral influence.

Our German ancestors have been of service to us in this respect; and it is much to be desired that we should also take pattern from them in the beautiful simplicity of their home-life, which stands apart and has a character of its own. The simple habits of the people; their pretty and tasteful customs; their observance of family anniversaries, such as days of birth, death, and weddings, — all lead us to look for exactly what we find, — a greater love for home, and truer appreciation of it, than most of the Continental nations possess. We find this view confirmed by William Howitt in his "Rural and Domestic Life of Germany." He says, —

"One thing, however, is certain, that there are not in the world more attached, affectionate, and domestically happy people than the Germans; and if their wives are not qualified to solve a mathematical problem with them, to discuss some point of history or politics, to enter into the religious questions of the day, or to decide on the excellence of some new work of taste; yet, on the other hand, they do not so much pester them with demands of expensive pleasures, huge parties, splendid dresses and equipages, and all the unsatisfying and greedy dissipations of a more luxurious state of society."

The simple and inexpensive manner in which they entertain their friends is productive of much social enjoyment; the toilet and refreshments of both being of so plain a character, that all are enabled to receive their guests, without that foolish rivalry as to dress or entertainment, which, with us, destroys so much innocent pleasure.

A simple cup of tea about six o'clock, music and dancing, with the lightest kind of supper, usually of cake and the cheap wine of the country, make up one of these evenings, not forgetting the vast variety of German games, which the young people enter into with much zest. These social evenings usually break up about ten or eleven o'clock. Thus cheerfulness and light-hearted gayety are promoted, without any of the ill effects of dissipation and late hours.

One cannot fail to be struck, in studying German life and customs, with the social nature of the people.

They seem naturally *gregarious.* They have their "Sing Vereine" and "Lieder Tafel," or Singing Unions and Long Tables; their various observances of festivals and anniversaries, — all resulting from this same social taste, — this assembling of themselves together for common enjoyment, rather than seeking it individually.

During their winters, which are long and cold, they

have at their museums, or public buildings for amusement, balls and concerts, as well as many private entertainments. We read that "family parties, with
dancing and simple games, make this gloomy and cold
season pass cheerily."

Their "Kranzchen," or, literally, *little garlands,* also
deserve mention. These are meetings held once a
week at the houses of those who compose them, in rota-
tion; thus, as it were, in their poetical tongue, forming
a wreath or garland of friendship, twined together with
the bright cords of love.

At these parties, or rather social gatherings, they
take tea, talk, read, of course knit, and dance or play,
as the taste or age of the guests may dictate.

But the crowning amusement of a German winter is
the sledging party: without this, they think there
can be no enjoyment, and to it they all look forward
as the greatest treat of the season.

Engagements for this wonderful affair are often
made as long as three months before; the gentleman
then engaging his partner, for it is strict etiquette that
no sledge shall contain more than the one couple. The
sledges are of all sorts and sizes, some very gayly painted, richly cushioned, and furnished with robes made of
the shaggy skins of bears, wolves, foxes, and deer.

Few more picturesque sights can be seen than one
of these sledging parties. First appears a troop of out-
riders, gayly costumed in colored jackets, caps, white

breeches, and jack-boots. Then follows the train of sledges, often amounting to forty. They go to some inn, a short distance from the town, where they amuse themselves with some simple German games until it is dark, for more than half the pleasure consists in returning by torchlight. Persons are sent to meet them with torches; and they enter the city with resounding whips, flaring lights, and much commotion, and once more traverse its whole extent, parading several times round the most public square. For here again the nature of the people is shown: they would find no pleasure in the party, if they did not show their train to their fellow-citizens; and the fellow-citizens, on their part, would consider themselves as defrauded of the spectacle.

We have alluded to the observance of anniversaries. Birthdays are specially marked. Garlands of flowers of the choicest kinds are sent in by friends. These garlands are often seen hanging in houses as grateful memorials of love; even in palaces these may be found, having been sent as proofs of affectionate regard. On the supper table, a cake in the centre is usually surrounded with as many wax-lights as the person has years whose birthday is celebrated.

But the great family festivals in Germany are the silver and golden marriages; that is, the twenty-fifth and the fiftieth anniversary of married life. These are kept in great festivity, much in the manner of birthdays.

A pretty feature in German social life is the language of flowers; which to them is so real that they are guided by it in every arrangement of bouquet or flowers, carefully using or avoiding certain flowers, according to their meaning. Garland-making is a distinct trade; and so particular are the makers to suit them to the occasion, that, to a practised eye, a glance is enough to decide whether it is intended for a marriage, a birthday, or a funeral.

We have dwelt at some length on these amusements and customs, because it is through these that the best traits of the German people are discovered. The very fact that they seek and find enjoyment in such innocent and simple pleasures shows how fertile the soil is for the good seed of the Gospel, could it take the place of the German rationalism, which floods the whole country with its dangerous errors.

Could we but combine the faith of the Gospel and the Bible observance of Sunday which mark the Anglo-Saxon nations, with the natural joyousness of temperament and genial characteristics of the Germans, we might almost hope to find that *rara avis* on earth, a perfect people.

There is something very beautiful in the manner in which the Germans cultivate the domestic affections. The custom, which we have already alluded to, of observing anniversaries, tends greatly to encourage this feeling. The birthday offering leads to a kindly remembrance of the season, a consideration of the taste of the person to whom the offering is to be made, and an effort to gratify that taste; whilst the floral garlands presented on these occasions, and selected with reference to their meanings, are necessarily productive of harmony and good will.

Much attention to education is given in Germany. The German student life, with its fascinations, has become almost a proverb; but we refer, at present, more especially to that earlier home-training of children, which, after all, is most important in forming the future character. The people are domestic, and thus exercise a most desirable influence in their families; the children being, as a rule, carefully trained to habits of neatness, thrift, and industry. The girls may almost be said to *knit by instinct:* for it would be quite impossible to say how early or when they acquire the art; and we sometimes feel inclined to think that it must be brought with them from some former state of existence, or to believe what they tell you, that a knowledge of it "comes by nature." The girls are also taught to spin very early, and no German home is complete without its spinning-wheel.

It is a favorite custom with the women to carry their spinning-wheels to some neighbor's house; thus accomplishing the double purpose of "spinning long yarns" with tongue as well as wheel. Another proof of their social turn of mind, thus seeking society during the absence of husbands and brothers at their work.

Some admirable hints upon the effect a mother has in the formation and development of her children's characters may be found in a work of Jean Paul Richter's, entitled "Levana, or the Doctrine of Education." But, whilst giving the proper priority to a mother's influence, he by no means detracts from a father's responsibility: he holds strongly that this God-appointed union can only act perfectly when it acts in combination.

Thus he says, "Only by the únion of manly energy and decision with womanly gentleness does the child rest and sail as at the conflux of two streams. Or, in another figure, the sun raises the tide and so does the moon; but he raises it only one foot, she three, and both united four. The husband only marks full stops in the child's life; the wife commas and semicolons, and both more frequently. One might exclaim, 'Mothers be fathers,' and 'fathers be mothers!' for the two sexes perfect the human race, as Mars and Venus gave birth to harmony. The man works by exciting powers; the woman by maintaining order and harmony among them. The man in whom the State or his own genius destroys the balance of powers for the advantage of one will also bring this overlaying influence to education; the soldier will educate warlikely; the poet, poetically; the divine piously; *the mother only will educate humanly.* For only the woman needs to develop nothing in herself but the pure human being; as, in an Æolian harp, no string predominates over the rest, but the melody of its tones proceeds from unison,, and returns to it."

II. — DINNER–PARTIES.

THERE are few better maxims in the world than that "any thing that is worth doing is worth doing well;" and we would add, that there is a right way of doing every thing, and it is always desirable to ascertain what that way may be in order to follow it.

The first direction we would give is the same with dinners as with other things, and perhaps more needed, because there is much temptation here for extravagance: let them be within your means; this is all-important. The second is, that refinement and taste should be apparent in every arrangement. There is nothing that adds more to the charm of good society than elegant *re-unions,* if properly understood and carried out.

Light and warmth are two great essentials to the enjoyment of a dinner. Nothing tends more to cheerfulness than a brilliantly-lighted room: it has an enlivening power of its own, whose assistance 'never should be undervalued. As for warmth, little need be said in our country upon that subject, for we are all too apt to have our rooms overheated. But, in England, dining-rooms are often uncomfortably cold: this has a *chilling* effect, in many ways, on a dinner-party, and should be carefully avoided. The comfort of the guests is always the first thing to be studied in every respect. With regard to

lighting a table, we would say that the manner of doing
it is even more important than the quantity employed.
The principal object is to throw as much light as possible
on the table, with sufficient on the faces of the guests.
Lights from chandeliers will be found more successful
than any lamps on the table itself. The rest of the room
must not, however, be left in darkness: side-lights may
be used, or lamps on the sideboard or side-tables.

A very elegant centre-piece for a dinner-table is desirable; not too high nor too large, either a silver *épergne*, or
some work of art of glass or china. Too great a display of massive silver should be avoided, as it always
looks ostentatious. The china, for elegant dinners, should
be French. Nankin and Canton china are not so much
in vogue for entertainments, although much valued for
private and domestic use.

The dessert-service should always be handsome, and
admits of greater elegance and variety than the dinner-
china; each plate very frequently having its own clus-
ter of fruit or flowers.

The cipher or the family coat-of-arms is also much
used on all china at present, or engraved on the glass,
which has a very good effect.

The napkins may be folded according to fancy, varying
much with the varying fashion. Sometimes they are
placed on the plate, with a roll of bread inside, and sometimes arranged in a fan-shape in the champagne-glasses.

We have alluded in a former article to the importance

of punctuality on the part of the guests; but a word is also needed as to the cook's duty in this respect, which is equally if not even more important. And to this matter the lady of the house should give the strictest attention, as her whole dinner may be disturbed and its comfort destroyed by an unpunctual servant.

Who has not suffered from that terrible time, in the drawing-room, when every one was assembled and waiting: minutes seemed hours, conversation growing more and more formal every instant, and yet no signal for dinner? At such times there always appears a strange conspiracy between mind and body. Mind refuses to give forth any of his stores till he sees body righted. We have often been amused to watch this understanding between the two, and to notice how, the moment body receives his due, mind hastens to make the *amende honorable*, and gives out as rapidly and lavishly as body takes in. Ah, well! it is not only at the dinner-table that one depends upon the other. They must always be on good terms and act in harmony, or we shall find ourselves the sufferers.

We have offered in this article a few directions, accompanied with several hints, for giving a dinner-party according to the usages of good society; but we would by no means be understood to imply that many pleasant dinners might not be, and are not, constantly given by those not furnished with all these appliances. We never meant that you should not welcome your friends to your house, at any time, without these elegancies; for, after all, true enjoyment never consists in such things, but in a hospitable, hearty greeting, and the consciousness that you are an acceptable and welcome guest. Goldsmith thus describes those dinners:—

> "Blest be those feasts, with simple plenty crowned,
> Where all the happy family around
> Laugh at the jests and wit that never fail,
> Or sigh with pity at some mournful tale,
> Or press the bashful stranger to his food,
> And learn the luxury of doing good."

HINTS.

1. A round or oval table for a dinner-party has been decided to be most conducive to comfort and conversation.

2. For comfort and elegance, we think not more than ten should sit down to dinner, and would give the preference to eight. Large dinners are rarely agreeable.

3. Two white table-cloths should be placed upon the table; the one on which the dinner is served to be removed when the dessert appears.

4. On the sideboard should be tastefully arranged the articles of plate for the dinner, such as silver waiters, candelabra, knives, forks, and spoons.

5. The wines must remain in ice till they are used; that is, such as require it: but neither red wines nor Madeira must ever be cooled.

6. Table-linen, napkins, &c., should all be of the finest

damask. The quality of these articles has a great effect upon the appearance of the table.

7. Silver dishes, where the means permit, should also be used; and also the finest kind of glass, — cut, never blown or moulded.

8. The dessert-knives should be silver, with handles to suit your taste, either of silver also, or agate, or mother-of-pearl.

9. Dinner etiquette varies. At present, at the most elegant dinners, no dish is either carved or helped at table. Every thing is brought from a side-table.

10. Flowers are a very important item in ornamenting a dinner-table. The arrangement must vary with the fashion : the present *mode* is to arrange them upon the table itself, perfectly flat and it has the advantage of not interfering with the view of your opposite neighbors.

11. The French custom of a bouquet at each lady's plate is a pretty one, and frequently adopted here.

12. Every dinner must begin with soup. The French say, " Without soup, there is no dinner."

13. Fish formerly followed as a necessity. At present, there is a difference in this matter.

14. The *entrées*, or made dishes, should be well arranged, well chosen, and well cooked.

15. The removes generally consist of poultry, in place of the roast, game, French dishes, &c.

16. A grand dinner is incomplete without a finishing salad, which must always be served alone.

18

17. Pastry has been said to involve "very high art," and requires much care to have it good.

18. Coffee should always be served before the guests leave the table, followed by a "*chasse café*," or small glass of cordial.

19. Servants should wait in white cotton gloves.

20. Finger-glasses should be placed by each person's plate at dessert. The water in them may be perfumed, or a lemon or orange leaf put into each glass.

21. If the finger-glass and doily are placed on your dessert-plate, remove the doily to the left of your plate, and place the finger-glass upon it, leaving the right for the wine-glasses.

22. Be careful to know the shapes of the various kinds of wine-glasses, to avoid making blunders. High and narrow or very broad and shallow glasses are used for champagne; large goblet-shaped glasses for Burgundy and claret; ordinary wine-glasses for sherry and Madeira; green glasses for hock; and somewhat large bell-shaped glasses for port.

23. Port, sherry, and Madeira are decanted. Hock and champagne appear in their native bottles. Claret and Burgundy should be handed round in glass claret-pitchers.

24. If any thing is to be taken cold, let it be as cold as ice; if hot, let it be smoking.

25. Servants must be well trained and instructed that the charm of waiting consists in its being done silently, almost noiselessly.

26. In short, rules for a dinner have been well summed up as follows: " The attendance should be rapid and noiseless, the guests well assorted, the wines of the best quality, the host attentive and courteous, the room well lighted, and the time punctual."

27. There is still a higher authority concerning these feasts, and one rule which has never been quoted: —

" When thou makest a dinner or a supper, call not thy friends nor thy brethren, neither thy kinsmen nor thy neighbors, lest they also bid thee again, and a recompense be made thee. But, when thou makest a feast, call the poor, the maimed, the lame, the blind, and thou shalt be blessed, for they cannot recompense thee; for thou shalt be recompensed at the resurrection of the just."

III. — POLITENESS AT THE TABLE.

> " La politesse est à l'esprit
>   Ce que la grace est au visage :
>   De la bonté du cœur elle est la douce image,
>   Et c'est la bonté qu'on chérit." — *Voltaire.*

DUCLOS says, " Politeness is the expression or the imitation of the social virtues."

Politeness is nothing but practical kindness. There is no politeness without kindness, benevolence, and a certain degree of sensibility.

Chesterfield defines good breeding, " the mixture of good sense and good nature."

These are, no doubt, the essentials; but there is something more that can only be acquired by instruction, or by the habit of mingling in good company.

To give some knowledge of these conventional forms is one object of these essays; and here it will not be amiss to introduce a story, given by M. Boitard as a warning.

The Abbé Cosson, a celebrated professor of the belles-lettres, and one of the most erudite men of his day, was invited to a dinner-party, composed of people of the highest rank and eminence. The good Abbe had not the least distrust of his knowledge of etiquette, and, in going home with M. Delille, boasted that there was nothing in the way of propriety which could have been objected to in him through the dinner.

"You?" answered Delille: "you are greatly mistaken; you did nothing but commit blunders from beginning to end."

"Impossible!" said the Abbé: "I am sure I behaved like everybody else!"

"Your presumption makes you think so: the truth is, you did nothing like other people, and I will prove it to you. Come, count on your fingers!"

1st. You unfolded your napkin, you spread it out, and fastened it by the corner to your button-hole. Nobody but you did such a ridiculous thing. The napkin is not to be opened out: it is to be kept in the lap.

2d. You ate your soup with your spoon in one hand

and your fork in the other.   A fork to eat soup! Good heaven!

3d. You sent up your plate twice, a thing never done out of the family circle.

4th. When asked what part of the chicken you would have, you childishly said *any part.* Do you not know that you are giving trouble and embarrassment to your hostess, by refusing to give her a simple answer, and by obliging her to reflect upon a trifle, interesting to nobody but yourself?

5th. Before beginning to eat, you wiped your knife with your napkin! What worse could you do in the most miserable tavern, where you distrusted the neatness of the house?

6th. You were very rudely officious with Baron R——— and myself. Every time wine was offered you, you took it into your head to fill our glasses before your own, without consulting us. Who told you that we wanted wine, or that sort of wine rather than another? How did you know but that, by special favor, the master of the house had intended for one of us a particular bottle of wine, which he knew we preferred?

7th. Instead of breaking your bread, which is always done at dinner, you cut it with a knife.

8th. You spread your bread with butter, a thing never to be done by well-bred people at dinner.

9th. At the dessert you slipped bonbons off the plate, and put them in your pocket. A horrible impropriety.

10th. You say you have a cold in your head; but is that a reason why, after using your handkerchief, you should, as it were, make a show of it? This is worse than impolite: it is indelicate.

11th. You eat slower than other people; therefore you should have eaten less, and not have kept everybody waiting after each course.

12th. Your coffee being hot, you poured it out by portions in your saucer, and drank it in that way. People always drink out of the cup, and under no pretext out of the saucer.

13th. To fill up the measure of your iniquities, before rising from the table you folded up your napkin, as if you thought it might be used again before it was washed, or as if you meant to come again to-morrow.

"You see, my dear Cosson," added Delille, "you are very much out of your reckoning, and that you have done nothing like other people." . . .

RULES FOR A DINNER-PARTY

1. Gentlemen should be particular to arrive precisely at the hour named in the invitation. If they desire, they may come from eight to ten minutes sooner, never later.

2. A lady who keeps a company waiting more than a quarter of an hour does it often to produce an effect; but it is generally taken in very bad part, as she would be well convinced, could she listen at the door before entering.

3. When dinner is announced, never hasten into the dining-room. Wait till the master or mistress of the house, whose part it is to enter first, give you the signal.

4. If the dinner be given to a lady, the gentleman of the house takes her in first, the hostess following, either with her husband or the person next in importance amongst the guests.

5. But if the dinner be given to a gentleman, and the lady of the house be present, the latter takes the lead, entering the dining-room first, with the most prominent guest of the occasion.

6. In taking a lady to the dinner-table, a gentleman should always offer his left arm, and lead the way, allowing the lady to follow without quitting his arm. In every other case, for a gentleman to pass before a lady is an impoliteness.

7. If the conversation be general, speak loud enough to be heard by every one ; if there are several separate conversations, speak low enough not to disturb your neighbors.

8. If you desire a glass of water, a knife, or bread from the servant, do not call " waiter," as you would at a restaurant, but call him by his name, or, better still, merely make a sign that you want him, without calling.

9. Nothing indicates a well-bred man more than a proper mode of eating his dinner. A man may pass muster by *dressing well*, and may sustain himself tolerably in conversation ; but, if he be not perfectly *au fait*, *dinner* will betray him.

10. Ladies should never dine with their gloves on.

11. Invitations to dine should be answered to the lady. Invitations to a ball should be in the lady's name, and the answer, of course, sent to her.

12. It is customary, when you have been out dining, to leave a card upon the lady the next day, or as soon after as may be convenient.

13. At some of the best houses, coffee is brought into the dining-room before the gentlemen leave the table, — a very good custom, as it *gently* prevents excess, the guests retiring to the ladies immediately afterwards: it also allows those who have other engagements to take coffee before they quit the table.

IV. — BALLS.

OUR articles on "good society" cannot be complete without some mention of one of the amusements imperatively demanded by it, and which those moving in its ranks often find themselves reluctantly entering into from the force of custom and the desire to give their children every social advantage.

We have already alluded to the innocent recreation of home dancing; but this is something quite distinct and apart from any thing of that kind. Social observances require that friends, or those whom we agree to recognize as such, by interchange of courtesies, should occasionally meet together for festive purposes. One such re-union leads to another, and, with the object of relieving monotony and promoting enjoyment, music and dancing are introduced; thus a ball *nascitur*, but whether it shall "*fit*" must depend upon various considerations which require some thought.

Let us look in at a bright, sunny parlor in —— Street, on a snowy February morning, and listen to the pleadings of the beautiful Emily L——, who is just enjoying her first winter.

"Ah, dear papa! please say 'yes.' Mamma says I may have just as large a ball as I like, if you will only agree; and you know I have been to so many! I really think that the least we can do is to give one; and, if we don't hurry, every night will be taken up before Lent."

Mr. L—— looked at the eager, animated face of his only daughter, and, as usual, allowed her to have her own way.

"As you will, my child. It upsets a house terribly; but I suppose I should remember that I was once young myself: and it is natural you should want it."

"Oh! thank you, dear papa. You are the dearest, sweetest man in the whole world," said Emily, as young ladies usually aver when they get their own way.

Permission granted, the next step was to arrange affairs promptly and judiciously; and here mamma's judgment was called into requisition, to be set aside, however, when it conflicted with any preconceived notion of the spoiled child.

"Mamma, how many shall we ask?" questions Emily.

"Not more than two hundred, my dear: our rooms will not accommodate even that number comfortably."

" *Two* hundred! O mamma! we must ask at least *five:* only about half ever accept. Mrs. Mortimer asked eight hundred, Ernestine told me, to their ball; and their rooms are smaller than ours. No one ever thinks in these days of how many your rooms will hold. Then there are the stairs, and the hall, and the conservatory, where they can escape; besides, the more of a crush the better; people always like a crowd, even if their dresses are torn." So five hundred is fixed as the requisite number for a pleasant ball, regrets being allowed for.

"Did you ever read 'The Hand-Book of Etiquette,' Emily?" said Mr. L——, coming back to the parlor two hours later, whilst the important discussion was still going on.

"Oh, no! papa: I never want a book to tell me what to do in such matters," said the self-satisfied maiden.

"I think you might find some valuable hints there about balls, and how to give them; but do as you prefer," and he once more sought his study.

We had not the pleasure of being present at the ball in question, and therefore cannot inform our readers whether it bore off the palm from all other balls given before or since; doubtless it did in Emily's estimation.

But Mr. L——'s remark has led us to look into the book
he named; and we agree with him, that it contains desirable information on many points connected with such
subjects.

We find that this writer's views differ from those of
the youthful Emily, inasmuch as he directs that no one
should invite above *one-third* more than the rooms will
hold, to secure the proper number of guests.

We are more inclined to take this view than hers, on
another ground: those who have provided themselves
with elegant and expensive dresses for the occasion
cannot as easily forgive their not been seen. How common to hear, after a crowded ball! —

"How was Miss So-and-so dressed?" and the answer,

"Oh, don't ask me how any one was dressed. It was
such a jam, I saw nothing but their heads!"

The arrangements are perhaps more important than
any other item to make a ball pass off pleasantly; and it
has been well said that there are six requisites to secure
this: —

"Good ventilation, good arrangement, a good floor,
good music, a good supper, and good company."

We are all aware how much social enjoyment is produced and promoted by brilliance and elegance of the
details, whilst beauty and dress are improved by proper
lighting; and pleasing effect is given by judicious management, and the concealment of every thing which does
not strictly accord with the scene before us.

One of the most important instruments in forming fine effect is the employment of shrubs, plants, and flowers: when this is done tastefully, and with some artistic skill, almost a fairy-like scene is produced; and one is scarcely aware what value this arrangement has in brightening and enlivening the company, and thus securing the grand *desideratum*: a "successful ball."

In Paris, where balls are generally considered to be more elegant than elsewhere, great attention is given to this branch: the balustrades of staircase and gallery are woven with evergreens, the fireplaces concealed by flowering shrubs, and the musicians send forth their strains from behind a flowery bank, themselves completely unseen.

Although, as we have said, the rules of good society demanded a few words upon balls, we would not be understood as advocating them in a general way.

The simple amusement of dancing in the home-circle is altogether different, and free from the objections attendant upon a crowded assembly, where, too often, the principal object in going is for the sake of joining in objectionable dances, which can never be innocent or harmless.

We have already given our views in a former article on dancing, as to its innocence, when properly conducted; nor would we by any means be understood as condemning balls *as balls*, but merely when improper and indecent dances are there introduced.

The queen of England and the ladies of her court may, and she must, by the requirements of her position, join in such amusements at any time, provided that demoralizing dances be excluded; and the case is the same with persons of means and social standing in this country. To obtain right practice, we must go a step further back. Mothers must so train their daughters, that they would be unwilling of themselves to join in any dance of the kind; nor should young ladies be permitted to go abroad to any social amusement not allowed them at home.

We do not propose to enter into any discussion of the merits of this much-disputed point at present; but merely to question whether the professed followers of Christ have not an obligation resting on them, by virtue of their profession, to show the world that they have come out from it, and have enlisted under another banner, and in the service of another Master.

It does seem to us, that, in the days when there is so little to mark any outward distinction between the Church and the world, a deep, earnest love for that Master must find pleasure in relinquishing some fashionable amusement, or even allowable enjoyment, for His dear sake who gave his life for us, thereby showing publicly that we are leading another life, and actuated by other principles, than those who have no such aim or purpose.

We are altogether opposed to that style of religious sentiment or religious practice which condemns those who, whilst striving, it may be, equally with ourselves, have arrived at a different conclusion.

Harsh criticism, even in a right cause, never yet benefited either criticiser or criticised; whilst consistent practice, gently but steadily maintained, leading by influence and example, unstained by bitterness, and unsullied by severe comment upon others, may win many to imitate a life from which such beautiful results are seen to flow.

HINTS.

1. The lady of the house should remain till supper-time near the door by which her guests enter the rooms.

2. A well-bred young lady will not dance in her own house until she has found partners for her guests.

3. A young lady should be very careful how she refuses to dance with a gentleman; and above all she must take care not to accept two gentlemen for one dance. Many duels have resulted from this thoughtlessness.

4. The right of introducing rests mainly with the lady or gentleman of the house, but may be done also by friends. On the Continent, no introduction is needed; the presence of any guest at the house being considered a sufficient passport to acquaintanceship for the evening.

5. In a crowded ball, it is desirable to have the supper-room on the first floor, as the crush in going up or down stairs is often extremely uncomfortable.

6. If the ball be a large one, it will be found convenient that numbered tickets should be given for the cloaks and hats, although, at present, this practice is generally confined to public balls.

7. Great care should be taken, in leaving a heated ball-room, to put on sufficient wrappings before going into the outer air. Many young and beautiful girls have lost their lives by inattention to this most important point. Over-fatigue should also be avoided in dancing at balls, or at the watering-places, during the extreme heat of summer.

V. — BLOTS ON THE LIGHT OF HOME.

SIR Walter Scott says, "The spirit of chivalry had in it this point of excellence, that, however overstrained and fantastic many of its doctrines may appear to us, they were all founded on generosity and self-denial, of which, if the earth were deprived, it would be difficult to conceive the existence of virtue among the human race."

The spirit of chivalry always gave reverence to God and honor to woman: this spirit we would awaken among our young countrymen. We have hitherto preferred to point out the bright side of the usages of good society, and their bearings upon the happiness of the home circle; but our subject would be incomplete if we did not look on the other side, and show the influence of such habits as swearing, intemperance, and the use of tobacco, — habits, which, if allowed to gain ascendency, will surely lead to selfishness and hardness, and thus lower or destroy the true nobility of American character and the virtues of home life.

The first two must be classed in the list of sins, whilst the latter is little more than a bad habit; and yet we have noticed it here, because it seems to us objectionable, undesirable, and not tending to increase the enjoyment of the domestic circle.

We shall come to this later, however.

Swearing, or any form of profane language whatsoever, is so repeatedly and strictly forbidden in Holy Writ, that any words of ours surely should be needless; and yet how many persons thoughtlessly make use of irreverent expressions in daily conversation, merely from a habit contracted in boyhood, and continued without consideration of the sin.

Swearing is considered so inadmissible in good society, or in the presence of ladies, that there is little danger of its being introduced in either; but let no one forget that the sin is the same wherever it is indulged. God is present everywhere, and He is outraged whenever his holy name is taken in vain. Mothers have a great responsibility in this matter. Let them watch and guard the expressions of their sons, and early inculcate the exceeding sinfulness of the practice.

We say of their *sons;* for we cannot bring ourselves to think of the pure lips of their daughters, or of any woman, indeed, unless fallen to extreme degradation, being sullied by the use of profane language.

Some one may ask, But, if unused in the presence of ladies, how does it impair the happiness of home? We answer, A man too frequently gives himself a license within the precincts of the domestic circle which he would most carefully avoid elsewhere; and thus it often comes that a slight difference or trifling altercation is magnified into a bitter quarrel by the use of violent and profane language.

Intemperance, with all its sad train of sorrows, — the deserted home, the lonely wife, the neglected children, — is doubtless a heavy sin, and one which entails prompt and present punishment upon the offender; but to my mind the guilt is by no means so great as that of swearing. Whilst there are many causes and excuses for the one practice, such as feeble health, great suffering, exhaustion from either mental labor or physical exertion, exposure to cold, &c., there can be none in palliation of the other.

The one sin seems a yielding (cowardly, it is true) to temptation; a feeble power of endurance; a weakness of the flesh: the other, a sin of the spirit, a moral stain upon the conscience, and a crime against the majesty and holiness of God. And yet, whilst intemperance, spiritually considered, is not so great a sin as blasphemy against the Lord of Heaven, we must never overlook the fact, that no one crime so desolates the home, and wrecks all domestic peace and enjoyment as this, the crying sin of our land. To prevent the spread of this evil, the law should go to the root of the matter, and stop the manufacture of distilled spirits, except for medical or scientifio

19

purposes. Wine and beer are, comparatively speaking, harmless; but it is the tremendous traffic in distilled spirits which works the main mischief. We can hope for no reform in this habit, so long as the very ships which are carrying out our missionaries to spread the light of the Gospel are laden, at the same time, with *New-England rum*, as the chief part of their cargo.

We may be met with indignant denial; but we do assert that club-life has vastly increased this evil in our midst. Nothing is more surely and certainly subversive of all true domestic peace, than the habit of passing days and evenings away from home, at such places of resort for idle men.

Often, at first, the habit is formed without any wrong intention; but look at the results! By degrees, the simple pleasures of home become tasteless and insipid; a craving for the stimulus of excitement is created, and gradually becomes a necessity; then for the sake often of drowning the reproaches of an accusing conscience, sharpened by the memory of a pale, patient, loving face at home, other stimulants are sought, and, as a matter of course, increased till the power of resistance is gone.

To all who prize home happiness, we would most affectionately and earnestly say, Never let any friend or any inducement whatever lead you to pass your evenings at a club: if you have leisure for a club, you have leisure for the home circle; and, depend upon it, you will find a **deep true** and exalting happiness in the one which the **other can never afford.**

We are aware that we are trenching upon dangerous ground, when we enter upon the large question of the use of tobacco; nor have we any idea of placing it on a level with the other habits of which we have been speaking.

The use of it is a world-wide custom; and it may be that (as is the case with many other things), its worst effects spring from its abuse. And yet our chief argument against it is drawn from the strange fact that those who are its strongest advocates in practice are also usually its strongest opponents in theory. Here is a singular thing.

Why are we constantly told, " Yes, I smoke or chew, or take snuff; but it is a miserable practice, a wretched habit: I never would let my boys do it if I could prevent it!" Then why do it yourself?

Having heard this testimony, not once, but frequently, from confirmed smokers, we have been led to look at the matter, and try to discover whether the use of tobacco was actually necessary to masculine happiness. We were assisted in this study by the remark of a gentleman in one of our steam-cars. As an apology for not offering a lady his seat next the window, as possibly more agreeable to her than the outer one, which she had taken, he mentioned his habit of chewing, which required that he should retain that seat.

By way of courtesy, the lady remarked, that she believed " the use of tobacco was a habit, which, when gentlemen had once learned, they found very difficult to give up."

"Pardon me, madam," said he, with some emphasis, "*gentlemen* never learn it; *boys* learn, and gentlemen continue the practice."

The remark suggests the duty to mothers of influencing their sons upon this point. A strict prohibition is not counselled as the best way; but a mother's influence against it, her wishes and preferences, not commands, exerted mildly and gently and persistently, may have an effect for which the future man will feel most grateful.

We find a great difference in the writings of the French and English on this subject. The French wage constant war upon it, on paper, whatever their practice may be, whilst the English as warmly defend its use.

We confess to no little amusement in reading, lately, a French work, containing a tirade against "*Le Tabac.*" After many severe strictures upon smoking, the author concludes by saying, "As for those who chew, they belong, generally, to the very lowest class of persons, of whom nothing need be said here!" Americans! what think ye of this French verdict? Could not our Senate Chamber or House of Representatives tell a different story?

An English work, now open before us, asserts, on the other hand, that tobacco is the cure of almost every earthly ill, — the soother of suffering, the preserver of the temper, society to the lonely, wife to the bachelor, and comfort for the sorrowful. It will thus be seen that varying opinions are held on the question on the other side of the water. In our land, we would refer to an article which lately appeared in one of our leading religious journals, strongly reprehending the use of tobacco by the *clergy*, as forming indolent habits, weakening the powers of concentration of thought, creating a great and wrong expense, lowering the spiritual tone of mind, and tending to irreverence by leading to the performance of the highest and most sacred duties, with the clothes still retaining the odor of the previous self-indulgence.

We were much struck with this article, and further reflection upon it led us to conclude that any reform in this habit must, in the first place, come from two classes, — the clergy and the women of our country. Let the clergy teach by that most powerful of all agents, example; and let the mothers, as we have proposed, discourage the practice in their sons, and the thing would be done, or, at any rate, one great step would be taken towards checking the fearful extent to which it is at present carried in this land of liberty.

VI.—THE HAND, AND ITS WORK.

THE hand — what wondrous wisdom planned
  This instrument so near divine?
How impotent, without the hand,
  Proud Reason's light would shine!
  Invention might his powers apply,
    And Genius see the forms of heaven,
  And firm Resolve his strength might try;
  But vain the will, the soul, the eye:
  Unquarried would the marble lie,
  The oak and cedar flout the sky,
    Had not the hand been given.
The frost's ice-breath the seas may block,
  An earthquake's arm the mountains shake,
The lightning's eye dissolve the rock,
  The heaving breast of waters break
    A pathway through the solid land:
  No form that Nature's force could take
  Such changes in the world would make
    As doth the human hand.

Its slender palm the forest clears,
  And sows the nurturing grain;
The harvest springs, the vine appears,
  And pastures dot the plain
Where flocks and herds secure may lie:
  Nor prowling beasts will venture nigh;
  They feel their Maker's stern command,
  And yield to man the cultured land.
  Then cities lift their stately spires,
  And orchards bloom, and household fires
  Are kindled up with song and glee;
    And art and taste their riches pour;
  And strong, swift ships have bridged the sea:
    While nations meet on either shore,
    Like neighbors stepp'd from door to door;

And savage hands, whose work was strife,
  Now clasped in social compact, prove
Justice and peace may govern life,
  If man his work perform in love.

WHEN we consider the wonderful doings of the hand, as seen in the ruins of the Old World and its remaining monuments, does it not seem strange that heathen philosophy never attempted to deify it, and build temples to the God of Work? The idea never appears to have entered the minds of the wisest among the worshippers of images, that the hand, as the organ which created all the visible forms of those idols, was a greater power and more manifest providence than the things it made and they worshipped.

It was reserved for this nineteenth century to unveil the wonders of the Hand, as the Christian philosophy of Sir Charles Bell has done; and also to this age alone must be charged the idea that a Carlyle has embodied in his philosophy, — " Work is Worship!" This apothegm has been seized upon and read, effectively as some writers seem to think, in exalting the natural condition of the human race, and giving to men the independence and liberty which are now so much coveted.

And so work is considered as worship of the God of nature, and therefore the glory of man; and its results are exalted as the exponents of the true civilization of the people, in which our own nation leads the world. But these are not the teachings of Divine Revelation.

The Bible doctrine is, that whenever work is put before man, by the position and circumstances in which it has pleased God to place him, let him do it honestly and faithfully, remembering, that, if done in His fear and favor, it exalts, never degrades. It is man's duty; and he should perform it as a duty, but not as worship.

Work is not worship, — work is obedience; and whilst we should be thankful to God for so graciously uniting it with advantages, and so frequently mingling pleasures with it, we must always remember that the exemption from *hard work* is a blessing. What Agur's prayer comprises, "Give me neither poverty nor riches;" what the poet means by an "elegant sufficiency;" in short, *gentility,* — was the normal state of mankind. The first man and the first woman were gentleman and lady by condition. No *hard labor* was required; only tendance, care, and pleasant help over what God had prepared for their enjoyment.

It was *sin* that brought HARD WORK on our race; and the necessity for this hard work on the "ground cursed for Adam's sake" (or sin), with the loss of Eden, and the favor of and intercourse with the Lord God, which was the privilege of Eden, that have led humanity in the downward road of misery, ignorance, and vulgarity. Read the first three chapters of Genesis: there you will find the true explanation of these enigmas.

Therefore, there is a real foundation in the nature of humanity for this superstructure of *gentleness,* or state of ease and enjoyment which is supposed to be the privilege of the higher classes. In our country, this state must usually be reached through industry; and this may be a real blessing: but we cannot count the need of hard work among the blessings of life. It was imposed as a punishment; it cannot of itself bring us any glory; it should be done, as we said above, as a duty, placed on us by Divine Providence, as one burden of the original sin.

We do not consider the convict who faithfully works out his penalty in the State Prison, as having gained *honor* by being placed there, although he has done well in submitting to the lot his sins have deserved. Just so should man do his duty in hard work, if such is his lot; but it is a hard lot, and shows that we have all broken God's laws, or such a doom would never have been laid on our race. The aspirations of the soul, the visions of the intellect, the longings of the heart, — these are never called forth by the holiness or the loveliness of hard manual labor.

Man's work is to subdue the earth; woman's to take charge of the home, to nourish and bring up children. Woman has her work and her duties: but these are neither man's work nor man's duties; and, just in proportion as he seeks to impose his own burdens upon her, will he find his own character degraded and debased by so doing.

In France, and also in Great Britain, women are thus burdened with labors which belong to men. There are districts in France where they are harnessed to carts with the ox and the ass. In Perigord, the women live in a state of filth and abjectness, which reacts on the whole family. In Picardy and Limousen, they serve their husbands at table without daring to seat themselves. In Brescia, they are mere beasts of burden. In Lower Brittany, all live together, eating black bread from the same trough with their sheep and hogs. A French writer, M. Aimé Martin, well says, "Everywhere is the degradation of the woman a sure proof of the brutishness of the man; and everywhere is the brutishness of the man a necessary consequence and reaction from the degradation of the woman."

We find, among the English statistics for 1861, that 43,964 women and girls were at that time agricultural laborers; besides all those confined in factories, and engaged in other trades properly belonging to men.

To the customs of our country, where man has done his own work of subduing the earth, — has shielded, aided, and protected woman, — do we owe it, that we have developed socially, intellectually, and religiously as a nation.

De Tocqueville, at the close of his great work on America, says, "If I were asked to what America owed her greatness, I should say, to the character of her women," or to this effect. If the justly celebrated Frenchman had considered his subject more closely in its moral relations, he would have given at least one-half of his compliment to the American men.

*It is not what women do for themselves, but what men
do for them, that marks the true greatness of a people,
and their real progress in Christian civilization.*

This subject may be discussed in another paper: now
I would say that women have a good work to do; and
perhaps the shortest way of explaining this is to give the
conclusion of the poem * from which a quotation was
taken to head this article.

    *   *****   *****   *****   *****   *****   *****

While thus to ceaseless task-work doomed to make the world his own,
Lest, in the struggle, sense should drag the spirit from its throne,
Woman's warm heart and gentle hand, in God's eternal plan,
Were formed to soften, soothe, refine, exalt, and comfort man ;
And win from pleasure's poison-cup to life's pure fount above,
And rule him, as the angels rule, by deeds of peace and love.
And so the tender mother lays on her soft nurturing breast,
With loving hand, her infant son, and lulls him to his rest;
And dries his tears, and cheers his smiles, and, by her wise control,
She checks his wayward moods, and wakes the seraph in his soul ;
And when life's work commands him forth, no more to dwell with her,
She points him to the HAND that saved the sinking mariner,
And broke the bread for famished men, and bids him trust that stay ;
And then her hands, unclasped from his, are lifted up to pray.

But man could never work alone; and, even in Eden's bowers,
He pined for woman's smile to cheer his task of tending flowers ;
And soon a fair young bride is sought and found to bless the youth,
Who gives, for his protecting hand, her heart of love and truth.
And now his work has higher aims, since she its blessing shares ;
And oft her hand will roses strew where his would scatter tares ;
And, like a light within a vase, his home enshrines her form,
Which brightens o'er his world-tossed mind, like sunshine o'er the
     storm ;

* Unpublished.

And, when she pleads in sorrow's cause, he cannot choose but hear;
And, when her soul with Heaven communes, she draws his spirit near.
And thus they live till age creeps on, or sickness lays him low;
Then will she gird her woman's heart to bear life's deadly woe,
And soothe his pain, and stay his head, and close his dying eyes;
Oh then, his work well done, his hand may rest in Paradise!

VII. — SUNDAY AND ITS REST.

HAST thou stood,
And watched Niagara's earthquake flood
Gather his might for the leap below,
And marked the rapids' whirlwind flow,
And heard the moan like muffled thunder,
  And felt the thrill of Nature's life,
When the solid earth was quivering under
    The tramp of the flood in his terrible strife? —
      Roaring and rushing,
      Gurgling and gushing,
Now like a troop of wild horses away,
  Over the prairies in headlong war,
Tossing their thunderous manes of spray,
  Rearing and plunging near and far.
Ha! the sea-serpents seize their prey!
      Writhing in horror,
      Trembling in terror,
      Quaking and quivering,
      Striving and shivering!
And ever, thus ever, day after day,
Rushing and dashing, away, away,
Whirling aloft a storm of spray,
The furious waters struggle and moan,
Then leap, and are lost in the dread unknown!

And thus in troublous toil and struggling strife,
Forever on had been the law of life, —

The doom of man, unceasing toil and care;
No freedom for the soul, no pause for prayer;
But urged by earth's tumultuous flood away,
Till death's dark gulf received its shrinking prey, —
Had not the restless flow of common time
Been stayed and calmed by Mercy's sacred chime,
Sounding one day in seven the tidings blest,
That God ordained the Sabbath's peaceful rest!

WHO can look abroad over the struggling world of mankind, and refuse to confess that marked and peculiar blessings attend those nations, which, since Christianity was established, have been most faithfully observant of the Sabbath, or Lord's Day? Rest and peace, as well as progress in goodness and intelligence, are characteristics of Sunday; and it is exactly these blessings we find wanting among heathen nations, where all knowledge of the true God and his laws are lost; and also among those nations that received the Gospel and its worship on the Lord's day, if they have thrown away or neglected these priceless blessings, show, in their institutions and characteristics, the irreparable injuries to humanity that have been inflicted on their peoples.

Even the most worldly-minded men in our land, while not caring personally for the sacredness of Sunday, must, if they are true patriots, desire its observance for the sake of its good moral influences, as contrasted with the corrupt effects of its neglect which are seen in other countries. The late Theodore Parker, who seems to have labored all his life to break down the Puritan Sab-

bath, in one of his last letters from Italy, made the confession, that, "rather than be cursed with the fearful dese-
cration of an Italian or Parisian Sunday, he would have
the old-fashioned Puritan Sabbath in all its strictness."

We should always bear in mind, that, in breaking the
fourth commandment, we are undermining the whole
Decalogue. We were struck with a passage upon this
subject, which we met with lately: —

"If any thing distinguishes the Christianity of Great
Britain and America from the Christianity of the Continent, it is the strict observance of the Sabbath, as a
divinely-appointed day of holy rest. Every earnest
Christian traveller and observer admits the superior
practical advantages of the Anglo-American Sabbath,
however he may differ from our *theory*. Even the zealous
Roman Catholic, Count Montalembert, derives the con-
stitutional freedom and national prosperity of England
from her sacred regard for the DAY which God gave to
man as a training school of piety, virtue, and self-government.

"Freedom is impossible without law and discipline.
The best men in Switzerland and Germany are now
laboring to introduce a better observance of the Lord's
Day, after the English and American example. Should
we retrograde and degenerate?"

It is well known, that, at the Resurrection, the first day
of the week took the place of the Jewish Sabbath; and
that all Christians, from that time, have observed the

festival of the Lord's rising, commonly called Sunday. This, as we say, is well known to every one; but comparatively few have looked closely into this matter, and asked the question, Do Christians keep the original seventh day, or Sabbath? Let us read the proofs.

"God blessed the seventh day and sanctified it." — GEN. ii., 3.

"That was setting it apart for a sacred or holy purpose, to secure it from violation." — *Webster*.

"The first Sabbath was the first of human existence, and of course the first day of the year. And we may reasonably conclude that this Sabbath was observed by the patriarchs. Adam lived till Methuselah was two hundred and forty-eight years old; and Noah was six hundred years of age when Methuselah died, which was the year of the Flood. Abraham was forty-eight years old when Noah died; so that there were only three between the days of Adam and Jacob, who was about thirty-five years old when Abraham died.

"The Jews go back in their chronology to the creation, but do not claim to be keeping the original Sabbath, as they acknowledge that to have been changed when they left Egypt.

"Now, the Jewish year is an ecclesiastical one; but, in instituting the Jewish economy, the length of the year could not be changed, and the ceremonial law was adapted to it. Every year begins a Sabbath as it had done; and each month has thirty days, except the last, which has thirty-five, making fifty-two weeks; and, once in twenty-eight years, there is a whole week thrown in to make up for leap-years.

"Now, as we have already said, every year began with a Sabbath; but, by referring to the twelfth chapter of Exodus, from the second to the sixth verses, we see that God gave the Israelites a new calendar, making a change from the fourteenth day of the month, or making the fourteenth the first, giving them the sixth day of the original week as their Sabbath, to distinguish them from the heathen throughout their generations, which means till the coming of Christ.

"And, as all the ceremonies of the Jewish law were done away at the Crucifixion, its types and shadows being fulfilled in the sacrifice of Christ, there was no longer any need of that distinctive Sabbath. And as God finished the work of creation on the seventh day, so Christ, by his resurrection, finished the work of his redemption on the seventh day: the disciples, understanding this, always kept the first day of the Jewish week, which was the original *seventh*, as the Sabbath."

If this calculation be correct, Christians have an increased obligation to keep Sunday as the day of rest from secular pursuits and amusements. It is the day hallowed, not only by divine example and blessing, but also the glories of creation and the mercies of redemption meet in its holy memories. Ought not Christian nations to keep it as the sign of their faith in the Bible, and the pledge that they worship only the living and true God?

Where there are no Sabbaths, there is no Christianity. We talk of Asia and Africa as "the Heathen World;" and so they are. Yet Asia was the native land of Christianity, and Africa partook largely in the early faith of the Gospel. Our Saviour and his apostles and evangelists were all Shemites, speaking the Aramæan and Syriac tongue. None of them were of the Roman race; none spoke the Latin as their vernacular. There seems to have been no Latin Christian literature until it was imported from North Africa, three or four centuries after Christ. Cyprian and Tertullian of Carthage, and Augustine of Hypo, were the fathers of Roman Christianity. "No Celt, no Greek, no Roman, no Teuton, no Slavon, was one of the originators and publishers of the Gospel. It was essentially Shemite and Asiatic. *No Shemite race in Asia holds it now!*"

Yes, Asia was Christianized; and, until about the seventh century, there was "a huge Eastern Christianity, estimated at seven or ten times the size of the coeval Christianity of Europe, Roman and Greek together."

In West Asia, there were eighty-four Christian bishoprics among the populous cities that then reached onward from the Mediterranean into the territories of Persia. In Palestine, there were forty-seven bishoprics; and all over Asia, within the Roman Empire, the Gospel had been preached and churches established before the fifth century.

Outside the Roman dominion in Asia, there was Armenia wholly converted to the Christian faith; and a multitude of Christians living in Persia, — so many, that when Sapor the Old, the greatest of the Persian kings, began his first persecution, he put twenty-five bishops to death at once : one of those bishops is said to have had two hundred and fifty clergy!

In short, the nations and peoples of the East had the Gospel-light for centuries; they had their Sundays, or "Lord's Day," their churches, their Christian civilization; but they must have become corrupt, and left the true faith, or they would not have been crushed, even by the terrible Mahomet, who, on the ruins of Christianity, built up his empire of blood and lust, and the worship of himself and of a god like unto himself.

Without the Bible and the Sabbath, hallowed by the spirit of the Gospel as the Lord's Day, the church will become a sham or a show (and thus it is now found in some European nations), or it will be a desolation and total loss, as in the once Christian East, now the " Heathen World."

What makes the greatest difference between the ignorant, miserable hordes of Asia, and our American people? Is it not that the former land has had the precious gift of the Gospel, and cast it away ; whilst — thanks be to God! — the Bible is sown broadcast over our great country? To the Bible we are indebted for the sanctities of true marriage, the blessings of home, and the SUNDAY REST.

PART SEVENTH.

I.—DESOLATED HOMES.

"In every government, though terrors reign,
Though tyrant kings or tyrant laws restrain,
How small, of all that human hearts endure,
That part which laws or kings can cause or cure!
Still to ourselves in every place consigned,
Our own felicity we make or find:
With secret course, which no loud storms annoy,
Glides the smooth current of domestic joy."

Goldsmith's Traveller.

AS the year draws towards its close, the beauty of Nature decays, and the glory of the visible world is dimmed. This is not desolation, only a suspension of that bounteous joy and life-giving happiness which we feel will revive when the next spring shall call forth the beauty of Nature in her gifts of love, life, and joy. But no such hope cheers *the desolated home:* for that no spring-time is in store; and when the leaves of love and trust are swept from the domestic roof-tree by the autumn blasts of dislike, discord, and divorce, we find no bud upon the branch, giving blessed promise of future brightness.

We have before us, in one of the leading religious newspapers of the country, the following notice:—

"About sixteen hundred divorces have been decreed in the State of——in six years; of which 584 were for desertion, 553 for criminality, 132 for cruelty, and 142 from other causes. It is known that 1316 were decreed in five years that ended May 1, 1865; and at the same rate, during the last eleven months, it may be assumed that the grand total is not far from 1600!"

On this the editor remarks:—

"We find this item afloat in the papers. It is probably prepared from official sources. If so, it is a sad and fearful comment upon the state of things. It is nearly five a week, from year to year. And this does not include those cases of separation which are the result of mutual agreement to disagree, where the wife or husband takes the law into her or his own hands, and *departs.*"

Now the question is,— In what State could such a fearful number of divorces have been granted? Will you guess?

No, it is not Indiana; yet that great State has been always considered the paradise of unhappily-mated couples, for there they could go and get unmarried half an hour after setting foot in the State. This is not done now: the present law requires that the parties must wait *one year.*

It is not Kansas: yet, at the first session of the first State legislature, over sixty divorces were granted; but the laws on this point are now rather more stringent.

No: it is not Kansas nor Connecticut; although the number of divorces in the land of steady habits is so fearfully large, that the governor has called the attention of the legislature to a consideration of the subject.

No, it is not Connecticut. Can it be believed that this is the *Old Bay State?* Remember Webster's words: —

"Massachusetts! There she is, — behold her, — and judge for yourselves. There is her history: the world knows it by heart. The past, at least, is secure."

The patriot poet, Pierpoint, thus alluded to her history: —

> " And that pale Pilgrim band is gone,
>   That on this shore with trembling trod,
> Ready to faint, yet bearing on
>   The ark of freedom and of God."

Can this be said of her at the present day? Is she still —

> " bearing on
> The ark of freedom and of God."

with regard to the laws of marriage? Or, rather, judging from the above record, which we have taken from "The New-York Observer," have we not cause to fear that she has divorced true "freedom" and "God," and, by seeking an unhallowed liberty, fallen into great and grievous sin?

"The laws of marriage," says a competent authority,[*] "are the laws of permanence and of mutualness, from which spring all its duties."

And, according to these laws, the one cause of divorce is adultery.

And the causes of misery in marriage-life are, "selfishness," "sensuality," and "self-will."

A sorrowful trio, truly! If these are the parents of divorce, does it not become a matter of serious importance to consider what has led to the great increase of this sin in late years?

Is it, as it would of necessity appear, from the increase of these qualities? There is something very terrible in the thought; but it does seem to us that the license which men allow themselves in every thing, and the unbridled freedom of thought, speech, and act, which characterizes the people of our land, have contributed not a little to the spread of this deadly poison in our midst.

Five divorces in a week! Five desolated homes! The mind recoils from the contemplation; the heart shudders as the vision rises of what these words portray. All misery in them, all wretchedness, all woe.

A desolated home! As we pause upon the words, there seems almost a paradox contained in the sad phrase. How can that centre of all joy and peace and love be desolated? Not by God's sending some bright messen-

[*] Rev. William Adams, D.D., author of "The Elements of Christian Science."

ger to bear one of its best-loved treasures to a fairer clime. This does not *desolate:* it does but add another link to our dear home on high, drawing us ever upward, and binding those still left on earth with holier, tenderer ties. Not by loss of fortune or place or station. These do not *desolate.* Often, most often, this has but served to call forth woman's true nature, which ever shines most brightly in adversity, leading her to fulfil one of her chief missions here, — to comfort and console; and thus the home is brightened, not desolated, by such loss. Sin, only sin, can cast that blight upon it. Satan alone can sunder those firm bonds which God hath joined: all other sorrows will but knit true hearts the closer.

Alas, for our humanity!

" We choose the ill, and let the blessing go."

For warning, not for pleasure, let us glance at one of these sad homes. Where there are five made weekly in Massachusetts, we cannot have much trouble in the search. Two hearts estranged; two warm, true, loving hearts — or so each deemed the other but such short space since — now evermore divided. Hard thoughts, or bitter words, or angry acts, now take the place of all those glowing visions with which the bridal pair, as youth and maiden, entered the bright portal of their married life; and Satan, having once gained admittance, rests not till he has worked his will, and they are parted. The vows so solemnly assumed, in sight of God, are broken; and they go forth each alone, with the burden of blasted hopes, and leaving a desolated home as the tomb of their conjugal happiness.

But where are the children? Where the little ones, God-given, and at their hands to be required by Him at the last day?

A contest usually occurs for their possession; but their lot is sorrowful, however decided. for, in either case, henceforward they must become half orphaned or bear a dishonored name; their father, a man who has been false to his vow to "love, honor, and cherish;" their mother, a divorced woman!

Five divorces in a week! Two hundred and sixty in a year in one State of the Union! Is there no means by which this can be arrested? No plan, no suggestions, which may lead those solemnly bound together for life to overcome the antagonisms of their characters, and strive to assimilate, as far as may be, in taste and feeling? Different qualities, tempers, and fancies may be harmonized by the all-powerful influence of love; and if a little more latitude were mutually allowed to varying opinions; a little more of the respect and consideration which we accord to the views of strangers were as freely exercised in the sanctuary of home, would not dissensions be more apt to decrease, and differences be done away? Why is it that we are so ready to yield gracefully in an argument with a stranger, yet urge it to the point of a quarrel when carried on within the limits of home? Why insist there upon a union of sentiments and opinions which we do not demand elsewhere?

The spirit of gentleness, of yielding, and of mutual forbearance; the recognition of each one's right to his or her own tastes and opinions, — would go far to prevent the entering wedge of discord. This is of no slight importance; for we all know how trifles grow and increase, and what mighty results spring from almost imperceptible causes.

In the daily intercourse of life, strive to find points of agreement; do not harp forever upon opposing interests. If you can alienate your friends or casual acquaintance, by dwelling forever upon the differences in your opinions and habits, how much sooner the daily companion of your life, with whom you are restrained by no conventionality, and towards whom, unfortunately, you do not consider yourself compelled always to exercise the Christian laws of forbearance and courtesy.

Try to overlook slight ebullitions of temper, called forth by the thousand petty irritations and vexations of daily life; these are magnified by notice or comment, or, worse, by heated or angry response. A smile, a playful word, or a jest, often turns the current of unpleasant thought, and restores a feeling of harmony and cheerfulness.

We do not mean to assert that this sin is confined to our land. We find in a work by Charles Boner, "Saxons, Wallacks, Hungarians, Transylvanians," some startling facts with regard to the extent of divorce among the Saxon peasantry, all Protestants. It is allowed upon the most trifling grounds, such as "antipathy," "groundless complaining," or even far more frivolous pretences. In a town of four thousand inhabitants, one hundred and seventy-one divorce suits were pending. The population, in other respects, seems to be moral; but the results of this habit of sin are apparent in thè decrease of numbers. According to Mr. Boner, this country stood at 302,204 in 1787; whilst in 1850 it was only 192,482.

It may seem unimportant, in comparison with our own vast country, to cite the habits of the Saxon peasantry in a small domain. But take the history of Ancient Rome. For the first five hundred years not an instance of divorce occurred. While the wife was honored, woman continued worthy of honor. Nor was it till the Roman men were banded together, and absent from their homes in their long wars, thus losing the softening, purifying influence of their mothers, wives, and daughters, that the frightful demoralization of the nation was reached. When men repudiated their wives, as Cicero did his, for no fault, but only to gratify his selfish propensities, and the multitude of divorces had created a virtual polygamy, in which the women participated, then the Roman Empire fell to rise no more.

And just as certainly would this proud republic fall, from the like causes, in like manner, were it not for the one safeguard, — the influence of Christianity, teaching, as it does, repentance and reformation.

What we need as a people is to recognize and obey the law of Christ in this matter, " Whosoever shall put away his wife, saving for the cause of fornication, causeth her to commit adultery ; and whosoever shall marry her that is divorced committeth adultery ; " for it is worthy of note, that, from a record now before us, we find the laws of twenty-two States (all that the record contains) permit divorces upon entirely different grounds than those laid down in the Gospel. New York is, we believe, the only State where a full divorce is not granted upon any other grounds than the New-Testament law.

We cannot better sum up this whole subject, than in the words of an eminent moralist : " Christian faith and Christian holiness can alone completely and entirely bring forth the marriage-vow in its beauty, and enable the husband and wife to estimate the marriage-state as 'holy,' 'sanctified,' 'honorable in all.' Christianity alone says, ' Husbands, *love your wives, as Christ loved the Church, and gave himself for it.*' This compares the marriage-union to that of Christ and the Church ; instead of ' civil contract,' makes it a vow before God, of mutual love, honor, obedience, affection, reverence, — in fact, love unselfish and unsensual."

II.—DOMESTIC ETIQUETTE AND DUTIES.

THE little community to which I gave laws, said the Vicar of Wakefield, "was regulated in the following manner: we all assembled early; and, after we had saluted each other with proper ceremony (for I always thought fit to keep up some mechanical forms of good breeding, without which, freedom often destroys friendship), we all knelt in gratitude to that Being who gave us another day. So also when we parted for the night."

Let me earnestly recommend that the precepts and example of the good old vicar should be followed and adopted by every newly-married couple.

With regard to the first, the courtesies of society should never be omitted, in even the most trivial matters; and, as respects the second, what blessing can be reasonably expected to descend upon a house wherein the voice of thanksgiving is never heard, nor yet protection sought by its acknowledged head?

On the wife, especially, devolves the privilege and pleasure of rendering home happy. We shall, therefore, first speak of such duties and observances as pertain to her.

When a young wife first settles in her home, many excellent persons, with more zeal, it may be, than discretion, immediately propose that she should devote some of her leisure time to benevolent plans and missionary societies.

We say, in all earnestness, to our young friend, Engage in nothing of the kind, however laudable, without previously consulting your husband, and obtaining his full concurrence. Carefully avoid, also, being induced, by any specious arguments, to attend evening lectures unless he accompanies you. Remember that your heavenly Father, who has given you a home to dwell in, requires from you a right performance of its duties.

Win your husband, by all gentle appliances, to love religion; but do not, even for the sake of a privilege and a blessing, leave *him to spend his evenings alone.* Look often on your marriage-ring, and remember the sacred vows taken by you when the ring was given: such thoughts will go far towards allaying many of those petty vexations which circumstances call forth.

Never let your husband have cause to complain that you are more agreeable abroad than at home, nor permit him to see in you an object of admiration, as respects your dress and manners, when in company, while you are negligent of both in the domestic circle.

Beware of intrusting any individual whatever with small annoyances or misunderstandings between your husband and yourself, if they unhappily occur. Confidants are dangerous persons; and many seek to obtain ascendency in families by gaining the good opinion of young married women.

Never seek to pry into your husband's letters or affairs, nor ask him questions about the business of others with which he may have been intrusted. It is foolish and wrong in a wife to seek information from her husband which has only been imparted to him in confidence and for professional purposes, and most culpable in a husband to disclose, even to a wife, knowledge thus acquired.

In all money-matters, act openly and honorably. Keep your accounts with the most scrupulous exactness, and let your husband see that you take an honest pride in rightly appropriating the money with which he intrusts you.

"My husband works hard for every dollar that he earns," said a young married lady, the wife of a professional man, to a friend, who found her busily employed in sewing buttons on her husband's coat; "and it seems to me worse than cruel to lay out a cent unnecessarily."

Be very careful not to spend more than can be afforded in dress: this must be settled by the style of living befitting your husband's means and wishes. A sensible woman will always seek to ornament her home, and to render it attractive. The power of association is very great; light, air, and elegance are important in their effects. No wife acts wisely who permits her sitting-room to look dull in the eyes of him whom she ought especially to please, and with whom she has to pass her days.

Above all things avoid bickerings. What does it

signify where a picture hangs, or whether a rose or a fern looks best on the drawing-room table? There is something inexpressibly endearing in small concessions, in gracefully yielding to the will of another, and giving up a favorite opinion; and equally painful is the reverse. The mightiest rivers have their source in small springs, and the bitterest domestic misery has often arisen from some trifling difference of opinion.

Lastly, remember your standing as gentlewoman, and never approve a mean action, nor speak an unrefined word; let all your conduct be such as an honorable and right-minded man may look for in his wife and the mother of his children. The slightest duplicity destroys confidence. The least want of refinement in conversation, or in the selection of books, lowers a woman far more than she can be aware of, in the eyes of the man who looks to her for a delicacy, particularly on such points, far superior to his own; and she should beware how she destroys such expectation.

In short, a wife's aim should ever be to deserve the beautiful commendation of Solomon. If she merits this, she need desire no higher earthly praise:—

"The heart of her husband doth safely trust in her: she will do him good, and not evil, all the days of her life. Strength and honor are her clothing; and she shall rejoice in time to come. Her children rise up, and call her blessed; her husband also, and he praiseth her." — Prov. chap. 31.

Having considered some of the important duties of a wife, I would now address a few words of counsel to you, young men, who have taken on yourselves the sacred and honorable names of husband, and head of the family.

These are stations that best show the true nobleness of manhood, if nobly sustained. You have formed a home to dwell in, and placed therein a gentle and confiding young bride, who has left for you all that was heretofore most dear; and you have vowed to love her only, to cherish her, and provide for her.

You have now, as a married man, a very different standing in society from the one which you previously held. Never forget that the happiness of another is committed to your charge, and strive to render your home happy by kindness and attention to your wife, and by carefully watching over your words and actions. If small disputes arise, and your wife has not sufficient good sense to yield her opinion, even if she seem determined to have her own way, do not get angry; rather be silent, and let the matter rest. Master your own temper, and you will soon master your wife's; study her happiness without yielding to any caprices, and you will have no reason to regret your self-control.

Never let your wife go to church alone on Sunday. You can hardly do a worse thing as regards her good opinion of you and the well-being of your household. It is a sad sight to see a young wife going to church unattended, alone in the midst of a crowd, her thoughts probably dwelling on the time when you were proud to walk beside her.

Sunday is a day of rest, wisely and mercifully appointed to loose the bonds by which men are held to the world; let it be spent by you as becomes the head of a family. Let no temptation ever induce you to wish your wife to relinquish attending divine service, merely that she may remain at home with you. Religion is her safeguard amid the trials and temptations of this world; and woe may be to you if you seek to withdraw her from its protection.

Much perplexity in the marriage-state often arises from want of candor. The husband ought frankly to tell his wife the real amount of his income; unless this is done, she cannot properly regulate her expenses. They ought, then, to consult together as to the sum that can be afforded for housekeeping, which should always be below rather than above the mark.

When this is arranged, he will find it advantageous to give into her hands, either weekly, monthly, or quarterly, the sum that is appropriated for daily expenditure, and, above all things, to avoid interfering, without absolute necessity. The home department belongs exclusively to the wife. The province of the husband is to rule the house; hers, to regulate its internal movements. Should your wife prove inexperienced, have patience, and do not become pettish and ill-humored. If too much money is laid out at first, give advice, kindly but firmly, and she will soon learn how to perform her new duties.

Let a man preserve his own position, and assist his wife to do the same: all things will then move together, well and harmoniously.

Much sorrow and many heart-burnings may be avoided by judicious conduct in the outset of life. Husbands should put perfect trust and cônfidence in their wives, and they will rarely have cause to regret it; whilst too often, from an error in this matter in the beginning, the unhappiness of years has arisen.

If your wife be diffident, encourage her, and avoid seeing small mistakes. Be pleased with trifles, and commend efforts to excel on every fitting occasion. It is unreasonable to add to the embarrassment of her new position by ridiculing delinquencies.

Forbear extolling the previous management of your mother and sisters. Many a wife has been deeply wounded, and even alienated from her husband's family, by such injudicious conduct.

It would be well for every young married man who wishes to render his home happy to consider his wife as the light of his domestic circle, and to permit no clouds, however small, to obscure the region in which she presides. Most women are naturally amiable, gentle, and complying; and if a wife becomes perverse, or indifferent to her home, it is usually her husband's fault.

Before a woman is your wife, you know very well, and she knows, where you spend your evenings. After that, you may know; but she does not. The first suspicion many a woman has of the waning of the honeymoon is the absence of her husband in the evening. Is there not many such a husband and many such a home?"[*]

We would recommend to all young men to practise some self-denial, and to remember that no one acts with a due regard to his own happiness, who lays aside, when married, those gratifying attentions which he was ever ready to pay the lady of his love, or those rational sources of home enjoyment which made her consent to become his companion through life.

III. — MISTAKES IN LANGUAGE.

WORDS are things of much import in good society. Ignorance of grammar shows a condition of mind to be pitied, but not always to be blamed or ridiculed. Those persons who have been untaught or ill-taught commit, unconsciously, errors in speech and writing; but bad taste in language, when opportunities of culture have been enjoyed, seldom deserves any toleration.

Among the errors of American speech and literature,

[*] See " The Home Gift," by John F. W. Ware.

none is so inexcusable as the practice of substituting the animal designations of sex or gender for the names or titles of humanity. To use the term *male* for *man*, or *female* for *woman*, degrades the idea of personality, and thus vulgarizes our language. More than this, it strikes at the root of Christian faith, — that man was made "in the image of God," — because it places human beings on a natural equality with animals in regard to sex. Scripture language never does this. There is no instance in the Bible where the word *male* is applied to *man*, nor *female* to *woman*, in connection with character, abilities, or attributes; nor as referring to heart, soul, mind, and imagination; nor describing any emotion or feeling, as love, pity, reverence, hope, joy : neither do the terms ever refer to any acquirement, as wisdom, skill, experience, accomplishment, — nothing, in short, that implies educational capacity in which human reason is to be exercised. The term of sex, when in the Bible applied to human beings, is always used abstractly or arbitrarily.

Is it proper to say *male mind, male capacity, male usefulness*, in reference to man. Might not the elephant, the horse, the ox, be included in the term ? Yet we hear and read every day about *female mind, female benevolence, female genius, etc.* Is such language correct ? Is the full idea of womanly humanity expressed in the animal term of gender ? Sex is not an attribute of soul, nor a faculty of intellect, nor a synonym for human beings. Sex belongs to animated nature. All creatures that bring forth young are *females;* and, lower still, it belongs to vegetable life, as many flower-bearing trees and plants have sexual differences.

The term *female* cannot, therefore, be a proper name for feminine humanity ; nor should it be used as an adjective, except in contradistinction to man as *male,* abstractly, in numbering like the census, or in institutions like prisons, penitentiaries, poor-houses, which have both sexes and all ages to represent. A celebrated English writer * is competent authority on this point : —

" Why should a woman be degraded from her position as a rational being, and be expressed by a word which might belong to any animal tribe, and which, in our version of the Bible, is never used, except of animals or of the abstract, the sex in general. Why not call a man a '*male,*' if a woman is to be a '*female*'? "

Perhaps a few illustrations may make these truths more clear. The poets are the best expounders of language, because they must use the most appropriate words in their truest, which is their noblest signification, in order to exalt, beautify, and perfect their themes of song. Let us take a few examples, changing the style in regard to *woman* to the vulgar mode of *female:*—

> I grant I am a *female*, but, withal,
> A *female* that Lord Brutus took to wife.
> I grant I am a *female;* but, withal,
> A *female* well reputed ,— Cato's daughter.
> > Shakspeare's Julius Cæsar.

* Henry Alford, D.D., Dean of Canterbury. See his " Queen's English," page 227. London, 1864.

For none of *female* born shall harm Macbeth.

Macbeth.

To whom thus Adam fervently replied:
" *O female!* best are all things as the will
Of God ordains them."

Milton's Paradise Lost.

O *female!* in our hours of ease,
Uncertain, coy, and hard to please,
When pain and sickness wring the brow,
A ministering angel thou.

Scott's Marmion.

Female! blest partner of our joys and woes.

Sand's Yamoyden.

Ah, *female!* in this world of ours
What gift can be compared to thee ?

George P. Morris.

Earlier than I know,
Immersed in rich foreshadowings of the world,
I loved the *female.*   Tennyson's Princess.

The absurdity of these substitutes is at once apparent;
and the beauty, as well as truthfulness, of the word *woman*, in place of *female*, must be acknowledged.   But
there is yet another and clearer demonstration.

If we are to be influenced by the letter of that particular verse of Scripture, "God made them male and
female," for the term to define the one sex, we are equally
bound to apply this rule to the other.   Let us see how
this would influence our classics.

He was a *male*, take him for all in all,
We shall not look upon his like again.

Hamlet.

> Oh! but *male*, proud *male*,
> Dressed in a little brief authority, &c.
> > Measure for Measure.

An honest *male's* the noblest work of God.
> Pope.

The lamps shone o'er fair *females* and brave *males*.
> Byron.

Male is but half without *female*. Festus.

O *male!* while in thy early years
How prodigal of time! Burns.

Then, if we come to the plain prose of common life, we should see accounts of the *males* who had robbed the mail being arrested; of a drunken *male* taken up for insulting a *female;* of an honest *male* returning some valuable article he had found; of a noble *male* who had given largely for the relief of the poor, distressed *males* thrown out of employment, &c.

Should this phraseology be adopted by journalists, and the term *male* for man be used, as *female* now is for woman, the ridiculous impropriety of the language would be seen at once. It would be a good subject for satire.

We have looked chiefly at the serious results of the misnomer. One is that it degrades the woman, and thus deprives her of the sympathy and respect of men.

Editors are not, however, the only writers in fault. Our swarming works of fiction are nearly all infected by this low taste of using *female* for woman or lady. The word occurs so often in some of these books, that it alone would give vulgarity to the style. Many, perhaps most of these works, are written by women, whose lack of self-respect in this is the more remarkable, except we consider that the writers are not aware of the effect of this style.

There is still another source of this popular corruption of words which we are considering, more important and more to be lamented than any we have mentioned. We allude to the almost universal habit of the clergy of our country to speak of woman only as a *female.* Thus, the term, "*female* hearers," "*female* converts," "*females* of the Church," "*female* Bible Societies," "*female* associations," &c., are constantly enunciated from the pulpit; while rarely is the beautiful Bible name of woman pronounced by a preacher of the gospel, except it happen to occur in his text.

Might not a Brahmin, if he could hear from our preachers this oft-repeated word "female," applying equally to all of that sex which brings young, from the elephant to the emmet, draw the conclusion that Christian ministers held the Eastern doctrine of woman's inferiority, even that she had no soul?

Has an animal a soul? Is it not strange that the order of men whose province it is to refine, purify, and exalt language as well as morals should adopt the lowest term of designation for the largest portion of their friends and followers? Christ did not speak thus. The apostle did not so teach. The terms they used were WOMAN and

LADY. These are the Scriptural modes of defining man's companion, not for earth only, but for an immortality of glory.

Would it not be as easy to say, "Women of the Church," "Women of the congregation," "Women converts," "Ladies' Bible Societies," "Ladies' Associations," &c., as to use the present vulgar style? We would humbly present this question to the clergy of the United States. They might, by their influence and example, soon correct the present improper, inelegant, and unscriptural modes of expression.

Nor is this a matter of small importance. Language is a powerful instrument for good or evil. Words are things of mighty influence. The manner of speech indicates the habit of mind.

If we seek to improve our taste, we must be careful that our expressions are appropriate and refined. A vulgar word will often destroy the good effect of a moral lecture: whilst "words fitly spoken are like apples of gold in pictures of silver."

NOTE.

Bonum nomen bonum omen. — Besides this proverb, that a good name is a good omen, we may say that the *right* name, when human beings are in question, is required both by reason and justice. Not only the name or synonym, but the best term that signifies the person, should be used. This correct mode of language is now especially required in designating places of education for men and for women, the profession, in which either sex may engage, and the offices which they may discharge. In these cases the masculine and the feminine should be so clearly distinguished by the name or title, as not to require an explanation. "Young Ladies' College," lately established in one of our cities: this is a definite title. You feel it is designed to give the advantages of high culture to the daughters of America who are fitted to gain admission.

"*A Female College*" is announced as re-opening on the next page of the newspaper. "*What Female?*" is the involuntary comment. The number of *female animals* so vastly preponderates over the *feminine human*, that, when the sexual term *female* is used to signify a woman, it seems to refer to the lowest class of human beings; as if only such as these would go to a *female institution.*

Bear in mind that the term *female* does not *certainly* mean a woman, and never designates a lady; and that a "School or College for ' Females,'" literally offers — even when we confine its meaning with or to feminine humanity — a place for all the sex, from little girls to aged women, married and single, and widows, — all are included in this term *Female.* Yet these seminaries and colleges are only intended for girls and young ladies, from twelve years old to twenty-five.

Why not be as careful in America to designate our institutions rightly, with good names, as we find is the rule in Europe? On the Continent such an absurdity as using *female* to designate the human *feminine* would not be tolerated. Nor in England is it found connected with education. There is a "College for Ladies;" also seminaries for "Maidens," "Girls," and "Young Women;" but not one institution is degraded to the animal level of "*Female.*"

When this class of seminaries was first commenced in America, it was but natural that those who began the gooa work should seek to distinguish it from the colleges for boys, and thus, without weighing the matter, bestowed a title intended to make such distinction; failing to see that they were lowering with one hand her whom they were seeking to raise with the other; for must it not be lowering to woman to confound her with the brute creation?

This bad custom is now changing. The new "colleges for young women" are rightly named; and several of the first class institutions, like Vassar College, have dropped the "*Female,*" from their titles.

IV.—OUR NATIONAL THANKSGIVING DAY.

"Then he said unto them, Go your way, eat the fat, and drink the sweet, and send portions unto them for whom nothing is prepared; for this day is holy unto our Lord: neither be ye sorry; for the joy of the Lord is your strength."—NEHEMIAH, viii. 10.

SUCH was the order given to the people of Israel. for the celebration of their *national and religious festival*, the "Feast of Weeks." We learn from this that a day of yearly rejoicing and giving of gifts was not only sanctioned but enjoined by divine authority on God's chosen people. Such yearly festival is not positively enjoined on Christians; but that it is both expedient and beneficial may safely be argued, when we find that the practice was approved by our God and Father in heaven.

Our day of thanksgiving represents, in many striking coincidences, the Jewish Feast of Weeks: only make our day national, and we should then represent the union of joy that was the grand proof of the divine blessing. Such social rejoicings tend greatly to expand the generous feelings of our nature, and strengthen the bond of union that binds us brothers and sisters in that true sympathy of American patriotism which makes the Atlantic and Pacific Oceans mingle in our mind as waters that wash the shores of kindred homes, and mark from east to west the boundaries of our dominion.

One of the coincidences to which we have alluded is the custom of giving gifts, and "sending portions to those for whom nothing is prepared." I venture to assert that there is not a public institution of any sort, charitable or reformatory, hospital or prison, which is not remembered at this time by a plentiful dinner, liberally provided by our citizens. Indeed, we all know that " *Thanksgiving turkeys*" have become proverbial; and there are few homes, no matter how humble, which cannot on this DAY boast of at least one, supplied either by generous friends, or prudent thrift during the rest of the year.

The Creator has so constituted the race of mankind that their minds need a moderate portion of amusement as imperatively as the body at times wants stimulating food.

This recreative joyousness, this return, if you please, to the gayeties of childhood, is good for the soul. It sweetens the temper, it brightens hope, increases our love for each other, and our faith in the goodness of God. There are individuals and nations who, from an unhappy state of things, — vice in themselves or in other persons, from poverty, or political oppression, — never " drink the sweet nor eat the fat," but drag on a miserable and starved existence.

Even thus, mental starvation from all the sweet joys of social intercourse and innocent merry-making has a wasting and deforming effect upon human character, similar to bad or insufficient diet on the bodily constitution.

God intended that all our faculties should, in the right way, be exercised; and neglect of such exercise changes us to incomplete creatures. One has but a lame existence who has lost or neglected to cultivate " the store that nature to her votary yields." Our busy, wealth-seeking people require to have days of *national festivity,* when fashion and custom will call them to the feast of love and thanksgiving.

The propriety and general advantages of a common DAY for our whole nation to express and acknowledge that " goodness beyond thought and as of power divine," which blesses the increase of the husbandman, and keeps ward for the safety of the city, have never failed to win the approbation of those who have thoughtfully considered the subject. Still, in our wide land, so many occupations and such varied interests and distractions, in the multiform demands of private as well as public life, abound, that men are apt to forget duties which are not brought before them with the regularity of dates and appointed epochs.

In order to overcome this difficulty, the editress of the "Lady's Book" has for the past twenty years been in the habit of urging upon the attention of its readers and friends, year by year, the plan of a NATIONAL THANKS-GIVING DAY.

We suggested *the last Thursday in November,* as the most suitable day to set apart by the governor of each State for this festival, which would then become a national jubilee. This time was selected because then the agricultural labors of the year are generally completed, the elections over, those autumnal diseases which usually prevail more or less have ceased, and the summer wanderers are gathered to their homes.

We have received letters approving this Union festival from governors of nearly every State and Territory who had, before the war commenced, approved the idea although all had not acted upon it.

On the last Thursday of November, 1859, the people of thirty-three States and Territories held and consecrated this new national holiday, as follows:—

Maine, New Hampshire, Vermont, Massachusetts, Rhode Island, Connecticut, New York, New Jersey, Pennsylvania, Maryland, Virginia, North Carolina, South Carolina, Georgia, Florida, Alabama, Mississippi, Louisiana, Texas, Arkansas, Tennessee, Kentucky, Ohio, Michigan, Indiana, Illinois, Iowa, Wisconsin, Minnesota, Kansas [then a territory], California, Nebraska Territory, District of Columbia.

Thus you learn that the governors of all the States have warmly approved the idea of a national thanksgiving day; so also have the missionaries in heathen lands. But there were obstacles.

Thanksgiving day has been an establishment of custom, not a law; without State legislation, there cannot always be unity among the governors. In 1862, all the States which observed the day, united upon the last Thursday in November, excepting Massachusetts and Maine: these two held their Thanksgiving the first Thursday in December, because it was the *anniversary of the separation of Maine from the parent State.*

Thus the unity of the festival was marred; and this would be constantly recurring, unless each State, by legislative enactment, made it obligatory on its governor to appoint Thanksgiving Day on the last Thursday in November. It might take a long time to bring about this State unity.

Is it not a better plan to have, in the first instance, the day appointed by a proclamation from the President of the United States? As head of the nation, as well as the chief of the army and navy, the authority rests with him; and by his action on this point perfect certainty of unity of observance would be secured.

The way is already prepared: the *last Thursday in November* has been observed as the American festival day for the last five or six years, not only on our own shores, but by Americans in European cities, and wherever our countrymen could meet together, — on board our fleets in the Mediterranean, African, and Brazilian stations; by our missionaries in India, China, Africa; and, in 1860, it was observed by our countrymen in Japan, and also in Constantinople, Berlin, Paris, and other places.

Our late beloved and lamented President Lincoln recognized the truth of these ideas as soon as they were presented to him. His reply to our appeal was a proclamation, appointing Thursday, November, 1863, as the day of national thanksgiving. But at that time, and also in November, 1864, he was not able to influence the States in rebellion, so that the festival was necessarily incomplete.

Since the close of the war, these obstacles have been removed, and President Johnson's Proclamation for the National Thanksgiving on the *last Thursday of November*, 1866, was observed over all the country. Thus the family union of States and Territories in our Great Republic was fixed and hallowed by the people in the ninetieth year·of American Independence.

No one can doubt the effect upon us, as a nation, of acknowledging God, at least once in a year, and returning thanks to him publicly for the infinite mercies so lavishly bestowed upon us. Nor only upon ourselves is this influence. Such an observance by us will not be unfelt by the nations of the Old World. There is something peculiarly beautiful in seeing a great people, of the most varying creeds and opinions, bound by no established faith, thus voluntarily uniting throughout our wide land to mingle their voices in one common hymn of praise and thanksgiving. Thus, and thus only, can we show to the world that America is indeed a Christian Republic.

Every thing that contributes to bind us in one vast empire together, to quicken the sympathy that makes us feel, from the icy North to the sunny South, that we are one family, each a member of a great and free nation, not merely the unit of a remote locality, is worthy of being cherished. We have sought to re-awaken and increase this sympathy, believing that the fine filaments of the affections are stronger than laws to keep the union of our States sacred in the hearts of our people.

We believe that our Thanksgiving Day, if thus fixed and perpetuated, will be a great and sanctifying promoter of this national spirit. Our whole people will then look forward to it, — make preparations to honor and enjoy it. Literature will take her part, and send her tribute of gratitude.

We are glad to see that this has already been done in a measure, and that the press has taken up the idea. One of our leading journals has an excellent article entitled "Thanksgiving Literature." The writer, after mentioning "certain well-meaning, but rather heavy hymns," which he says is all we have on the subject, goes on to wonder that American writers should have failed to see what a vast theme might be here opened to them, — family affection, the bringing together of the scattered, the tender recollection and renewal of old ties, in short, a countless throng of pleasant topics on which to weave romance or song. All this is a step in the right direction.

22

" Let Thanksgiving, our American holiday, give us American books, — song, story, and sermon, — written expressly to awaken in American hearts the love of home and of country, of thankfulness to God, and peace between brethren."

I have thus endeavored to lay before my readers one of the strongest wishes of my heart, convinced that the general estimate of feminine character throughout the United States will be far from finding it an objection that this idea of American Union Thanksgiving was suggested by a woman. The enjoyments are social, the feastings are domestic; therefore this annual festival is really the exponent of family happiness and household piety, which women should always seek to cultivate in their hearts and in their homes. God gave to man authority, to woman influence: she inspires and persuades; he convinces and compels.

It has always been my aim to use my influence in this womanly way. And now I feel, that, under the blessing of God, I am indebted to the efficient aid of good and patriotic men, who have accomplished this idea of establishing *the last Thursday in November* as the set time for the people of the United States, wherever they may chance to be, to celebrate and hallow as the AMERICAN NATIONAL THANKSGIVING DAY.

V. — EVENING RECEPTIONS.

A MONG the fine arts that embellish life, none gives more pleasure, or is of more advantage in every age and in every situation, than the art of conversation.

Some people have from Nature the gift of eloquence, as we see persons have a natural turn for painting or for music; but as the genius of Mozart could not have shone, had he been confined to a Jew's-harp, so wit and facility of speech are stifled by ignorance. Even learning and cultivation lose their charms when their possessor has not the proper words and the best turn of phrases to express his knowledge and define his meaning.

Conversation, like all arts, needs culture, which should begin in the home-circle; but the place where it gains its perfection and power, and also where it gives and receives its greatest pleasure, is in good society. Now, here it is that woman begins to exercise that precious influence which extends from her family to the city she inhabits, to the country where she dwells, to the very era in which she lives.

To the *Hôtel de Rambouillet*, to the Marchioness de Rambouillet and her daughter Julia, France has been indebted for that *esprit de société*, and that series of remarkable conversationalists who have rendered the *salons* of Paris the centre of intellectual *causeries*, or easy talking (only the French word expresses the true meaning), ever since their day.

At the *Hôtel de Rambouillet*, the great Corneille read his early plays; here, too, the wonderful orator, Bossuet, in their re-unions, took his first steps to fame. In England, there have been women who have illustrated their own times by drawing together men of genius and women of appreciative powers.

Mrs. Montague and Mrs. Vesey conferred more benefit on English society than did the court of St. James. Mrs. Thrale's charming parties, so vividly described by Madame d'Arblay, show what could be done, even in that exclusively aristocratic age, by a woman of talent and good nature, to cultivate literature and help intellectual advancement.

Mrs. Delany, in her pleasant correspondences, shows how acceptable a woman can make herself to minds of the highest order in society when she aims at pleasing by what is elevated and truly interesting.

The Correspondence of the Miss Berrys, a very charming work, lately published, gives a picture of sensible women, whose extensive sphere of usefulness should be a pattern to others of their sex, who fritter away life, often a burden to themselves and very little pleasure or comfort to others.

Our American society, to become something worthy of the name, should not be left entirely to dancing boys and girls; neither should it be confined to those who think "to live is to eat."

Some years ago, there lived in one of our cities a widowed lady with an only daughter. They were not rich in acres or stocks; but they had "spirit, taste, and sense." They tried the experiment of collecting ladies and gentlemen in their parlors who had the culture and powers to make themselves agreeable, — people who were amusable as well as sensible. The artist was there with his sketch, the musician with his song or his inspired fingers, and ladies who could listen as well as talk.

The *savans* learned the way to that pleasant house, where there was every Thursday evening a social circle composed of people worth seeing, and where ceremonious and extensive toilets were neither required nor observed.

The clever author, the popular poet, the celebrated man of letters, — such were the people who had, one by one, been welcomed to these pleasant receptions, or *soirées*, where there was neither finery nor feasting, but where good sense, genius, accomplishments, and genuine hospitality, which gave the best it had, shook hands, and enjoyed the pleasures of refined, witty, and intelligent conversation.

It need not be added, that, as the evenings went on from year to year, those who frequented them were made better and happier, and more useful. Many a bright idea, struck out by discussion in those unpretending rooms, has cheered a listening public by its wit, or moved a crowd of spectators by its truth, or opened the hearts of the people by its tender pathos.

Why cannot this way of receiving company be more frequently tried in our own free land? Why cannot our ladies feel that good conversation is as attractive in its way as dancing, dressing, and devouring? There is a time for the *galop;* but, beyond that time, why may we not derive happiness and amusement from the exercise of higher faculties? Why should we not improve as well as please ourselves by fancy, imagination, wit, knowledge and all the intellectual *agréments* to be got from the clever and the educated?

I have known people who refrained from inviting their friends because they could not entertain them with a luxurious supper and expensive wines. There seem to be notions in many minds that the table must be loaded with eatables, or there is no welcome.

Such men might be legitimate descendants of Penelope's lovers, who thought there was no enjoyment at a party, unless "whole beeves" were slaughtered for the occasion. Was not this a very low state of civilization? In the dim chronicles of the old Greek Republics, Milo might have gained honor by carrying a heifer of four years old on his shoulder, and then eating the whole of it in a single day; but now, when a chop or a steak would be all that the most hungry "suitor" would demand of his "Penelope," shall the lady at home, when inviting her friends to pass an evening in social conversation, be expected to serve up *bouilli* with brilliancy, game with gravity, or mutton with mirth?

The growing fashion for expensive dress is another obstacle to hospitality and home enjoyments. When people go out to be looked at, of course they are obliged to make a display themselves, as the feast of the eye demands elegance and variety. But one can talk agreeably in the simplest raiment; and, when we meet for conversation, the pleasures of intellectual society should be the great attraction.

Mere fashionable display is out of place: nothing external is required to constitute the good society of an evening reception, except that personal neatness and appropriateness in costume which marks the true lady and gentleman in every home-circle. For this reason, a reception may be as well given in a log-hut as in the grandest home of wealth and luxury. Wit will sparkle as brightly, mirth will flow as easily, deep problems will be studied and solved as readily, where "rafters rise around" as where silk hangings drape the walls. We doubt not our Great West could attest the truth of our words, could it give in its experience, and tell us of what has already taken place there.

No doubt, if this fashion were tested, of having *soirées* characterized by the qualifications of the guests, and the character of their conversational abilities (to be a good listener is an important requisite, and indispensable for a woman), rather than by fine clothes and expensive suppers, there would be good progress in intellectual enjoyments, moral refinements, and social pleasures.

There would surely be great abatement in the vanities of life and the vexations of spirit which now disturb the harmony of society.

HINTS.

1. The most important requisite to make receptions general is, that they should be inexpensive; thus putting them within the power of every one. Let mind, character, and conversational ability, be the qualifications, — not costume and eating.

2. The subjects of conversation may embrace every thing but polemics and politics, and, of course, all irritating controversies. The aim is to unite, in conversation, information with amusement; and whatever most tends to promote this should be cultivated.

3. Upon the lady of the house must depend, in a great degree, the character of the receptions. Thus we find that Madame de Rambouillet, who established this style of *soirée* during the reign of Henry IV., is said to have given "a moral stamp to the society she founded." This is the more remarkable when we consider the low state of morals of the times in which she lived.

The Miss Berrys, living plainly in Curzon Street, London, yet surrounding themselves with wealth of mind and luxury of talent, and the widow lady already named, on the one hand; on the other, Mrs. Harrison Gray Otis of Boston, and Mrs. Rush of this city, whose hospitality will long be remembered by Philadelphia (both

ladies of most ample means and high social position)
the one at her *soirées* offering but tea and cake, the
other, at her morning receptions, giving nothing eatable
of any kind, — set a beautiful and most useful example of
how mind may be exalted over matter, and of what may
be done for the elevation of society by the influence of
educated and cultivated women.

4. Every woman should know how to *elicit* information
as well as to bestow it. This is quite an art, we might
almost say a gift.

A question intelligently and accurately put, an interested, appreciating manner of listening, will often call
out a valuable store of facts and fancies, which will be
of far greater benefit to the hearer than any display
of her own conversational talents could ever become.
We read that Madame Récamier spoke little, but always appealed to any one in the circle who was likely
to have any special knowledge; thus constantly adding
to the stock of her own information.

VI. — BOOKS FOR HOME-READING.

WHAT is the greatest earthly blessing of human beings? Is it not a happy home, where comfort, order, and improvement are enjoyed and made sure by the
faithful affection of husband and wife for each other, and
by the wise and loving performance of all their duties?

Love, then, is the only sacred and sure power of developing and sustaining the home; *love* secures the blessings of earth, and opens the gates of heaven. The books that best portray the nature of this pure love, and show the way in which it can be righteously enjoyed, and through the whole world of life diffused in joy and peace and goodness — these are the books for home reading.

There is but *one Book* that can make good and happy homes. Take from the world the BIBLE, and the knowledge it has given to mankind, and what would our homes become? Would they not be like the Chinese, the Hindoos, the Arabs? And worse, far worse than these; for the glorious light of the Holy Bible has illumined each one of these, scattering the thick darkness which must of necessity envelop any and every spot where its blessed presence never comes.

Women require that their moral and religious feelings should be early and constantly cultivated by the Bible. The foundation stone of their temple of learning must be the Gospel of Jesus Christ. Woman without the Bible is but a doll or a slave. The fire of her genius can only burn clear and bright when placed on the altar of the true God.

"Our religion is that of our mother," says a celebrated French writer; and he might have added, this religious medium prepares the human soul for the reception of all its ideas. The mind cannot be healthy when surrounded by moral miasma. Go, then, to the source of truth. Be-

gin with the Bible; and, though it may be you have read
it many times, you can never exhaust its information or
its interest. It is the earliest history. It contains the
first and most sublime specimens of poetry; and one of
the first poets was a woman. Its narratives, for true pathos and beauty of sentiment, are unequalled. Where,
in all the ancient writers, can be found tales of such tender and thrilling interest as those of Esther and Ruth?
If these were now published for the first time as translations from the French of some popular writer, how they
would be seized upon and read without a pause in a fever
of admiration!

And yet though there are few, if any, women in our
land but believe that the Bible is the word of God, containing the oracles of divine wisdom, truth, and love, and
revealing the hope and the way of eternal life, is not this
book of books too often laid aside and forgotten for the
last new novel?

At the present day, great conflicts of opinion are going
on with reference to the foundation truths of our faith.
Foremost amongst these is a denial of the divinity of
our Saviour, the very corner-stone of the whole structure,
without which it must of necessity fall to the earth. To
those interested in this vital question, we would earnestly recommend a work by a Scotch lawyer, "The
Christ of History."*

His object is to prove the divinity from the perfection

* Published by Robert Carter & Brothers, 530 Broadway, New York.

of the manhood; and the whole argument is a masterly one, worked out in quite a new, powerful, and original manner.

An eminent English critic says, —

"This work belongs to the best class of the productions of modern disciplined genius. We may describe this little book as one of the best works in modern English for introducing us to the knowledge and life of Jesus of Nazareth."

Respecting family reading, we speak what we *know:* it is the most convenient, the most improving, and the most unfailing of pastimes. It is also the best for family enjoyment, as it admits of those useful and pleasant womanly pursuits, necessary in home life, during the readings.

Let the young married pair consecrate their new home by some plan of mental improvement together: the good results will be sure and far more important than they may then imagine. On the wife usually devolves the arrangement for these readings, which should be held at least on two or three evenings of each week. Take up some regular course of reading or of study, — botany is a delightful science for home-study — and pursue it steadily, till that real improvement is gained which will make you love and remember what you have learned. A married pair thus engaged together in mental pursuits have interesting subjects of conversation in their daily life. The man's reason will enlarge the knowledge of the woman materially and intellectually; and her ideas (usually intuitive) will enlighten his moral sense, and refine and strengthen his emotional nature. Thus both may derive pleasure and profit from these different-sided views; whilst love, the great solvent of prejudices, as it is the perfect magnet of virtue, will draw their minds and hearts into closer communion, and thus, cultivating the moral sentiments, lead them, let us hope, to the study together of the "Book" of divine wisdom which shows the way of perfect love and immortal life.

Americans should first acquaint themselves with the history of their own country, its literature, arts, and science, as the stand-point for acquiring such knowledge of all other countries as may be most interesting and beneficial.

Great Britain, of course, stands as the ancestral fountain from which we have drawn the pure waters of moral and intellectual knowledge, that have made our "green forest land" rich in the best fruits of the Old-World civilization, even whilst we are apparently but entering on our career of national life. To run (the way we have done) this career in that "righteousness which exalteth a nation" requires in each individual a well-informed mind and well-disciplined character. Much of this knowledge and discipline is gained from the written knowledge and wisdom of the past.

The following list of books for family reading does not

pretend to be, in any respect, exhaustive. It consists rather of simple compendiums of knowledge on various subjects necessary to be known, or of great and popular works, ignorance of which might justly be held a disgrace to any American of common education. We have selected the list upon the principle of giving as much prominence as possible to American publications; and, above all other considerations, furnishing suitable studies for Christian homes and American citizens.

History. — Taylor's Universal History, Dr. Smith's smaller History of Greece, Mrs. Markham's History of Rome, Hallam's Middle Ages, Goldsmith's Pictorial History of England, Goldsmith's Pictorial History of France, Mrs. Willard's American Republic, Lossing's Field Book of the Revolution.

Those who have leisure for a more thorough course should read, consecutively, Grote, Arnold, Merivale, Gibbon, Hallam, Hume, Froude, Macaulay, Bancroft, Prescott, Motley.

Biography. — Boswell's Life of Johnson, Johnson's Lives of the Poets, Memoirs of the Duchess of Abrantes, Lockhart's Life of Walter Scott, Barry Cornwall's Life of Charles Lamb, Southey's Life of Cowper, Irving's Life of Columbus, Irving's Life of Washington, Mrs. Hale's Distinguished Women, Stevens's Women of Methodism.

Science. — Consult the most recent encyclopædias on

the separate subjects. Geology — Hitchcock. Physiology — Prichard. Astronomy — Nichols's Architecture of
the Heavens. Mrs. Somerville's Mechanism of the
Heavens. Philology — Trench; Müller. Botany — A.
Wood. Physical Geography — Guyot. Natural History — Good's Book of Nature; Martin's Natural History.

Moral Philosophy and Metaphysics. — Combe on the
Constitution of Man, Sir William Hamilton, Paley, Way-
land's Moral Science.

Theology. — Butler's Analogy, Bunyan's Pilgrim's
Progress, Stanley's History of the Eastern Church.

Travels. — Africa — Livingstone, Baker. Assyria —
Layard. China — Huc, Doolittle. Palestine — Kinglake's
Eöthen; Stanley's Sinai. Arctic Voyages — Kane, Bay-
ard Taylor's Travels.

Fiction. — Walter Scott; the earlier novels of Dickens;
the later novels of Bulwer; " The Newcomes " of Thackeray; Cooper; Hawthorne; Miss Austen; Charlotte
Brontë, "George Eliot;" Mrs. Gaskell; "The Gaywor-
thys," and "Faith Gartney's Girlhood," by Mrs. Whit-
ney.

This may seem meagre to the novel-devourer; but let
these become familiar books in the household, to form
the taste and cultivate the judgment respecting works of
fiction; then the serials of Mrs. Oliphant and other
good writers in the magazines will keep up the supply.

Poetry and the Drama. — This field is too large for

selection in a concise list like this; therefore we will say, read Shakspeare, Milton, Mrs. Browning, and the great poets of England and America in general: each person must read for his or her own enjoyment. The best introduction to the style and characteristics of the different writers of "poesy," as well as the best compendiums of their works, are Dana's "Household Book of Poetry," and Palgrave's "Golden Treasury." Keble's "Christian Year" will be a favorite with all who love the great themes of religion and spiritual life.

Miscellaneous. — Chambers' Cyclopædia of English Literature, Essays of Elia, Disraeli's Curiosities of Literature, Mrs. Jameson's Shakspeare's Characters, Carlyle's French Revolution, Hallam's Literature of the Middle Ages, Burke on the Sublime and Beautiful; Age of Fable, Bulfinch; Age of Chivalry, Bulfinch; Irving's Sketch Book; Holmes's Autocrat of the Breakfast Table.

These suggestions may be of some use for those who find plan as well as purpose is required in a well-ordered home. It will be easy to enlarge the list of books; thousands on thousands have been published in our land during the last six years. These, as yet, belong rather to the present than the past; so we must leave the selection to individual judgment and taste.

The mass of "current literature" and "juvenile books" have some remarkable specimens of excellence. The works of Mrs. Charles deserve particular mention. Her

"*Chronicles of the Schönberg-Cotta Family*," and "*The Song without Words*," should be in every household. Still it seems to us that what is rightly denounced as "Sensation Literature" has its root and growth in the habit of "fast" and promiscuous reading, now forced upon children by the pressure of 'juvenile books." The subject is important; but we cannot here discuss it, and only name it to draw the attention of writers who are competent to deal with one of those evils which beset and mar our best efforts for doing good.

VII.—MEN AND WOMEN.

IN every time and every nation, the hearth of home is in the care of the women. And, if ever a nation shall deserve to present to the world a new and higher phase of home-life, it must be that people in which woman is treated with the highest regard and true chivalry; where she is permitted to become all that Nature intended her to be. We believe in Europe that this people is to be found in the United States of America. — *Miss Bremer.*

As far as exemption from the hard work of "subduing the earth" (which God has expressly laid on men), the women of America are freed from all oppressive toils; and their homes are made more comfortable and pleasant than those of any other women. There is not now, nor has there ever been, a nation where the men are so careful to provide for their families, and devote such thought and skill for domestic appliances intended to lighten the tasks of women; and the love and liberality of fathers and husbands are apparent in the comforts and luxuries of home-life, and in the personal appearance of their wives and daughters. All this is well done; but is not something more needed before that shining phase of home-life which our Republic should assume can be fully displayed?

Men, besides their superiority in physical strength, have the mechanical ingenuity which discovers the natural laws of science, and how to apply these to their own inventions and constructions. What wonderful talents of power and usefulness God has intrusted to men! and what wonderful things they have done in the world during the last hundred years! The cultivated nations of Christendom are, in their knowledge of scientific truth, and in their appliances of this worldly wisdom, seemingly raised to their empire of sovereignty over earth, and the natural capacities of happiness for mankind.

Are the people better or happier for this knowledge, as they have hitherto applied its results? Does not every advance in material prosperity and intellectual power bring in its train an increase of degradation and misery to a large class of society, and new devices of crime and sin to darken history and discourage hope?

We are slow to learn that the real progress of humanity

must have its root in moral goodness; and we are yet
more dull in comprehending the need of early tending
this root of excellence in the minds of little children,
training its tendrils, and turning them to the divine light
of the Gospel, that these moral virtues may be purified
and vivified by faith in Christ, till they bear the full fruits
of righteousness in the characters of men and women.
Carlyle has, in his photograph style, happily embodied
the idea of this necessity for childhood culture: —

"It strikes me dumb to look over the long series of
faces, such as any full church, court-house, London tavern,
or miscellany of men, will show. Some score or two of
years ago, all these were little, red-colored, pulpy infants;
each of them capable of being moulded into any social
form you chose."

Thus far the philosopher sees clearly; but neither he
nor any man seems as yet to have comprehended that
this work of moulding humanity rightly *must be done by
women.* Never will the best capacities of human nature
be developed in a healthy state, and directed heavenward,
as the "living soul" should tend, until the feminine sex
are fitted for their duties, and honored when performing
them faithfully, — duties the first, the highest, the holiest,
which the Creator has intrusted to human beings. I place
woman's office above man's, because moral influence is
superior to mechanical invention. *Man is greater than
his work;* and woman's mission is to mould mind, and
form character; while man's work deals with material

things: both equally need the cultivation of their intellectual powers to fit them for their duties.

I do not agree with those who would place women in competition with men in their industrial pursuits. Such a course would not only deteriorate the feminine nature, but fatally injure society, because giving material things a still greater preponderance over moral goodness than is now to be found in Christendom.

Radical changes are not required in American life. What we need is to increase the power of good influences now active, and to restrain and banish those which are evil. For the first, we need better means of education for women. The higher, that is, the more thoroughly trained, the mother has been in all branches which her children will need to study, the better able she will be to form their minds for the reception of culture. On the right ordering of households depend the health and comfort, the improvement and enjoyment, of every human being. Does not the lady who presides over the duties and destinies of family life require the aid of a thorough education, mentally as well as morally, in order to become capable of using her faculties to the best advantage? John Ruskin, in his lectures on education, places a higher estimate on the capacity of the feminine mind, and says that, in the education of a young lady, "all such knowledge should be given to her as may enable her to understand and even to aid the work of man."

And yet in America, while the young men have schools

and colleges, richly endowed by public and private boun-
ties, to fit them for all manly-professions, there has never
been an institution in our land founded and endowed by
State or national bounty for the young women. Nor is there
but *one* endowed institution in all our wide country: "VAS-
SAR COLLEGE" stands alone in its just design of giving
"to the young women of America an education as thorough
as our colleges are accomplishing for young men."

The founder of Vassar College has the glorious honor
of leading in this, the right way of individual and national improvement.

Moreover, women have never yet had any suitable
means of education for their household duties. *Domestic science*, far more important to the health, happiness,
and morality of mankind than any other sort of scientific
learning, has never yet had a college or school founded
to teach its arts, rules, methods of practice, and deep
mysteries of knowledge. Congress has liberally given
millions of acres of public lands to found agricultural
colleges for working-men : working-women have no recognition in this national bounty. Is it not time to begin
the experiment of fitting woman for her own work? She
certainly has many things to do. Among these duties,
there must be some of importance to the public weal.
Do not the daughters of the Republic require more in
their culture than the elementary education of the common schools?

Medical science belongs as surely to women as to men.

Woman is the preserver; the study of the laws of health
and of the healing art would harmonize with her feelings
and her intuitive faculties.   She has a right to this knowledge and to the means of acquiring it, so far as her own sex
and children are concerned.   The profession of "Doctress
of Medicine" should be considered, like the duties of
mother and nurse, which it closely resembles, a proper
sphere for educated women, if they choose to enter it.

And, while these beneficent changes for women are in
progress, legislation must be invoked to suppress those
vices and crimes of men that destroy the happiness of
home where woman's world centres.   Drunkenness, gam-
bling, licentiousness, — these are the blasting sins that
now defy law, and disgrace the manhood of American
citizens.   Surely there are enough good and true men,
would they unite, to accomplish all these reforms in our
country.

The bayonet or the ballot-box must govern the world.
Wherever the latter bears rule, moral power is in the as-
cendant, and there the influence of woman predominates.
Would it not be better if the sex were admitted to participate directly in the administration of government,
voting and holding offices equally with men?   No: I
reply unhesitatingly, no!   Feminine power is not coer-
cive, but persuasive.   However salutary moral influences
may be, yet in civil governments the laws must, in the
last resort, be upheld by material force.   This duty women could not perform; nor could they share in the gov-

ernment, unless the other sex permitted. When men are prepared, from their appreciation of feminine goodness, to do this, they will be 'good themselves, and therefore better fitted, by their masculine power of sustaining law, to uphold and discharge all the duties of government than women can possibly be. Besides, our American women have the controlling power over their homes, their children, and social life: it is but just that men should enjoy a separate theatre for the cultivation and display of their own talents and virtues.

Would the true wife desire to supersede her husband? Would the good, intelligent mother, who has trained her son to the glorious ambition of serving his country, and gaining a noble fame, — would she, were it in her power, pluck the laurel from his brow, and place it on her own? Would she be willing that any woman should enter the lists against her son? If not, is it right for this mother to encourage the competition of her own sex against the sons of other mothers?

Greatness is most perfect when it acts with the least reference to *self;* power is most efficient when moving the will through the heart. Let us American ladies cultivate the virtues, the knowledge, the accomplishments, which will influence, imbue, and aid men to do the work of the world to the glory of God; then the woman will truly shine forth as "the glory of the man."

In the first paper of this work (see Love), I alluded to the precepts of Christ as the foundation rules of conduct and character, when we seek to refine and dignify human nature. And now, when the year has come full circle, and we are at the close of the fifty-second paper, this *Gospel etiquette of love and duty* comes again before us as the perfect pattern for that home-life and social improvement which the men and women of America are, as we all hope, destined " to present to the world."

The real worth and glory of American institutions can never be understood nor appreciated, until we, as a people, teach, by our example, that Jesus Christ, in making men "free," subjected them to His truth.

> In thy place, O tender woman!
>   Teaching faith and hope and love,
> Thine to guard and guide the human
>   In the way that leads above.
>
> In thy place the nearest heaven,
>   When creation's chain was done;
> To thy seed the promise given
>   Gives us heaven through the Son.
>
> . . . .
>
> Man, thine arm with strength is gifted,
>   And thy will the world may bind;
> But with power and pride uplifted,
>   Wouldst thou deify the mind?
>
> Grant thee learning, wealth, and talents,
>   Can these gifts salvation give?
> 'Tis the heart that holds the balance,
>   Love alone in heaven will live.
>
> Ay, and Love, o'er earth extended,
>   Must his sovereign sceptre sway,
> Ere the reign of sin is ended,
>   Ere the just enjoy their day.

Thou who, calm, Heaven's will awaitest,
  On thy soul these counsels bind, —
Gentle things work changes greatest,
  Faith when true is found most kind.

Wouldst thou draw the angels nearer,
  Make the woman's lot more blest;
Wouldst thou read Heaven's wisdom clearer,
  Holier keep the Sunday rest.

————————

VIII. — MERRY CHRISTMAS.

WHEN the blessed anniversary of GOOD TIDINGS to the world is at hand, what heart so sad, what life so lowly, that a thought of cheer and of joy does not lighten the load when we feel that Christmas is so near us all!

Christmas is a sweet bond of confidence and brotherhood in the hearts of all who believe the Bible. Beyond the sea, Americans meet and rejoice together in their Christian faith and in the free land they love so well. American artists gather in Italy for the sake of study; yet not less fondly do they meet their countrymen, and identify themselves with all of home that can be obtained in those old cities. These Christmas meetings, Christmas dinners and celebrations, keep up the feelings of patriotism and the memories of home, which might, perhaps, wither without freshness of thought imparted at such re-unions.

"Recreation," says Bishop Hall, "is intended for the mind as whetting is for the scythe, to sharpen the edge of it, which otherwise would grow dull and blunt. He that always toils and never recreates is ever mowing, and never sharpening his scythe, — laboring much to little purpose. I would so interchange that I be neither dull with work nor idle with recreation."

For the purpose of proper amusements, holidays are especially useful in our working-day country, and above all others the Christmas festival. This best answers the object ; and it must be a very narrow, if not cold, heart that cannot become warm and open then as a blossom in spring-time. To help the poor, cheer the mournful, gratify the demands of friendship, and make happy the dear ones of the domestic circle by gifts according to your means, and congratulations and kind words as your generous heart prompts, — are not these enjoyments the bread of life and the wine of love, that strengthen the best energies of the soul, and give beauty and enjoyment to our homes and worldly possessions?

In the happiness of Christmas rejoicings, there is an element of religious feeling that tones down merriment, and prevents it from degenerating into riot or even levity. The soul is raised to something beyond unmeaning mirth, and the character is improved by the exercise of generosity, and the heart tranquillized by the solemnity of the church services. This is the sober side. It has its merry scenes also.

Christmas is the bright household festival that comes to gladden old winter, bring joy to life, good cheer, family gatherings, and tokens of love. To children especially it is the happy epoch, to be joyfully anticipated and joyfully remembered. Merry Christmas! The words are full of happy meanings to warm every heart. Even when gloom darkens the minds of the elder members of a family, when sorrow or adversity has checked their pleasures, there is ever a little reserve of Christmas merry-making for the young folks. "We must not, on this day, throw a gloom over the children," is every wise parent's thought.

And so the Christmas-tree rises in its glad greenness, laden with its glittering presents, and bright with the tapers that display its rich fruits. And the stockings are hung up for Kriss Krinkel, and filled with such wonderful treasures as fairy lore never exceeded in the fancy of the little ones, who pull out the toys and presents of the season. Wise and good mothers take this time of Christian joy to teach the little hearts, made happy by home cherishing, to remember the poor and desolate, and that it is more blessed to give than to receive.

THE QUEEN'S BOOK.*

As Christmas is the season for presents of the best books, a remarkable volume, not named in my list for family reading, deserves notice. It shows pictures of

---

* Queen Victoria's Memoirs of the Prince Consort. — His Early Years. New York: Harper and Brothers.

human nature so noble in aspirations for the good, so true and pure in love, and so lofty in ideals of duty, that it should become a standard work in our family literature among all classes of people who love and honor virtues that exalt a nation.

For young men and women it should be a favorite study. The character of Prince Albert, the hero of the history, is a model of excellence in real life that no examples of romance heroes can parallel. And then it is not a fanciful or unattainable excellence set before the world. Albert's noble resolve to do good in his life-work, and his patient perseverance in duty, by which he won the highest renown of human greatness, — the title of "Albert the Good," — these opportunities of resolve and action are open to every boy and young man in the United States. In American homes, be they ever so lowly, the princely virtues of truth, patience, self-denial, and perseverance in the right, may find room and scope and reward.

Queen Victoria also in her home-life, so far as revealed (the aim of the book is to portray her "dear Albert," not herself), is a beautiful example for all young wives. In reverence for her husband, and submission to his will as head of the household, we see the divine root of domestic peace and mutual love in the royal family. They lived in conformity with God's law of marriage: the husband gave honor to his wife, and loved her as himself; the wife loved, obeyed, and reverenced her husband; this made the perfect confidence of their conjugal affection, the happiness that no royal rank or earthly splendor could have conferred.

In such a marriage-union, the good promoted in each other by the faithfulness of both in duty exalts the tender affections and private virtues into ennobling influences on social life and national character. Such marriage-unions should be the rule in America, where the highest greatness that moral virtue and material wealth can reach may be won.

Two examples of married life in the Anglo-Saxon nations should be put on record, as beacon-lights in the progress of Christian civilization. The personal examples of this domestic excellence are found at Mount Vernon in America, and in the royal palaces of England, where Queen Victoria and Prince Albert had their home.

Washington's household example, the model of goodness, has its honored place in this volume, as it should have in the hearts of every family of his race. Prince Albert's youth, and "first year of married life," are portrayed in the "Queen's Book," and now come to us as a new revelation of the power of personal goodness and the loveliness of domestic harmony. The marriage took place before the Queen or Prince was twenty-one: as youth and maiden their troth was plighted, and their perfect example of true love and self-sacrificing devotion to each other are the models we wish to set before all the young people of America.

How truly the Queen and Prince kept their promises of love and vows of marriage we all know. Death has sealed their domestic history, but only to show, as by a light from heaven, the glory and dignity which may be won in the practice of domestic virtues and the faithful discharge of private duties.

The greatness of Prince Albert was unique. He has set a new star in the galaxy of man's glory. He won his high place among the leaders of mankind by his perfect obedience to God's law of marriage. This obedience he illustrated in his life, as the great apostle expounded the sacred ordinance, which is the foundation of human law, and, next to the requirement of "love to God," the foundation of moral law. Prince Albert "loved his wife as himself." He gave honor to her as the "weaker vessel" by devoting himself, with all his powers of mind and sympathies of heart, to her exaltation and happiness. He was the Prince Paladin of faithful husbands. No Knight of the Round Table has such a record of noble deeds for a noble purpose, as this God-obeying example of the husband of Queen Victoria, in his devotion to his wife, has left to the men of Christendom. And Queen Victoria, the royal mourner, will remember her lost husband. More than this: her whole future will show how deeply she reverences his memory, how tenderly she cherishes every token of respect to him, how religiously she follows every word of his counsel. She will live for him, to carry out his ideas, to fulfil his wishes; to keep *his name* identified with her own, will be the ruling thought in all that she plans or performs. The marriage-union thus illustrated in its perfection is one of the noblest triumphs of human reason and virtue. It shows the goodness of God in making the earthly happiness of mankind attainable in household affections within the reach of all. It foreshadows the purity, happiness, and glory of the redeemed in Heaven. " As Christ loved the church, so the husband should love his wife."

Wooings and weddings are seasons, that, in every condition of life, make or mar the happiness of human beings. It is only in loving homes that the real pleasures of Christmas can be enjoyed, as it was by the Queen and Prince the first year of their married life. We find in his "memoirs," — page 289, — this pleasant description.

" Christmas-trees were set up in the Queen's and Prince's rooms, — a custom continued in future years, when they were set up in another room for the young princes and princesses, — and in the oak-room for the household. It was the favorite festival of the Prince, — a day, he thought, for the interchange of presents, as marks of mutual affection and good-will."

CHRISTMAS-TREES.

We are glad to notice that every year the German custom of making Christmas-trees for children is becoming more common amongst us. Few things give greater delight to the little ones, or link happier recollections with the season and the home. As an easy manner of constructing them may not be known to all our readers, we insert a sketch of the German mode, written by an American lady.

Before giving the description of this wonderful tree, I would say a few words of warning to those who decorate it with their loving gifts, which make its sweetness and perfect its beauty. Do not load its green boughs with the *sugar candies now "made to sell."* You can adorn your Christmas-tree with the healthful gifts of Nature — apples, pears, grapes, nuts, and other fruits that the little ones love. You can add lumps of real sugar, white and clean as crystal, if sweets are indispensable; and there are sugar candies honestly prepared from good sugar, and made beautiful without coloring. But pray do not allow your children to eat *"white earth"* colored with *carlot!*

HOW THE TREE WAS MADE.

"The first winter German servants were in my house, as Christmas drew near, Augusta came to me one day, with her countenance glowing with enthusiasm, and making her usual little curtsey, said, 'Will the mistress please have a Christmas-tree?'

"I cannot give her pretty broken English. 'A Christmas-tree, Augusta? I do not know how to arrange one.'

"'Mine bruder will do dat.'

"The brother was a carpenter; so I consented to the proposal, and invited a party of children for Christmas Eve. The day before Christmas, the ' bruder, ' Gottleib, appeared, looking as though he had come from the wood of Dunsinane, with a tree upon his back, a beautiful spruce, seven feet high. This was to be set up in the back parlor; but how was it to stand upright?

"The carpenter had brought for that purpose a board or plank, a *foot square and an inch and a half thick:* a moulding, merely for ornament, was on the edge of the board. In the middle of this square, which was prettily covered with moss, was a round hole, into which the trunk of the tree, cut for the purpose, was tightly fixed. To my surprise, it stood firm and steady, balancing itself, the board not even nailed to the floor.

" Small wax-candles, red, green, yellow, and white, were then fastened to the tree in little rims of tin, that had clasps to attach them to the branches, in such order as not to endanger the boughs above them, and cause a general conflagration. Then, small glass balls, gilt and colored, were hung on by strings, looking like ripe and beautiful fruit. The most valuable fruits, however, the Christmas gifts, were then suspended from the branches, excepting books and boxes too heavy for that purpose: they were deposited on the nursery carpet, at the foot of the tree."

To children, Christmas is a peculiar delight: they never tire with its repetition. The Christmas-tree is, in their eyes

24

the perfection of beauty, — the wonderful show they have been looking forward to for weeks, every day of which is counted. What happiness it gives them! The elderly people feel young in witnessing their joy. Yes, Christmas is for children and the childlike.

Perhaps some of the many happy families where this volume — as I hope — will be welcomed, may like to read a lyric I wrote some years ago for a Christmas celebration where children were the singers.

CHRISTMAS SONG.

Hail, hail, the happy morn
When Christ our Lord was born!
   Sound, sound His praise!
The Prince of Righteousness,
He came our world to bless,
The glorious hymn of "Peace"
   On earth to raise.

Angels the song began,
And then to ransomed man
   The strain was given.
Hark! joining sweet and wild,
The voice of little child,
Blessed by his Saviour mild,
   May sing of Heaven.

Peace, peace! What blissful sound!
Let joy and hope abound
   This happy day!
We praise Thee, God above;
Our lives Thy blessing prove;
Thanks for Thy light and love,
   Our souls would pay.

Sound, sound the loudest strain !
Let earth and sky and main
    The anthem raise !
Father, Thy Love we bless,
Saviour, we ask Thy " Peace, "
Spirit, we beg Thy grace,
    When God we praise.

IX. — TIME'S LAST VISIT.

I.

THE night was a dark and stormy one,
    And the year was running low,
When Time threw his travelling mantle on,
    As he were about to go.
He cast on his glass a rueful look :
    The sands will be out, he said,
Seizing his memorandum-book,
    And these visits must be made.
Yet it does little good the fools to warn ;
    I nearly lose my labors :
They treat my message with idle scorn,
    Or think it meant for their neighbors.

II.

Last year my duty was faithfully done:
    I traversed this city through,
Revealing to every devoted one
    I had come for a final adieu.
Why, they treated my warnings as Europe treats
    The groans of the dying Poles ;
Or thought 'twas to save — how this avarice cheats ! —
    Their money, and not their souls,
That my hint of a speedy departure was given,
    Though I bade them farewell like a lover ;
And few there were who prepared for Heaven :
    I can easily reckon them over

III.

And first to a banker's house I hied,
   Though I knew he was often surly ;
But these Rothschilds, one must humor their pride,
   So I hastened to warn him early.
I found him within at a sumptuous feast ;
   An Apician sauce was before him :
Its flavor he praised to each smiling guest, —
   'Tis Death,— thus my warning came o'er him.
Oh, how his eye glared as he bade me flee !
   I was off, like a twinkle of light ;
And he ate at that dinner enough for three,
   And he died of a surfeit that night.

IV.

And next I tapped at an editor's door :
   It sounded so like a dun,
He scattered his papers about the floor,
   As he made a motion to run.
But soon he resumed his studies again,
   When he found no sheriff drew nigh,
Searching old books for a New-Year's strain :
   I whispered, *The year to die !*
He started, — " ah, 'tis a lucky thought,
   " And I'll rhyme it out," said he :
" My patrons may fear that Death is near,
   And repent of their debts to me."

V.

I hurried away to a doctor then,
   Though I knew I might spare my pains, —
That he thought of disease as the end of men,
   And of death as the doctor's gains.
" My patient must die," he was maundering on,
   As he glanced a fee-bill o'er,
" And his money will go to his graceless son :
   My bill might be something more.

The youth will never take trouble or care,
   Though I charge five visits a day."
So he figured away, while I hissed in his ear,
   Remember, my visit's to pay.

VI.

I told an old man it was time he should go,
   And he was too deaf to hear.
I called at the play on a dashing beau,
   And he was too gay to fear.
I paused in a merchant's counting-room,
   And a dunce was I to stop :
Scarce would he have heeded the crash of doom,
   While reckoning his ledger up.
There is one demand, I began to say :
   He burst, with a hurried breath,
" Show me your bill ; I've the cash to pay."
   —I left him to settle with Death !

VII.

And then I went to a poor man's shed,
   And thought 'twould delight him so :
I knew he often wished he was dead,
   But he flatly refused to go.
And oh ! the wild agony of his eye,
   As he begged me one year to give,
And said 'twas hard that a man should die
   Who had struggled so long to live.
That his wife was weak, and his children small :
   I whispered, *Charity !*
He turned his face to the low, damp wall,
   " 'Tis a broken reed," sighed he.

VIII.

I had fared so ill with the lords of earth, —
   Of earth they had proved indeed, —
That I turned to the sex of gentler birth,
   And hoped more kindly to speed.

On a beautiful belle I made a call :
  Her milliner's girl stood by ;
She had brought a new dress for the New-Year's ball
  I breathed a sepulchral sigh,
And the rich, red flowers seemed ghastly white :
  "How odd ! " cried the beauty in sorrow ;
"These do not become me at all to-night,
  But bring me some brighter to-morrow."

IX.

And then, — but why continue the list
  So fraught with chagrin to me ?
Who likes to remember the times he has missed,
  When recounting his archery ?
I called, in fine, on the old and the young,
  Fair, ugly, sober, and gay :
The chorus the same to the tune they all sung,
  They would not be hurried away.
There were some who hated the world, to be sure,
  And called Time an old villanous cheat ;
But heaven was so distant, so holy, so pure,
  They had no inclination to see't.

X.

Worms of the dust, I murmured in wrath,
  As reaching a princely home,
And following the clew of my fateful path,
  I entered the nursery room.
The little ones slept like nestled birds ;
  And she, the sweet mother-dove,
With a face too happy to paint in words,
  Was sorting her gifts of love
For the New-Year's morn.   I touched her cheek ;
  She knew Death's ice-cold chill,
And lifted her eyes with a smile so meek :
  "Our Father, do thy will."

XI.

Yes, woman should always be willing to go:
  She has nothing on earth but love, —
A dowry that bears little value below,
  But is priceless transferred above.
Oh ! lavish it not on thy brightest joys;
  'Tis folly, 'tis all in vain :
I never bestow them except as toys
  I mean to resume again.
Even now I shall gather a thousand fair things
  I gave when this year was new ;
And the hopes for the next, that I shake from my wings,
  Will prove as deceitful too.

XII.

But why should I preach ? Who'll the wiser be ?
  The young are engaged in pleasure ;
The elderly cut all acquaintance with me ;
  And nobody else is at leisure.
They may learn if they will ; though life is brief,
  Some monitor ever is nigh, —
The fading flower, the falling leaf,
  The year about to die :
These speak to the hearts of the humble and just ;
  For the earthly and obstinate,
My visits to such are labor lost,
  So I leave them for aye to their fate.

X. — THE THREE SCEPTRES.

A VISION.

Nation shall not lift up sword against nation, neither shall they learn war any more. — ISAIAH.

"Bring forth the sceptres of command!" —
　That awful Voice I heard —
"And let the subject nations stand!"
　The waiting world appeared.
Then drew the sceptre-bearers nigh :
Old Asia first crept cowering by ;
Next Europe, with her troubled eye ;
　Then young America.
Each placed her sceptre, passed, and then,
Unveiled before the sons of men,
A Sword, a Crosier, and a Pen
　Upon the altar lay.

Again the Voice uprose, and loud
　As battle-cry it came ;
And wildly, from that heaving crowd,
　Echoed the shout, "For Fame!"
Brother 'gainst brother fiercely stood :
The earth was graves, the waters blood,
Kingdoms were crushed, as wasting flood
　Had swept o'er crumbling clay ;
Till 'mid the din a dove appeared.
The angel's song of "Peace" was heard :
I looked, and with that heavenly word
　The Sword had passed away.

Then, like a storm of ashes, hurled
　From Ætna's burning height,
A thick dark cloud rolled o'er the world,
　Blotting mind's blessèd light ;

And men sunk down in utter dread,
Mailed warriors weak as infants tread,
And monarchs, with uncovered head,
    Bowed low the Cowl before;
And Superstition's iron reign
Has seared the heart and shrunk the brain.
Ha! Thought's strong grasp has rent the chain:
    The Crosier's sway is o'er.

Pure as the light on altar glows,
    Lit up by prophet's prayer,
A small, soft, steady light arose
    On earth, on sea, on air:
It shines as shed from seraph's wings,
Withering all vile, old, useless things,
Like scorched flax from the grasp of kings,
    The reins of empire sever:
It burns from Craft his mask of night,
Intemperance blasts with holy light,
And shows the Ethiop's soul is white:
    " The Pen — the Pen forever ! "

Thus rang the Voice: its trumpet tone
    Burst like a swelling river;
From land to land went sounding on,
    " The Pen, the Pen forever ! "
I saw earth's joyous millions move,
Justice their shield, their banner Love,
While Freedom's eagle soared above,
    Watched by Faith's steadfast eye;
Cool springs gushed forth 'mid burning sands;
Bright flowers bloomed out in barren lands;
And bands of Peace, in angel hands,
    Were linking earth and sky.

American Women: Images and Realities
An Arno Press Collection

[Adams, Charles F., editor]. **Correspondence between John Adams and Mercy Warren Relating to Her "History of the American Revolution," July-August, 1807.** With a new appendix of specimen pages from the **"History."** 1878.

[Arling], Emanie Sachs. **"The Terrible Siren": Victoria Woodhull, (1838-1927).** 1928.

Beard, Mary Ritter. **Woman's Work in Municipalities.** 1915.

Blanc, Madame [Marie Therese de Solms]. **The Condition of Woman in the United States.** 1895.

Bradford, Gamaliel. **Wives.** 1925.

Branagan, Thomas. **The Excellency of the Female Character Vindicated.** 1808.

Breckinridge, Sophonisba P. **Women in the Twentieth Century.** 1933.

Campbell, Helen. **Women Wage-Earners.** 1893.

Coolidge, Mary Roberts. **Why Women Are So.** 1912.

Dall, Caroline H. **The College, the Market, and the Court.** 1867.

[D'Arusmont], Frances Wright. **Life, Letters and Lectures: 1834, 1844.** 1972.

Davis, Almond H. **The Female Preacher, or Memoir of Salome Lincoln.** 1843.

Ellington, George. **The Women of New York.** 1869.

Farnham, Eliza W[oodson]. **Life in Prairie Land.** 1846.

Gage, Matilda Joslyn. **Woman, Church and State.** [1900].

Gilman, Charlotte Perkins. **The Living of Charlotte Perkins Gilman.** 1935.

Groves, Ernest R. **The American Woman.** 1944.

Hale, [Sarah J .] **Manners; or, Happy Homes and Good Society All the Year Round.** 1868.

Higginson, Thomas Wentworth. **Women and the Alphabet.** 1900.

Howe, Julia Ward, editor. **Sex and Education.** 1874.

La Follette, Suzanne. **Concerning Women.** 1926.

Leslie, Eliza . **Miss Leslie's Behaviour Book: A Guide and Manual for Ladies.** 1859.

Livermore, Mary A. **My Story of the War.** 1889.

Logan, Mrs. John A. (Mary S.) **The Part Taken By Women in American History.** 1912.

McGuire, Judith W. (A Lady of Virginia). **Diary of a Southern Refugee, During the War.** 1867.

Mann, Herman . **The Female Review: Life of Deborah Sampson.** 1866.

Meyer, Annie Nathan, editor.**Woman's Work in America.** 1891

Myerson, Abraham. **The Nervous Housewife.** 1927.

Parsons, Elsie Clews. **The Old-Fashioned Woman.** 1913.

Porter, Sarah Harvey. **The Life and Times of Anne Royall.** 1909.

Pruette, Lorine. **Women and Leisure: A Study of Social Waste.** 1924.

Salmon, Lucy Maynard. **Domestic Service.** 1897.

Sanger, William W. **The History of Prostitution.** 1859.

Smith, Julia E. **Abby Smith and Her Cows.** 1877.

Spencer, Anna Garlin. **Woman's Share in Social Culture.** 1913.

Sprague, William Forrest. **Women and the West.** 1940.

Stanton, Elizabeth Cady. **The Woman's Bible** Parts I and II. 1895/1898.

Stewart, Mrs. Eliza Daniel . **Memories of the Crusade.** 1889.

Todd, John. **Woman's Rights.** 1867. [Dodge, Mary A .] (Gail Hamilton, pseud.) **Woman's Wrongs.** 1868.

Van Rensselaer, Mrs. John King. **The Goede Vrouw of Mana-ha-ta.** 1898.

Velazquez, Loreta Janeta. **The Woman in Battle.** 1876.

Vietor, Agnes C., editor. **A Woman's Quest: The Life of Marie E. Zakrzew-ska, M.D.** 1924.

Woodbury , Helen L. Sum n er. **Equal Suffrage.** 1909.

Young, Ann Eliza. **Wife No. 19.** 1875.